About Orca Boy

Joshua is a tall 17 year old geeky martial arts champion with a near genius IQ.

Samantha is a stunning 17 year old kayaker with a Golden Retriever named Sadie .

Pepper is a ten foot juvenile killer whale that is best friends with Sadie, and follows Josh like a puppy.

The story takes place in the beautiful San Juan Islands and includes: corruption, poaching, forensics, cyber crime, high seas adventure, young romance, attempted murder, and s'mores.

ORCA BOY

This novel is

DEDICATED

To

The young at heart among us

who enjoy romance, adventure,
intrigue, and have a soft spot for

Orcas

ORCA BOY

Chapter 1 – Pepper

"It's okay guys," says Josh, his heart pounding, but his voice clear and steady. "I'm not going to hurt you, and I kinda want you to not to hurt us—do we have a deal?" He stops rowing and the boat drifts. Slowly they inch past the battered snout of the bigger of the two killer whales.

"Never mind, don't answer—that would just freak us out. Especially if you have a deep radio announcer voice, or a minnie mouse cartoon voice, that would do it too. Anyway, my name is Josh; this other fellow in the boat is my Uncle Charley, and we live in that big old house up on the hill. Over there, on the dock, is my Aunt Maggie, she's the one taking your picture, and next to her is Sammie and Sadie. Sadie's the golden lab, it was her barking that brought us running to help you."

Josh's constant pitter-patter is meant to calm the huge animals and bolster his own courage. So far, his heart rate has increased, and he's sweating bullets, but luckily the orca's appear to be in full control of their emotions.

The two killer whales have brought an exciting, yet nervous calmness to the cove, and then without warning, they both explosively spout—thus ending the peaceful silence. First, the big one, then the little one, exhales a foul smelling steamy mist high into the air. Their industrial breath erupts for ten long seconds from fist size blowholes on top of their heads. The spouts catch everyone by surprise. Charley swallows hard and dry; his neck muscles knot and won't cooperate.

They pause after exhaling, much like after Yellowstone's *Old Faithful* geyser erupts and then calmness returns. Then, after a few more seconds, their blowholes suddenly flex open and they draw in fresh air. Their guttural inhales sound like the earth herself is sucking in a breath.

"Hey momma," says Josh, trembling, while her watery blue green eye looks him over. "That was way cool and very impressive up close like that. Like I said earlier, I'm Joshua, and we are going to help your baby. I think that's why you came here—to get help—right? Do you have names? What do you call each other? Has anyone ever told you your black and white outfits look formal? You know, like a penguin looks. This conversation is totally one-sided, but that's okay, we covered that already. I know—since you are both black and white, like salt and pepper, I'm calling you Pepper, and mom, it doesn't sound right calling you salt, so how about we just stick with big momma?" Josh pauses the chatter for his own calming deep breaths; the quiet moment is Sadie's cue to bark and whimper her concern.

Pepper moves her flipper fin in a circular motion pushing her blowhole and eyes back above the surface. She is resting, half perched on momma orca's outstretched six foot fin. Without constant swimming or her mother's support, the heavy net and weights entangling her body will pull her to the bottom drowning her. She bravely watches the rowboat drift closer, her mom's massive size beside her gives her courage, but fear overtakes her and she shakes as a trapped animal quivers when they are cornered.

"This isn't good," says Charley, "she's shaking, she's about to panic."

Fifty feet away on the dock, Sadie whines, Sammie rubs her neck soothing her, maybe Sadie senses something, maybe dog and orca connect in a way humans can't hear or don't understand. Sadie was certainly drawn to the cove and the orca's like a dog on a mission, bringing Sammie and Josh running. Sadie's whines turn whimpering and then she rises up and barks twice at Pepper before Sammie quiets her.

The puny little boat offers little protection should Pepper and big momma suddenly thrash about. Josh rows directly in front of Pepper; with unblinking eyes, she watches him pull the oars in, and reach for his hiking stick. Her left eye is dark blue the other is dark green. Above each of her small eyes is a large white eye-patch, Mother Nature's subtle disguise and attempt at trickery. She is black on top and white on her belly, the black and white markings duplicated on her mom. Like mother, like daughter, Pepper is a ten-foot version of her twenty-three foot mother.

"Well Charley, so far so good," says Josh, "It's okay Pepper girl, I see you're nervous, and probably scared too. Chill awhile; I need to keep from banging into you and your mom so I'm going to touch your mom lightly with this stick, that's okay with your mom—right?" Charley holds his breath, he squeezes the edge of the boat so hard his fingers hurt and his knuckles turn white. Josh exhales slowly through pursed lips, and reaches the stick out to momma—he gently pushes.

"Oh jeez," says Josh trembling again, "this is scary stuff—pushing on her is like shoving on a piling or dock covered with old truck tires. This momma is definitely a serious animal." The rowboat rebounds backwards. Momma's eye follows them; ever so slowly, she strokes her fin on the far side. Under water, she flexes her broad tail fluke—Josh freezes while holding the stick hovering over her.

"It's okay momma, Charlie and I are your friends, I'm going to rub this stick over here on Pepper's back." He lightly touches the tip of his stick on her back between her blowhole and dorsal fin. "Would you like me to scratch your back, Pepper?"

He rubs the stick back and forth, wondering what to do next.

"You really are a brave girl Pepper; let me scratch you a little bit over here by your big back fin."

Josh slides the stick over the ropes that are cutting into her skin and scratches in front of her long pectoral fin.

"What the heck is that noise," says Josh, "Pepper, is that you squealing? No, you're whistling—you sure are. You like this scratching, don't you?" Josh lifts the stick and raps it in one spot like when Sammie smacks Sadie on her haunches as part of a good-dog back rub. Pepper's whistles continue with an occasional clicking *eck eck* sound.

"Josh, I think that whale likes you," says Charley, loosening his death grip on the boat while the strange almost unbelievable sight unfolds in front of him. "If I didn't know better I would say Pepper is purring."

"Uh, I hope not, I once had a cat that purred when I rubbed its back, but then it bit me."

The scratching, whistling and clicking eck eck's continue while momma orca supports Pepper on her extended flipper fin. Her gentle fin and tail strokes hold their position opposite the floating dock in front of Sammie, Sadie and Maggie. His courage showing, Josh experiments and rubs the stick on different parts of Peppers body. He carefully shoves and manipulates the area where the ropes are cutting into her thick skin. She shows no preference nor displays any pain or displeasure; she tolerates his touching and doesn't seem to mind the boat bumping against her. Occasionally she double ecks when he scratches near her dorsal fin. Momma orca is motionless just feet away; she could be asleep except her eye is open, watching.

Josh and Charley lock eyes; it's time to get on with it. Charley shakes his head, "Look Josh —you don't have to do this. We can just paddle away."

"Yes I do, Uncle Charley, now more than ever, I can't not help them." He clenches his jaw, steals a pensive look at Sammie and then with his bare hand, he slowly reaches out and gently rubs his fingers along the white patch above her open eye. While comforting the small orca he makes an unspoken silent commitment to her. *You can count on me.* With his other hand, he wipes tears from his own wet eyes.

Using the hooked pole, he reaches into the water underneath Pepper and snags a piece of net. He pulls the snarled mass to the surface. With his Leatherman tool lanyard securely looped on his wrist, he slices into the netting. He saws the serrated blade through seaweed-encrusted line. He hooks more gobs and cuts through fifteen or more lines before coming to an extra heavy rope holding a lot of weight. It takes both him and Charley to pull the taught rope to the surface. Josh braces himself up on one knee and leans out over the ten foot orca.

"This is horrible Pepper, how the heck can you swim with all this junk hanging from you?"

The knife cleanly separates the stretched rope releasing hundreds of pounds that suddenly sink to the bottom of the cove. When the weight falls, Pepper, Charley, Josh and the rowboat all rebound at once. Big momma's huge supporting fin snaps upward like a catapult unleashed, lifting and tilting the boat. Charley falls over backward in the middle of the boat and rides it out, but Josh's precarious position is impossible to recover from, and he sails over the side flopping onto Peppers back. Her dorsal fin trips him up and he slides into the water between mother and daughter. Sadie jumps to her feet barking her alarm. Sammie pulls her down clamping a hand over her muzzle quieting her. Maggie yells Josh's name. Charley with the boat hook still in his hand pulls himself up and looks for his nephew.

"Oh my god," says Charley, eyes wide, fresh adrenalin replacing stale fear.

"It's okay Pepper," says Josh, "It's okay momma, just a little mishap—everyone remain calm."

Josh has slipped between the two killer whales, one arm resting on Pepper, the other forced upward over the much higher mom.

"Charley, you aren't going to believe this, I'm kneeling on her fin. I'm going to climb over Pepper and get back in the boat." He crouches, in waist deep freezing water ready to stand and straddle Pepper. His fear totally under control, he closes the hanging knife, and then reaches out and rubs his hand along Peppers head, his fingers stroking beside her blowhole, she exhales a quiet sigh.

When he stretches for the boat, he doesn't quite make it and falls on her again. With both arms, he pushes off ungracefully rejecting sitting on her. He lands with a flying crash back in the rocking boat. The two orca's watch and remain motionless, unlike Charley, their emotions and fear is still in check.

"Oh boy," Says Josh, able to breathe again, "I thought that was going to do it, and we would be smashed to bits, or big momma's tail would toss us over the dock."

"Are you okay," says Maggie, "what happened, did the big whale hit you?"

"No, everything is fine," says Charley, "we just got off balance." Focusing on the job at hand, Josh says. "That last cut released a ton of weight, but it didn't loosen these two tight ones around her body, we have to keep fishing for hanging lines."

In the next fifteen minutes, Josh and Charley manage to make another dozen cuts, removing a lot of netting and line but no more significant weight like the gob that threw him into the water.

"Okay, we're almost done, this is the one digging in, I'll slice— what the!! This rope has a wire inside it, it's dulled my knife, I can't cut it."

"I should have told you," says Charley, "some fishing nets are made with a wire cable in the top line."

Chapter 2 - Sammie

Yesterday— 24 hours earlier.

"Hi!—Hellooo...... I said Hi!—"

"Oh . . . you're talking to me?" *Oh geez, you dweeb, what a dumb answer.*

"Well yeahhh," she says, while twisting and winding her sun-streaked hair around a finger. "Do you see anyone else on the top deck of this ferry boat?"

"Well when you put it that way, just me I guess." *Wow, she's kinda pretty, her blue eyes sparkle—think, think, say something not too stupid, offer her a tic tac.*

"My name is Sammie, what's yours?" She looks straight into his face, he holds her stare for a second, and then looks down. His legs shake, his chest quivers, his head swims. She lets go of the hair twirl, setting the ringlet free, and starts another twist. She tilts her head trying to make eye contact again. His face flushes, and his cheeks burn.

She's wearing a purple Orcas Island baseball cap with sunglasses perched above the sharply curved bill. Her twirled hair ringlets hang below her shoulders cascading over a Columbia Windbreaker. The jacket is zipped to the top fending off the wind chill, but she is wearing shorts and sandals. She could be a cover girl for an outdoor magazine.

"It's Josh," looking up he forces himself to return her smile, "I mean my name is Josh. Isn't Sammie a boy's name, do you know where this ferry is going?" *That was so lame, I can't believe I said it.* "Is that your dog?" *Oh jeez, more stupid, of course it's her dog.*

"Her name is Sadie, do you think I look like a boy? It's going to Canada, I saw you down on the dock looking at the line to the other ferry."

"Canada!—oh crap, oops sorry," he grabs his mouth, "I'm on the wrong ferry, I gotta get off." *I can't get more stupid than getting on the wrong ferry.* Joshua grabs his backpack off the ferry deck and runs for the stairs.

Sammie and Sadie bolt after Josh, "Hey, where are you going?"

"To the other ferry, I'm supposed to be going to Orcas Landing."

"Wait—that's this ferry." Hearing that, he stops at the top of the stairs.

"But you said it's going to Canada!"

"It is—right after we get off on Orcas Island where I live. At least where I have to live all summer with my stepmother."

"Oh wow—me too! I wouldn't..."

The ferry horn drowns out any more talk; it blasts out a long ten-second warning that it is about to move away from the dock. Immense power surges through the ship, shaking decks and railings. It's massive twin propellers churn ocean water into a frothy wake of sea creatures and kelp pushing the 400-foot vessel away from shore.

"I wouldn't have made it—the other ferry I mean. I was panicked—I mean I live on Orcas Island too, not with your mother. I will be living there now, I guess. With my Aunt and Uncle. I haven't been there by myself, in a long time. Well—I guess I've never been there by myself, actually—" *I should shut up, she must think I'm dumber than dumb.* "Do we go to Orcas Landing or Orcas Island first, I don't want to miss my stop and end up in Canada. Do you want a tic tac," shaking the container, "it's really just candy you know."

Sammie holds out her hand, and he carefully shakes out two. She contemplates his anxious question and considers telling him they are really going to Canada to see if he faints. *He's cute, I can't be mean to him.* She leans against the heavily-painted railing, her hands behind her back, she rocks back and forth, fidgeting, and watching.

The ferry picks up speed and plows down Guemes Channel and into four-mile wide Rosario Strait toward the San Juan Islands. Cold seawater chills the wind keeping most passengers inside warm cabins. Sammie's hair streams behind her, the ferries speed providing a twenty knot breeze. Soon she crosses her arms and tucks her hands for warmth. Her bare calves and thighs double goosebump. She watches Josh's panic subside, he's no longer super amped over what is really just a boring bus ride, but she catches him shyly sneaking peeks at her. She kicks off one sandal and shoves it between her backpack and duffel bag. The backpack is bulging and has a water bottle hanging from a cord, the duffle bag is adorned with a peeling *save the whale's*• bumper sticker, another sticker proclaims, *caring counts,*•and an old•*earth first*•button dangles precariously. The zipper is broken, and it's tied shut with a frayed red bungee cord with knotted ends.

Sammie rests her bare foot on Sadie's back, digging her toes into the sleek golden fur while watching the boy show off. Josh treats the railing as a playground toy. In her presence, he acts ten instead of almost eighteen. Sadie is enjoying Sammie's attention, she has laid her head on the duffle bag, but leaves one eye open. Her long Retriever fur splayed on the deck is almost the same color as Sammie's twirled ringlets.

Finally, she says, "You didn't answer my question."

"What?" *Oh boy—what question?*

"I asked you if I look like a boy?"

"No—I mean heck no." —*excellent answer!* He looks directly at her, and when their eyes meet, she looks away. Goosebumps run up both her arms.

"Good," she says, hiding her smile.

"It's confusing," says Sammie hugging herself, rubbing her arms. "But it's the same place, Orcas *Landing* is like a bus stop for ferries, and it's the only stop on Orcas Island. It's the only way on or off the island, except flying, swimming or kayaking. It's short for Samantha."

"I would like to try it sometime," he gets instantly red faced, and then blurts, "kayaking—I mean. I have an app on my phone, it does white water kayaking, but I've never done it, you know, for real." *Oh jeez, I'm sounding like an idiot, I should just stop talking.*

"Want another." He shakes the tic-tac container.

"Sure." She holds out her hand, palm up. He shakes one out from six inches, and misses her hand. The tic-tac bounces once, and skitters across the deck and out the ships scupper to the sea fifty feet below.

"Oopsey," says Josh. *Oh god I said oopsey!*

"Here, let me show you." She takes the plastic container in her hand, and holds Josh's hand with her other. Carefully jiggling two white mints into his hand, she takes one for herself, before pressing the container into his palm, and closing his fingers. "There," she says, looking up at him, "that's how you do it, any questions?" She holds his hand in hers for a second longer than necessary, and watches his reaction.

"I got it, I think." *Oh my gosh—her hands feel nice.* Her look goes right through him, to avoid melting into the steel deck he quickly looks seaward, and that's when he spots the pod.

"Look," pointing, "out there, a bunch of dolphins." Sammie turns and follows his pointing in time to see a far-off orca spouting before going under.

"Those are orcas, *Killer Whales*," she says.

"They're fantastic; I hope they come around Orcas Island?"

Sammie is about Josh's age, he's taller at close to six feet and not rail thin; she has already sized him up and decided they could be friends. He doesn't seem pretentious or needy. Just shy and tongue-tied. He's not bad looking, his hair is a mess, it needs cutting, or at least a good brushing like Sadie, but he looks fit and not at all wimpy. She thinks his hands could use some lotion and he's tan enough to have been outdoors more than once. Most importantly, he's not saying crazy things, or dude and awesome all the time. He's just really nervous traveling on his own, she suspects her outspoken personality has him a little taken back; she has a similar affect on all boys she meets, not so with girls though, girls try to compete and get snitty around her, especially the made up trampy ones.

"They hang around the straits," says Sammie, "like out here. I teach people how to kayak and sail, sometimes we see orcas, but mostly seals. My stepmother, *Sandy,* owns the—*Islander Grand Re-*

sort Bed and Breakfast—and I work for her. So I also have to put fish bait on hooks, scrub toilets and change bedding."

"Wow, sailing instructor, fishing guide and maid, all in one. Your stepmom is lucky to have you help her. I don't know what I'll be doing, but I don't want to go back to Portland, so I guess I'm starting new today. I'm going to live with my aunt and uncle, they seem nice, but I only know them from holidays and at my mom's funeral."

"Your mom's gone, that sucks, where do your aunt and uncle live?"

"I guess where I'll be staying—Pearson's Cove."

"You're kidding," yells Sammie, "oh my gosh, you're Josh Pearson."

"Yeah, I know," says Josh looking puzzled like something more is coming.

"We're neighbors—I know Maggie and Chuck—I send my newbie kayaker's to your cove for practice runs, I guess I mean your grandfather's cove." *Finally, someone my age to hang with.*

"Really—were neighbors?— that's great." *You being my neighbor is better than great, it's awesome.*

Chapter 3 - Orcas Landing

The steel vehicle and passenger ramp winches down and drops with a clang just as the deck-man drags the safety chain to one side. With a wave, he motions the waiting foot passengers off the ferry and the captain blares *Orcas Landing* over the ships loudspeaker.

"See," says Sammie, "*Orcas Landing*, last stop before Canada, let's go."

They trudge up the boarding ramp, both kids loaded down with backpacks, and hauling all their worldly belongings. They blend in with the rest of the foot passengers filing off the ferry. Everyone sports a backpack, and half of them are pushing bicycles laden with camping gear.

"Joshua, up here, Joshua."

"That's my Aunt Maggie." He waves to her, and so does Sammie. "I guess it's time to say goodbye, I'll see you around Sammie," says Josh.

"I'm glad we met," says Sammie, "Let's do something sometime if you want, or maybe I'll see you out on the water, I have lots of kayaks."

"That would be great; I'd like that, what's your number, I'll send you mine?" A second or so after entering Sammie's number into his phone and pushing send, Josh hears her phone chirp, and then he disconnects. "There you've got mine." He takes the steps two at a time up the long flights of stairs to the upper parking lot where his Aunt is waiting and waving; Sammie cuts across the street and nabs the front seat in the *Islander Shuttle Service* minivan. His words still echoing in her head, Sammie can't help smiling—*That would be great, I'd like that, we traded numbers too. I like that!*

"Hi Joshua, we are really excited you're here, do you remember much, I think it's been nine or ten years, hasn't it?"

"Oh, I guess about that, I remember the ferry dock, and the smell of creosote, those big winches and the steel ramps clanging with every car are pretty impressive to a six year old. I remember Grandpa's cove, I didn't know it was called Pearson's Cove until I saw it on my GPS."

"Well it hasn't always been, we just call it Grandpas cove, it used to be West Cove, and Whale Cove, or maybe it was Whale Bay, but as the story goes, one day a county guy asked your grandma what it was called so he could paint a street sign. She and your grandpa were renting rowboats to tourists back then, so she told him if he didn't mind, to make it Pearson's Cove with an arrow pointing towards the marina. Now it says *Pearson Cove* on all the maps."

"I saw you walking and talking with a girl; did you meet her on the ferry?"

"That's Sammie, she works at the *Islander Grand Resort Bed and Breakfast*, she gave me a scare when she said the ferry was going to Canada."

"That's Samantha—wow, I didn't recognize her, she's a foot taller since last summer. We should have given her a ride, we drive right by the *Islander*. But, I guess it's just as well, I want to run to town and get some groceries, and I'm sure her mother is expecting her anyway."

"Correction—Stepmother."

"She told you stepmother huh."

"Yeah, she made it clear; I don't think she likes working for her too much."

"What makes you think that?"

"She said she had to be here all summer, like it was punishment or something. Sammie is different from other girls I've known, but she's just normal I guess. Most of the girls I've been around at school are super intelligent basket cases pretending to be something they're not. They are always on the edge of reality, needing to prove something. Sammie is different, she's just nice, I don't mean she's dumb; she's not, she's quick, and she's, she's …nice."

Maggie doesn't say anything, but she suspects that living next door to Samantha will have a profound affect on Josh.

After stopping at the store, she takes the long way to Pearson Cove; she pulls the rusty old pickup truck into a scenic viewpoint giving Josh a chance to see the islands. They see the ferry making its way across Haro Strait, trailing a wake of white foam headed for Canada. Maggie points to some of the hundreds of islands and waterways surrounding them and lists off mostly useless names. Lopez, San Juan, Blind Bay, Shipwreck. Squinting westward into the afternoon sun, she points to *Pearson Cove* and the *Islander Resort* out on the point.

"Uncle Chuck is waiting for us," says Maggie, pulling back on the road "he's got the barbecue going, and we have the buns."

Chapter 4 – Pearson Lodge

"Hey Josh," says Charlie Pearson when Maggie shuts off the truck.

"Hey Uncle Chuck."

"It's good to see you again, did you have any troubles getting here?

"Nah, for a second I thought I got on the wrong ferry."

"Well, were sure glad you're here," shaking hands, but turning it into a shoulder hug. "We have plenty of time to talk or do whatever, or do nothing at all, you are not a visitor here, it's your home for as long as you want, sound ok?"

"Sure Uncle Chuck."

"I need to know one thing." Says Charley seriously.

"What's that?"

"Where are the buns? Let's eat, you must be starving." Charlie motions for them to follow him over to the large rock terrace where a beat up stainless steel barbecue and a handful of shoddy old deck chairs face the cove. Charlie hands him a sizzling hotdog and points Josh to a tray of condiments.

"You know, I have always called you little Josh, but you're taller than me now, and nobody on the island calls me uncle anything. Why don't I drop the little part, unless were around your friends, and you call me Charlie, Chuck, or Charles depending on how serious the discussion is."

I'll try, but mom and dad have always called you guys Aunt Maggie, and Uncle Chuck."

"I don't mind Aunt Maggie, it makes me sound important."

"No it don't," says Charlie, "it makes you sound like someone's out of town relative. Josh, you can eat all want, or go inside and get situated, we figured you would like the room on the right upstairs, but there's others, or if you want, you can bunk out on the dock or in the boat house, it's your place."

The old *Pearson Cove Lodge* was a real showplace when Josh's grandparents were alive, and big. Grande fireplace, big wood stove in a huge country kitchen. Josh gets a big old guest suite with its own bathroom. He tosses his backpack on the king-size bed, flips the light switch on in the bathroom and stares at his reflection in the mirror.

"Well, little Joshua?" He says to his reflection, but he doesn't answer.

Then he wanders around the house making his way back downstairs taking in the view from the big window in the great room. He keeps saying, "Wow," to himself, "everything is big," as he discovers one thing after another, all of them big. He spots the rowboat pulled up on the beach, upside down on the dock is a little sailboat, its mast missing. There's a dilapidated outbuilding by the gangplank begging to be explored, there's bleached driftwood on the agate pebbled beach, trails lead into the woods and around the point. He knows one trail goes to the *Islander Resort,* where Sammie lives.

Out in the cove, he sees flat water and a group of diving birds, beyond is the main channel, the incoming tide mimics a slow flowing river. Farther out, across the channel are some of the islands he saw from the viewpoint, in reality, there are dozens more; it's hard to tell where one island ends and another begins. *Wow, getting lost in a small boat is a real possibility. I should have paid more attention when Maggie showed me the big view.* He sees powerboats, their curling wakes following them. Crossing the channel heading into the sun is a group of half a dozen kayakers, their dripping paddles flashing jeweled sparkles with each stroke.

Josh rejoins Maggie and Charlie lounging on the patio, the first thing that he says is, "I'd forgotten how cool this place is, does the ferry go by here?"

"No—no ferries, just the rest of the world, we see everything sooner or later," says Charlie. "Our passage is off the main route, but between the islands out there," pointing toward Shaw Island, "you can spot the inner island ferry heading for Friday Harbor."

"I saw some kayakers' way way out, where are they going, is it safe out in the middle?"

"Safe?—that's up to them, but they could be going anywhere, there are twenty state parks paddling distance from here, we meet people that are thirty miles from where they started out. Just around the corner," pointing off to the right, " is Rock Island and Mutiny Bay State Park, It's got campsites, fire pits, a little cove with a dock, you should take a kayak and go exploring. It's just a teensy little island, perfect for a modern day Robinson Crusoe. It's also where your dad proposed to your mother. Has he contacted you today?"

"Twice so far."

"He's pretty busy, coming home unplanned for the funeral and all like he did probably put the job behind, he'll catch up to you when he can. They don't come any better than Ray."

"He texted me twice this afternoon, once on the ferry to tell me the captain wouldn't leave unless I got off at Orcas Landing, and then ten minutes ago to tell me to move into the Sunrise room, and that the seventh step squeaked."

"Oh, seventh step huh, did he tell you about it?"

"No, but I figure it has something to do with getting caught sneaking out at night."

"You're close—he got caught sneaking back in at 4 am, the step squeaked, and grandma met him at the top of the stairs. He said he miscounted, but she said he never miscounted, cause she always heard every step, when her boys came in late. She said he just wanted to talk about going away to school and couldn't wait for morning. I had already moved out, dad was off Island, so she was all he had to talk with.

"That's funny," says Josh, becoming somber with thoughts of his own mother.

"There's a lot of family history here Josh, and a lot more to come now with you here.

"Why haven't I heard about the seventh step?" Says Maggie.

"I guess it never came up before."

"Anything else, I would be interested in?" Says Maggie

"Of course—boys will be boys, but I'm not talking."

"While you two are hashing out old times, is it ok if I take that rowboat down there for a spin."

"Sure Josh," says Charlie, "there's life vests in the boat shed, be sure to take one—right?"

"Yes Uncle Chuck,"

"I'm sorry Josh, its hard to let go of *little Joshua.*"

"It's ok, I don't mind."

ORCA BOY

The boat shed is a children's treasure trove of, ropes, floats, paddles, wooden pulleys and decades of collected gear. Josh picks out a life vest he wore when he visited once years earlier, the label reads, *child's under fifty pounds,* he hangs it back on the peg and picks out an adult size.

He spots a gnarly piece of driftwood leaning in a corner and remembers when he was only five years old finding it on the beach and giving it to his mother. She saved it saying it was beautiful. A flood of pent up emotion is unleashed and he tears up. Josh looks out the door toward the house; he doesn't want to be seen crying. Aunt Maggie and Uncle Chuck are still sitting on the terrace. He picks out two matching oars with brass oarlocks and quickly makes his way over to the beach. His eyes are blurry, he hurries to shove off before anyone notices, and wants to comfort him. The last thing that he wants is someone telling him *it's alright*, or *let it all out.* What he wants is to be left alone.

The aluminum boat is above the high tide line, a fuzzy weatherworn rope ties it to a rusty iron pipe set deep into the beach gravel; probably his grandfathers work. Josh works on the knotted loop, it hasn't been untied for a long time, turning it over and pushing on it, he quickly gives up, and lifts the loop over the top of the pipe the way it was intended. Flipping the twelve foot boat right side up is a two handed affair but he manages it with ease. Fiddler crabs scatter, disturbed before their normal high tide foraging foray.

Josh half carries, half slides the lightweight dinghy down the steep beach. He pauses for a second at the water's edge to snap the life vest buckles, and knowing that Charlie and Maggie are watching and waiting for any clue they might be needed, he gives them a quick look and wave, but mostly he wants to assure they stay put and not rush down to the beach. Thankfully, they are still in their chairs and too far away to see him still tearing up.

He was a little boy when he learned to row a boat, but never was able to handle the adult size oars, however he did learn what was required, and now a decade later, he effortlessly pulls the oars in long deliberate sweeps. Each powerful stroke propels him farther from embarrassing condolences and well-meaning words. In seconds, the middle of the cove becomes his refuge where he is alone and secure with his thoughts.

The water is fifteen feet deep and clear as an aquarium, except for his own rowing disturbance, the water surface is flat as a pancake. Bottom creatures and the occasional fish, parade just for him. He stops rowing and watches the underwater scenery unfold while he drifts over his personal gallery of nature's artwork. Glancing at the moving shore only fifty feet away, he becomes aware of the slight current. It has pulled him back, to where he started. Josh resumes rowing, intent on following the curving shoreline all the way around to the narrow entrance.

He remembers being afraid of the big waves in the mile wide channel outside his grandfather's cove. Today the water out in the channel is not the beast of his childhood, instead it is enticing and welcoming, prompting him to keep rowing.

"Expect building waves in the morning, highs 60, lows 40," he mimics a typical weather forecast, his mood greatly improved.

To the left is the *Grand resort* where Sammie lives and works. Maybe tomorrow he thinks, remembering her long ringlets, tan face and sparkling blue eyes. She is probably in the middle of a reunion with her stepmother right now or already hard at chores, she never mentioned her dad, he must live there too, that would explain why she leaves her mother to live with her step mom that she doesn't like. He wonders if her mom is married again. He thinks about his dad, wondering if he will he get married again. If he married Sammie's mom, she would be his sister.

To the right Josh will have to row against the current, and not too far is Rock Island. The shoreline beyond Pearson Cove is dotted with little bays, sandy beaches and vacation cabins hidden in the trees. He turns to the right and puts his back into the job; soon he is around the corner out of sight. Rowing hard, he is captain of the skiff, and owns the ocean. He quickly masters what he learned years earlier, but wasn't big enough to handle. Pulling hard one of the oars creaks almost breaking, years of weathering have weakened the once stout wood. Josh backs off, breaking an oar will make rowing difficult, but not impossible, he knows the current will carry him back, but with only one oar he would paddle in circles.

Like most rowboats, he sits backward and must keep looking over his shoulder to see where he is going. Facing backward also allows him to judge how far he has rowed; soon the cove is hard to see blending with the shoreline, but the point, a quarter mile beyond where Sammie's resort is, sticks out like a sore thumb.

While watching he sees a lone kayaker, its silhouette shoots out from shore. It's Sammie, he sees long hair, *who else could it be?.* For a second he considers turning around, but doesn't want to explain any red eyes. He needs to stay alone with his thoughts, so he puts his back into another long stroke when snap. The oar has broken clean off, right at the oarlock.

Oh crap, the first thing I do is break Uncle Charlie's oar. I'll have to get a new one. Using the remaining oar like a canoe paddle he awkwardly makes it over to the floating broken tip and fishes it out of the water. The current drags him backward toward Pearson Cove. He paddles, but the single oar only spins him, turning him in circles. Josh learns very fast that a rowboat is almost useless without two oars; He screams out in frustration that he can't make it go in a straight line. Eventually he gives up paddling and is satisfied to let the current bring him home.

The lone kayaker is headed his way and closing fast. Josh is sure it's Sammie and there's no doubt she's a pro. Her long deep strokes are picture perfect; each effort propels her slim kayak two-boat lengths. She streaks past Pearson Cove intent on catching up to Josh.

"Hi Sammie, I hoped it was you. Boy you sure look great. I mean your paddling looks great. Oh geez that didn't come out right. You look great too."

"Thanks Josh, I know what you mean, where's your other oar, when I saw you take off from the cove you were really moving."

"It's right here," he holds up the broken blade, "I guess I pulled too hard, do you know how I can get another?"

"Sure, get on the ferry and go back to Anacortes, there is a chandlery supply store there, or you can order it online, UPS delivers here every day. You know that's not your fault, oars shouldn't break, let me see it?"

The kayak and rowboat drift side-by-side, each of them with one hand on the others boat. They are facing each other and sitting in the boats closer to each other than when they were on the ferry. Josh hands her the broken blade, and while Sammie studies it, he studies her. She seems different now, more natural. On the ferry she was a smart ass, a pretty face putting on a show, now she is just herself, a likable confident and competent self. He notices right away that she has traded her windbreaker for a bathing suit, but she is covered up with her life vest, her smooth legs disappear into the kayak. Her hair is pulled back and tied with a sea shell and band, she has pearl ear studs, he smells perfume, and her cheeks seem softer, less wind burned. Josh crosses a line when he leans slightly forward for a better view.

"Stop it," she says with a sideways glance at him.

"What."

"You're staring at me."

"No I'm not." He says meekly, like a little boy caught sneaking a peek.

"Liar—look—see this," Sammie shoves her trimmed and polished fingernail into the soft wood, "You shouldn't be able to do this. The wood is old and rotten, and see this line here? It's been broken before and glued back together." What Josh see's is nine manicured nails, glistening polish and perfect fingers. "You're staring at me again."

" Sorrrry—I saw your broken nail, is that such a crime?"

"No, but if you don't quit looking at me and pay attention," pointing behind Josh, "you're going to drift right by the cove, and then I will have to tow you in."

"Oh my gosh, the current is strong." He gets busy paddling fast with the one oar; otherwise, he will still be answering Sammie's pointed accusations. Accusations she is happy to make because she is enjoying, making him squirm, and thrilled that he is checking her out. She tosses the broken oar into the open rowboat and shoves her kayak clear of Josh's splashing flaying oar. He stands up in the boat to get a better angle and immediately loses his balance, dropping to his knees to keep from going over the side.

"Nice recovery city boy, let's race." She unleashes a flurry of powerful strokes and flies into the cove where she drops a tip and spins the kayak sideways to better watch him struggle with the single oar.

Uncle Chuck watches from the terrace and eventually makes his way down to the floating dock.

"Hi Sammie, welcome back," says Charlie, "are you here for the summer?"

"Hi Charlie, yeah, I came in this afternoon and met Josh on the ferry. He's doing pretty good with only one oar." They both watch, as Josh floats the final distance in the smooth water.

"That's my fault Josh, those oars are rotten, I should have warned you to take it easy on them. Bring the boat over here, I'll take care of it, do you want to grab a kayak, it looks like Sammie needs a paddling buddy?"

"If it's ok with you, that would be great."

The two of them clear the cove and are back offshore in a few minutes, they head into the same current that brought the disabled rowboat back only this time Josh is chasing after Sammie. No longer dwelling on himself or sad memories, he is lost in the moment, and right now, his only interest is in keeping up with the pretty girl effortlessly leading him in a friendly chase. Josh paddles furiously and gains on her only to find he can't keep a straight line. He is veering off to the side, losing control and spinning around, wasting energy getting back on track. Sammie paces herself staying close but playing with him.

Thinking of him sneaking peeks of her earlier brings a smile to her and makes her look herself over. Earlier when she unpacked in front of the mirror, fixing herself up, and putting on some scent, she hoped to run into him kayaking. She lifts her fingers for inspection, and then follows her legs until they disappear in the kayak.

Sammie takes two or three strokes and rests, then glances over her shoulder at his progress and paddles some more. Unlike Josh, she is comfortable and in her element, and she can keep at it all day, and the next. They travel along the shore for half a mile staying out of the main current and the few boats that ply Orcas Passage.

"Hey," says Josh, "let's take a rest."

"What's wrong tired?" Sammie pulls next to Josh resting her paddle across both boats, holding them steady.

"No," he lies, but his grin and panting betrays him. "I'm doing fine, do you have any water?"

"Yeah right here," she flashes him back a happy smile, and hands him a sport bottle. "You are doing pretty well for never having been in a kayak before; I mean a real one, not a virtual one."

"Thanks, why do I have a hard time keeping it going straight. You look like you're hardly working and you're going straight as an arrow."

She is happy, and grinning again, he has asked her for help; Josh is saying all the right things, he respects her ability and isn't hung up on being bettered by a girl.

"You are almost able to keep up with me Josh, and that's pretty good, except I'm taking it easy on you. Once you learn a few strokes and master them you will have better control and be able to steer somewhat, but you will never catch me in that boat."

"Why not." He snaps, his competitive side suddenly coming to life.

"Simple, my boat is built for speed and long distance; yours is built for crashing into rocks and maneuverability. This one has a keel and foot controlled rudder, plus it's a lot lighter than yours."

"Here's the water, let's go," says Josh ready to prove himself.

"Hold on, remember what I said earlier about keeping the paddle centered for balance, most people capsize when they are just resting like we are doing right now, they forget they're in a kayak and over they go. Watch me dip my paddle, see the angle, now watch again, the higher the angle the closer you can stroke and move forward. With a lower angle, the stroke turns you, which is wasted effort if you don't want to turn."

Josh just received a thirty-second paddling lesson, but in the last ten minutes, what he has learned most is that he likes hanging with her.

"That's the park right up there isn't it, let's go." He doesn't wait for an answer, and takes off with strong strokes, turning back and forth, he leads the way. Sammie gets the challenge, but instead of racing off, she takes her time adjusting her seating position and drinking some water. She lets Josh get way ahead of her before finally taking her first few gentle strokes. She accelerates and then settles into a steady rhythm, her kayak slices through the water and she effortlessly matches Josh's speed following his erratic course. He is frantically paddling as fast as he can, throwing water in all directions including all over himself. She's cracking up watching the show.

About halfway to the island Josh slows down thinking his macho effort has sealed the race. Sammie allows herself to close the gap just a little but holds back about a hundred feet. She sees Josh glance back at her, and she makes sure he sees her paddling and not coasting. The approaching island has a small cove with a dock, and a steep gravel beach. Once inside the cove, Sammie stretches out reaching forward doubling her stroke length, rapidly catching up to Josh. The next time he checks she is right on his tail about to overtake him. To keep the lead he puts all he has left into it, but Sammie takes some coasting strokes so she doesn't pass him.

Josh is first to the beach and slides straight up the pebbly gravel lifting the kayaks bow. He realizes his mistake when the boat rolls; he drops his paddle and is dumped protesting into the three inch deep water beside the half-beached boat. Sammie stops short and with a little sideways curtsey lets her momentum take her to the beach. She carefully uses her paddle to push her kayak until it grounds out, and then she nimbly steps onto dry beach—pretty and picture perfect.

While Josh struggles, wet and with sandy gravel clinging to him, she reaches down and picks up her kayak, and carries it above the high water mark in the driftwood. Josh is panting hard, more than half-soaked standing in the water, his paddle is floating nearby.

"You're getting it," coaches Sammie, "but don't throw your paddle
like that, use it to keep upright.

"Very funny."

"No!—I'm not being funny, if you would have hung onto the paddle, and shoved it down into the gravel, you wouldn't be dripping wet right now. Come on let's hike the shore trail."

Chapter 5 – Proposal Rock

When Sammie releases the buckles opening the front of her life vest, Josh panics, he looks away, but not before she sees him watching while she pulls on a tee-shirt top. They toss their life vests into the kayaks and scramble over driftwood up to the trail.

"According to family legend, or Aunt Maggie, my father proposed to my mother somewhere here on this island."

"Really, that's so romantic," says Sammie, "do you know where?"

"No."

"You should ask your dad, is he around, can you text him?"

"He's in Europe, working on a project."

"Is that why you're staying with Maggie and Charley"

"Yeah, I guess so, we didn't really discuss it, with my mom gone he and Uncle Chuck just decided and told me.

Josh's text:
''Hey dad, I'm here hiking on Rock Island, where did you propose to mom?

Ray's text, two minutes later:
"On the rock on top."
"Ok, thanks, btw I broke Uncle Chucks oar. bye."

"Well, what did he say?" Asks Sammie, getting anxious, crowding next to him trying to read the screen.

"He says on the rock on top."

"I know where that is, it' a big boulder at the highest point on the island, it's a glacier erratic that rode in on an ice sheet during the ice age a billion years ago. We can hike up there in twenty minutes."

"Let's go then."

They follow the shore trail, dodging drop offs and climbing over down trees, soon a trail branches off, climbing steeply up the bank. They gain a surprising amount of elevation in a short distance. Josh sets a pace Sammie struggles to match. Part way, they end up stopping in an open level spot to catch their breath and share some water.

"I know what you're doing," says Sammie.

"I don't know what you mean."

"No seriously, if you want to race to the top, fine, game on." She finishes her drink," screws the cap on, yells, "thirsty—go get it," and tosses the half-full water bottle over the edge of the trail where it skids to a stop thirty feet below them. She tears up the trail in full sprint mode leaving Josh scampering down through loose rock while she disappears up the hill.

"Hey, that's not fair," But she's gone, out of sight. Josh recovers the bottle and bounds up the trail after her. Two steep switchbacks later he runs into an open area and finds Sammie stopped at a lookout. She is standing with her back to him watching a pair of eagles ride thermals.

He pulls up beside her, opening the water bottle before he takes the last step. Sweat beads run off his face in the late-day sun and he catches breaths in pants while he gulps down his first of the water.

"I've waited long enough,' says Sammie, "let's go." She takes off at a dead run again.

"Wait, hold up, I don't want to race, your right, I was pushing you." He hands her the bottle hoping she doesn't launch it off the cliff.

"Eagles mate for life," says Sammie, "those two have a big nest over on top of that snag. They ride updrafts thousands of feet up and soar for miles, never flapping their wings. They can snatch a fish out of the water without getting wet. "

The view out over the water is spectacular. They can't see around the corner back to *Pearson Cove* or the *Grand Resort*, but they can see out into Haro Strait and beyond to Canada. In the strait, they see sailboats, their big colorful spinnaker sails flying like kites high above them.

"The suns getting low, let's keep going," says Sammie. Sandy will call the Coast Guard."

"You can text her." Josh holds out his phone.

"No, she won't really, she doesn't care, but she'll get upset if I'm late for work in the morning."

"Really—she doesn't care? I'll bet she cares, she just doesn't show it."

"You haven't met her, what do you know; your dad shipped you off to live with relatives too." Sammie abruptly heads up the trail.

"Look, I'm sorry; I didn't mean to say anything bad." He follows her up the trail in silence. A few minutes later, they have walked several hundred feet, mostly up, and reach the summit. The top is an open grassy flat area, that would make a great backyard picnic site. The summit rolls over in all directions, so it is obviously the top. There are a few trees scattered around partially obstructing the view but the trees give the area a distinct sense of privacy.

"There it is," says Sammie, proudly pointing to a big glacier erratic. It's the size of a small car, and looks totally foreign and out of place, as if a helicopter delivered it to the top of the island for some kind of funny joke. There are no other rocks in view and the ones down on the beach and along the shore are sandstone and much smaller. This boulder is solid granite and came from Montana claims Sammie.

"One our guests knew all about these glacier erratic rocks and said the whole San Juan's area is covered with them and it's true, when we head back you can see little ones scattered along the shore, but none are sitting on the very top of an island. He said, a billion years ago when the sea was higher or the land was lower, a big floating iceberg with this rock riding on it had to run aground right here and then melt away leaving this boulder behind, how cool is that?"

Josh listens to Sammie's geology lesson, but mostly he is intent on climbing on top of the eggish shaped boulder. Finally, he gets on top and sits. Sammie backs up, and then runs up the side in two steps plunking herself down next to him. Side-by-side, almost touching they stare out over Haro Strait.

"I wonder if this is where they were," says Sammie, "sitting here like we are." She leans into him touching shoulders.

"What?" *Oh geez, not again. What—I may as well have said Duh.*

"You know, the proposal."

"OH— ah, I don't know, I guess I could ask him, but wouldn't that be prying."

"No, it would be romantic." Josh stares, Sammie Stares, his heart rate increases and he flushes, he is sure he's about to say something dumb, if he can even speak. The sun is moving toward the horizon, but on top of Rock Island, except for budding teenage chemistry there is no movement. Then, Josh is saved, when out in Haro Strait an orca breaches, and then another.

"Did you see that," Josh yells and points, "some whales jumped."

"I saw it; look at the others, there must be ten more."

"There he goes again, this is awesome. Do they come into this area?"

"Why—are you afraid? All we have are kayaks."

"No . . . well yes, I guess, it's smart to be afraid, those are *killer whales* right."

"They're orcas, just like we saw from the ferry, and yes they come in here, but usually they stay out in the big straits."

"Where are they going?" asks Josh, ever more impressed at Sammie's knowledge.

"They circle the San Juan's, they follow the tides feeding during incoming upwelling currents. They eat fish and seals, but mostly fat salmon. They live here, just like us. Some are fifty or eighty years or older."

"How do you know all this?"

"I've been reading about them, and going to the whale museum in Friday Harbor, I think I may go into marine biology."

"That's way cool."

"They talk to each other; they have their own language using clicks and whistles. They even remember people's faces and voices, they also hold grudges, and have been known to get revenge."

"You mean like in Moby-Dick."

"I think that was the other way around, what I meant is, they get revenge on one another. Apparently it's not all laughs and good times in the pod."

"They're way cool, says Josh. "I don't see them anymore, we should head back anyway." He jumps off the rock, and then turns offering her a hand. Their palms come together in a high five, fingers lock and fold over. Trusting him, she jumps. Both kids are keenly aware this is the first time that they have touched intentionally. She lands lightly facing him; his other hand goes to her waist steadying her, her free hand lands on his shoulder. They are facing each other in front of proposal rock. Her eyes and perfume capture his senses. They are close enough to kiss. The setting sun warms him, his face heats up, he looks into her eyes.

Josh lets go first and looks away relieved. He doesn't see her smile fade, turning to pouting lips.

The hike back down to the beached boats takes mere minutes; they jog most of the way. Josh detours and leads her out on the floating dock.

"Why didn't we come in here, then I wouldn't have gotten wet."

"The beach is easier if you do it right," she pokes him in the ribs laughing, "try it sometime, you will see."

The paddle back is over much too quick; the current whisks them along, while they float next to each other talking the entire way. The setting sun reflects off cabin windows hidden in the forest. The afternoon thermals have cooled and quit. Noisy gulls line the beaches and float with them hoping for a handout. By the time they get back, they have shared secrets and deep feelings cementing their friendship.

"Let's have a beach fire tomorrow." Says Sammie, before she peels away at the cove.

"Sure," says Josh, "where?" Having only seconds to make plans before the current pulls her away.

"Anywhere, text me." Josh waves his ok. Sammie waves too.

Chapter 6 - S'mores

"Good Morning Josh, are you hungry," Says Maggie, "I'm making pancakes."

"I can eat, if you have enough, hi Charlie."

"Hey Josh, if we don't have enough we can make some more, how do you like the presidential suite?"

"It's ok, sure a lot more room than I have at home, I slept really well, I guess I was tired."

"This place does that to you."

"Do you have any plans for today?" asks Maggie, "we could drive around and check out the island, drive up to the top of Mt Constitution or something.

"Not really, except Sammie asked me to a beach fire."

"When?" asks Maggie.

"I don't know, I'll ask her."

Text message: I had fun yesterday, when do you want to do the fire.

Text from Sammie: "Me too, I have to help Sandy today, sorry."

Josh's text reply: "Maybe later."

"Well, I guess the beach fire is off, she has to help Sandy, so I'm ready whenever you want to go."

"How about around lunchtime, I'll make sandwiches and we can eat when we are hungry."

Riding three across in the rattling old pickup, is no fun. Maybe if they were his mother and father and he was ten years younger, it would be fun, but uncle Chuck and aunt Maggie filled the bench seat leaving little left over. Luckily, he got shotgun and hung out the window. The grand tour as Charley called it went pretty well and was mildly entertaining, but mostly he listened to Charley talk about when he and his dad were kids growing up. He found out that *Pearson Lodge* is owned by his dad and Charley equally, which means, in a way it is half his. Charley and Maggie are supposed to keep the place up and pay a small rent to his dad in exchange for living there. The house is okay, but everything else is falling apart.

The afternoon went by fast. He didn't think much about home, or his mom and dad. Sammie was another thing, he thought about her a lot and how he almost kissed her on top of Rock Island. He was making plans, hoping to have an evening campfire and hang with her.

"Can we stop by the store; I want to buy some marshmallows." Says Josh, when they circle back through town.

"Of course," says Maggie, "I think we have some at the house, but they are probably hard and stuck together."

When they get home, Charlie spots the delivery on the porch right away. It's hard not to recognize the distinctive shapes from across the yard.

"What the heck, someone left some oars by the door." Prompting everyone to look towards the house.

"I saw the Anacortes delivery van on the road, he must have just dropped them off." Says Maggie.

Josh is first to pick up one of the new oars.

"These are nice, feel how light and strong this is," handing it to Charlie.

"Your right, the shipping label says Pearson boys, Pearson Cove, Orcas Island."

"This one says the same thing," adds Maggie. "I wonder where they came from."

"Well they came from the Anacortes Chandlery, it's their sticker, and it was their van we passed.

"I mean who sent them?"

"It was dad," says Josh, "I texted him from Rock Island yesterday and mentioned I broke an oar, he must have ordered them."

"That's amazing," says Charley, "there's half a day's time difference, it must have been the middle of the night when he got your text, and then he got a hold of the boat store when they opened this morning our time, in order to get them here now."

"I didn't think about the time, I probably woke him up."

"I glued that broken oar last night," says Charlie. "Boy this baby is strong, you're not going to break one of these Josh; the skiffs oar lock will break off first."

"What time do you think it is over there where my dad is?" says Josh after he types out—*"Thanks dad, the oars are perfect."*

"Oh, I suppose about midnight or so." Says Charlie.

Josh pushes send, *sorry dad, get used to it, you're all I've got.* Next he types into his phone *Sam,* and Sammie appears before he gets the m entered, in the message area he enters, *"What's up, I got some marshmallows,"* and pushes send.

Sammie texts back twenty seconds later, *"I've got a fire pit, come over in about an hour."*

He enters, *"Ok."* and hits send. *Oh my gosh, she's inviting me over, I wonder if her mom and dad will be there, I better dress nice. I wish she would've said let's meet at the cove or out on the water. I'll wear long pants and shoes, but first get a shower. I wonder why she said about an hour.*

"I just told Josh Pearson to come over in an hour," Sammie says to Sandy, "were going to burn marshmallows over the fire pit if that's ok with you."

"That's fine, I want to meet him, there's some guests coming in sometime later this afternoon, so they may join you around the fire."

"Ok, but don't interrogate him, he's really nervous, I don't want you to scare him away, there's no one around here my age."

"I don't interrogate, why's he so nervous?"

"See!" says Sammie, "he's shy, just don't ask him any questions."

"Ok, ok, I'll try to behave, but your dad should be back by then, he may ask him something, you know, like, how's your day going Josh?"

"That's ok, just don't ask about his mother or dad or something nosey."

"You like him don't you," says Sandy. "That's why you want to protect him from the evil stepmom."

"NO, I just don't see any reason to be mean to him. Yes, I do like him, I guess, or his marshmallows.

"What did you say."

Laughing, "I told you, were roasting marshmallows and he's bringing them, what did you think?"

"Nothing." Says Sandy

"I'll tell dad what you were thinking."

"Go ahead, and I'll tell Josh what you said, and he can talk to your dad about it, and then your dad will chase him away."

"Ok, you win. I'm going to go find the roasting forks and get them cleaned up."

"Clean up all of them sweetie, if it's not too much trouble, would you please."

"Sure that's what I'm here for."

Josh stands in front of Maggie and Charlie. "Well, what do you think?"

"Wow you cleaned up really well, Sammie won't recognize you," says Maggie.

"You look good Josh, but what's the occasion?" asks Charlie.

"No real occasion, were just going to sit around a fire and eat marshmallows, and I thought I should clean up. What's Sammie's stepmom like?"

"Oh--now the truth comes out, you're cleaning up because you're meeting her parents. Don't worry, they don't bite, you will do just fine."

"Just be yourself, but don't spit or swear." Adds Charlie.

"Ok, I'll try to remember, don't spit or swear—thanks see ya later."

"Have fun Josh," says Charlie, "hey, why don't you take a flashlight from the drawer by the fridge, that woods trail can get dark after sunset."

Josh picks out a working led flashlight and goes out the side door. He could take the gravel path straight ahead that disappears into the woods; instead, he turns down the flagstone path toward the dock and makes his way along the shore toward the *Islander Resort.* Following the shoreline is longer, harder and uses up more time. A glimmer of red in a flotsam pile catches his eye, so he stops to investigate and pulls out a perfectly good crabbing float, its tether still attached. The next pile offers up a perfectly good stick, so he ties the float on to it. In spite of dragging his feet, he ends up at Sammie's. Dawdling is not tiring but he takes a deep breath for courage, and then trudges forward.

Unlike *Pearson Lodge*, the *Islander Resort* is modern and much newer, not much over fifty if it's a day. Sammie's stepmom *Sandy* runs the struggling business, employing locals to help with endless chores. The open beamed main building has soaring two story, tinted windows facing the ocean. Overnight guests are treated to stunning views while protected from the bite of stormy weather. The lodge sits on a craggy outcrop jutting out from the mostly flat shore. The low-lying point interrupts flowing currents, forcing tidal waters into dangerous tide rips, and confused back eddies that push winter driftwood high onto the rocky shore. *Sandy's* oversized bed and breakfast is complete with paved parking areas, and small sleeping cabins dotting spacious manicured grounds. Guests enjoy upscale barbecue's, buffet meals and rustic beach fires.

He makes his way down the beach and scrambles over a big driftwood log below the lodge. Sammie is on the upper terrace organizing the brick fire pit.

"Hey Sammie, I made it."

"Hey Josh, I'm glad you thought of a marshmallow roast."

"The fire was your idea, I just got the marshmallows."

"I've got hot dog forks, firewood, matches, what else?"

"Can we have a fire down on the beach; we can sit on that log?"

"Sure, why don't you drag some rocks into a circle, I'll bring down the kindling."

Josh quickly arranges a small circle of ten-inch round rocks and then picks out a scrappy looking piece of dry driftwood. He opens up his pocketknife and using the blade sideways scrapes off a softball size pile of fuzz. Sammie sets down an armload of kindling and then while holding some newspaper watches the knife flash in Josh's hand. In moments he hands her a healthy handful of dry tinder. Next he picks a small piece of kindling the size of a hammer and sniffing the straight grain pronounces it to be cedar, he then slices long thin shavings as if peeling a carrot until the entire end of the stick looks like a bristly scrub brush. He does the bristle brush treatment to several kindling pieces.

"I've got some paper and matches to get it started." Says Sammie being helpful.

"Oh good, I can use them; you can help me down here." He crouches down next to the rock ring and places three pieces of wood next to a rock where it's shielded from the slight breeze.

"Ok, put the ball of shavings on top of those pieces and squish it down with some of those sliced up sticks, leaving them on top."

"Like this?" asks Sammie.

"That's great, now move back a little and don't freak on me, it's gonna be bright."

Next, Josh scrapes the back of his knife blade along the length of a three-inch flint. The single strike creates an eruption of fiery sparks; in one smooth practiced motion, he flicks the fire starter sparks into the ball of tinder igniting it, in short order the cedar is in flames, and Josh is carefully arranging some larger pieces of wood to grow the fire.

Until now, he has concentrated on doing the fire, and has not looked at Sammie, but he senses she is staring him and not the fire.

"You're staring at me, I can tell."

"No I'm not, you're paranoid."

"Now you're the one lying." Josh looks her in the face confidently for the first time since they have met. Sammie can't hold herself, she breaks into her mile wide grin returning his look. She is excited, she is seeing him in a new light.

"I'll take that paper now," extending his hand. He lays half the paper on the ground and kneels on it protecting his clean pants, with the other half he fans the flames, supercharging them into an inferno.

"That's why you needed the paper, to kneel on it?"

"Well sure, and to fan the flames, what did you think I was going to do, read it?"

"You're funny." Says Sammie, and she kneels on the paper next to him, their knees touching, their arms and shoulders touching. Josh smells her perfume it's the same as she had on yesterday.

"You have the same perfume on." *Notice her perfume, that's good.*

"I know, I put it on every day. I like it, don't you?"

"It's ok I guess." *I guess, oh jeez.* "No, I mean I like it, it makes you smell good. No wait, I didn't mean that, I mean it makes you smell better. I'm sorry, you don't smell bad."

"It's ok Josh, I know what you mean." She nudges his shoulder. "It looks like you are going to meet my parents."

He looks up from the fire, a little relieved he won't be botching another quick witted compliment, instead, maybe he can insult her mother and father.

Sammie looks up too, Sam and Sandy have been watching quietly from the top of the stairs, being acknowledged is an invitation to join in.

"Hey, that was quite a trick," says Sandy, I've never seen anyone light a fire that way except on TV. Sam heads down the steps followed by Sandy. Josh is very aware that he and Sammie are touching shoulders, or even leaning against one another. He thinks he may be too near Sam's daughter, so he suddenly stands causing Sammie to lose her balance almost falling over.

"Oops, I'm sorry." He moves towards her hand outstretched but then backs away and waits for her father.

"You must be Josh, this is Sandy and I'm Sammie's dad, Sam. That was an impressive piece of fire building; it looks like you've done that before."

Sadie charges down the steps barking and greets Josh by jumping on him leaving sand on his pants, and then she tears across the beach and back before sitting when Sammie tells her to sit.

Josh faces the approaching parents, Sandy extends her hand first.

"Thank you," says Josh, but it was Sammie that got together the dry cedar kindling. All I did was scrape up a little tinder."

"Your being modest Josh, I saw how you threw the spark, the first time, that wasn't beginners luck."

"Well thanks; you noticed I threw it, most people don't realize you can throw the spark right into the tinder, it's about the only way to light a fire in the wind." He hands the fire starter to Sam.

"This is magnesium," says Sam hefting the fire starter and examining its mahogany trimmed edge, "and well used, you've done this a bunch, but you used shavings just now instead of magnesium scrapings, how come?" Sam, turns the flint block over several times and reads the inscription on the side. *For my Eagle – Mom*

"I don't like dulling my knife shaving the magnesium, it's super hot, but burns up in a hurry. If it's wet, sometimes you have no choice. Mostly, all those cut marks are from when people borrow it for practice. I don't mind if they use their own knife. I mostly just use the flint."

"You're a scout?" Josh glances at Sammie like his darkest secret was just discovered, and he is waiting for her reaction.

"Hi Dad—over here." She waves four fingers in the air getting his attention."

"Hi Honey," says Sam, "thanks Josh." Sam turns giving Sammie his full attention, she is nearly as tall as her dad, when they embrace, she throws her arms around his neck and hangs from him like a little girl. She leans her head on his shoulder, and lowers her long eyelashes after making sure Sandy is watching.

"I brought the forks you set out on the table Sammie." Says Sandy. "It's nice to meet you Josh, please say hello to Maggie and Charlie. Come on Sam, you can throw sparks some other time, and there's only enough roasting forks for the two of them."

Sammie hangs on about three seconds beyond comfortable, and then pecks her dad on the cheek before letting go. She takes the roasting forks from Sandy with a minimal thank you, and hands one to

Josh. Sam and Sandy crunch across the gravel beach and retreat back up the stairs, leaving the kids alone with their campfire and Sadie.

The two of them sit on the big log, it blocks the wind and makes a place to set things and sit.

"You dad seems nice," says Josh, "too bad he couldn't stay; he acted like he wanted to hang-out."

"He's just a big older kid, you impressed him lighting the fire, and you impressed me." Sammie stares at the fire, Josh is staring at Sammie, both are silent for a moment and a little uncomfortable in their mutual admiration. Sammie breaks the spell, and looks at Josh, for a few moments their eyes meet, but his confidence wanes and he looks away at the fire.

"Lighting a fire is easy," he says, "but only if you have the right materials, and don't rush the steps. I try to test myself and not use paper so I stay in practice. You never know when it may come in handy, plus it's a way to show off and impress people." He sneaks a peek at her.

"Well it worked."

Josh rearranges the fire exposing cooking coals for the marshmallows. Sammie pokes at the fire with her fork causing more sparks to erupt.

"Do you like S'mores?" says, Sammie.

"Who doesn't like chocolate and graham crackers?" *Finally something right, and perfect timing too.* He hands her the paper bag he has been lugging around. "Maggie sent this for you."

Sammie unfolds the crisply folded sack and looks inside.

"Oh, I don't believe it, s'mores, she is so sweet."

ORCA BOY

Chapter 7 - Pepper

Sammie is first spearing a marshmallow, and she sticks it right into the flames so it catches fire, but Josh blows it out in seconds.

"Hey!—what did you do that for?" yells Sammie.

"It was on fire."

"I lit it on fire on purpose." Says Sammie patiently, as if her knight in shining armor has just saved her, except she didn't want saving, but he's still her knight after all.

"Why do you want it to burn?"

"So I can pull the outside off, eat it, and then do it again."

"But it's burned, and charcoal is bad for you—here, let me make you one." He carefully works his roasting fork over the hot coals staying clear of the flames. Deftly, he rotates the marshmallow turning it a light brown, the surface begins to swell with bubbly soft insides. It takes about 30 seconds before he presents Sammie with a perfectly toasted marshmallow.

"Pull that off," he says, "I'll have the next layer ready in sec." *This is so cool, I'm cooking for her.*

"Thank you," says Sammie, before stuffing the sugary treat into her mouth. She watches Josh repeat the toasting, but she is looking at him, not the fire. He intently watches the next layer turn brown, but he's fully aware that Sammie is looking at him.

"You're staring at me again." He says without glancing up. "If you think you can distract me into burning this, it won't work." *Oh man I'm going to burn this.*

"I am not staring, but I can distract you if I want." She slides over until their legs touch, she leans toward him and lightly blows in his ear. The marshmallow bursts into flames, but he lets it burn awhile before putting it out. "See," I made you burn it."

He scoots over enough to turn to her and says, "No you didn't, I made it your way." He holds up the charred ember on a fork. "Hungry?"

Sadie is lying next to the log, dog napping, but she raises her head and barks her standard all in one, *woof woof* announcement, and hello greeting.

"Be quiet Sadie, these aren't for you, and I don't want to be cleaning marshmallow out of your fur." She lays her head on her paws, and whimpers, her eyes focused offshore.

"Woof, woof." Sadie stands and takes a step toward the water. "Woof woof."

"What is it Sadie, what do you see?" Says Sammie. She and Josh scan the water, but don't see anything. Sadie keeps barking and Sammie moves over to stand behind her trying to see where her dog is looking.

"There's nothing out there Sadie, it's your doggy imagination." Sadie quiets, and sits in the gravel watching anyway. Josh has tossed the ruined marshmallow in the fire and started a new one; soon he has a perfectly toasted marshmallow sandwiched between two grammys with a piece of Hershey bar.

"Look, this one is perfection, no wrinkles, and it has a non sticky cover, plus a hidden surprise." He hands her a s'more, "Compliments of Maggie."

Sadie barks again, only this time, she lets out a long string of woofs, and jumps to her feet. Sammie and Josh both look in time to see the spout.

"It's an orca ," says Sammie, pointing. "You were right Sadie." She bends down to pet Sadie and reassure her that everything is Ok.

"What's it doing here, I thought you said they stay out of the inside waters.

"Well they do, most of the time, but we're right on the edge, and they don't have rules or anything. Maybe it's following some yummy school of fish. Look its spouting again, you can see its moving left to right, its coming this way, probably just to clear the point here."

"How do you know it's an orca , aren't there other whales out there."

"Well, I can't be sure unless it gets close enough to see it, or it breaches, but we have orcas that live here year around, and its spout looks like an orca spout. Other species are supposed to look different, but I've never seen any whales except orcas and the ones on Nat. TV."

"We could jump in a kayak a paddle out there." Says Josh.

"Are you serious, I thought you were afraid of them."

"I am, but you said they don't eat people."

"Well it's a bad idea, they don't have to eat you, they can squish or drown you, besides, it's against the law."

"I was just kidding, look there's two spouts, this is so cool, we have killer whales in our back yard."

Ever since Sadie first barked bringing attention to the orcas, she has been whimpering and watching, now she is pacing back and forth along the water's edge, looking out at the whales, whimpering and barking. Every so often, she barks and then jumps up to see better. The whales are at least a quarter mile away, and if they hear her barking, they will stay away. It doesn't take very long for them to make their way around the point. Sadie stays alert and on guard, watching and listening.

"We still have light for a few more hours, do you want to hike down the shore trail," asks Josh.

"Sure, which way do you want to go?" Sammie was hoping to hang with Josh, going Inside with Sandy and her dad is boring.

"I would kind of like to go back towards the cove, and maybe see the orcas again, that's the way they went, we can hike as far as we want and then come back on the road."

At the foot of the stairs is a red painted bucket hanging from a rusty hook. Josh fills it half full of seawater from a tide-pool and then dribbles it on the burning logs. Steam rises from the fire pit making a mini cloud enveloping them. Hissing and popping sounds come from the rocks as the water boils cooling them. Suddenly a loud bang precedes breaking rocks as thermal shock rips apart one of the smaller stones that was under the fire.

"Let's go Sadie, this isn't safe." Sammie stands and Sadie charges off the way the orcas went.

"Don't you want to tell Sandy or your dad." Asks Josh

"I don't need to ask permission for everything I do."

'I don't mean ask permission, I mean let someone know where you are, you know in case something comes up."

"Like what?"

"You know, like an earthquake or tsunami or something." Sammie rolls her eyes and exhales loudly, but agrees with Josh, and then dashes up the stairs with Sadie bounding behind her. She's back in about one minute, and with two water bottles.

"That was quick." Says Josh.

"I met Sandy on the path, she was on the way down with these," she toss's Josh a water bottle, "let's go."

Sadie leads the way, running down the beach, and then sprinting back to see what the slow down is. Sammie and Josh take their time; they carefully make their way, talking and picking at things. The beach trail winds its way into the forest with drops back to the beach, but mostly stays above the high water mark left by storms.

Josh digs around in a driftwood pile he passed by earlier and pulls out a strong lightweight stick to use poking at stuff and as a hiking staff. He uses the new stick like an extra hand. Helping Sammie, he braces himself in a good spot and holds the stick for her to hang from, lowering her down a steep section.

With four real legs and boundless energy, Sadie runs up and down the steep banks as if they are her personal stairs. She discovers a perfect stick and drops it at Sammie's feet, using her nose she shoves it against Sammie's toes until she throws it.

Last winter's storms have turned, churned and washed up flotsam to checkout. Sammie reaches into a shallow pool and moves a flat rock to see what's under it. Tiny little fish and hermit crabs scatter as she sorts through some small rocks, and then she brings up several agates. She holds the translucent gemstones up to the sun looking for interesting inclusions, and then shows them to Josh before slipping them into her pocket.

Josh pokes his stick into a curious suspect pile of seaweed, plastic, and wads of fishing line, and then he uncovers a broken piece of Styrofoam.

"Probably part of an ice chest someone tossed overboard or left on a beach," says Sammie, "people are such asses, fish and whales and seals eat all this crap, beer cans too. I've seen sport fisherman toss sacks of garbage over the side of their beautiful spotless million dollar boats. This stuff doesn't go away, what doesn't sink collects in tangled messes and floats around forever. I've read that out in the middle of the Pacific are drifting islands of floating garbage that stretch hundreds of miles."

Sadie has momentarily left her stick on the beach, and is wading in two inches of water, watching and whining, staring out beyond the point.

"Look at how concerned Sadie is," says Josh, "I bet she hears something we can't hear."

"Or smells something," says Sammie.

"Maybe those killer whales are still out there somewhere, let's work our way out, and take a look."

The falling tide has exposed a shelf that extends out hundreds of feet from the high water shoreline. Walking is easy but they slip and slide on the green seaweed with every step they take. Josh probes suspicious spots with his stick looking for hidden pools, Sammie forges ahead and steps in hole after hole, sometimes up to her knees. Sadie seems to be able to spot high spots and runs over the entire area.

"Sometimes our guests get a real surprise out here," says Sammie, they come out at low tide in their long pants and $200 running shoes, and don't realize how fast the water comes back in. They get busy looking in a pool full of sea life, and the water comes in behind them, cutting them off from shore. They end up wading through a foot of water and then falling in the pools we are avoiding. *Laughing.* When they get back to the lodge they are soaked, sometimes totally head to toe. The great part is that they are thrilled that they survived a dangerous ordeal."

"Dangerous," says Josh, "give me a break. What's dangerous is being one of these little animals we are stepping on as we walk around out here. If they don't get squished by people at low tide they eat each other at high tide. Urchins, anemones, barnacles, and a whole bunch of crawly little things make this their homes.

"You're compassionate for tidelands," says Sammie.

"It was my mother's passion; I just think we should give little things a break."

Stopped by deep water at the furthest point out, they can see the mouth of Pearson's Cove about a quarter mile or less farther on. While they watch, a whale spouts off the coves entrance. Sadie barks several times, and lowers her head onto her outstretched front legs like she is pulling back a slingshot ready to fire. She whines and carry's on like the whale is stealing her stick or refusing to throw it as fast as she brings it back. Her bark is not fearful, or like her territory is being invaded. She's not growling that low snarly growl dogs do when a strange dog trespasses. Her bark is more of a welcome to my yard, let's play kind of bark. Pearson's Cove is clearly part of her yard and she needs to get over there ASAP.

Sammie gives her permission saying, "Go Sadie." She takes off on a mission; she bounds back across the drying seaweed beds, and streaks up the crumbly scree slope leading into the woods and the trail.

"Wow, look at her go, we better get over there," says Josh, "You don't think she would go out on the dock and jump in do you."

"I don't know, she's just barely not a puppy anymore, and more eager than smart. She's not stupid, but she likes the water, she'll jump in to get a stick. We need to hurry, I should have told her to stay with us."

It only takes them five minutes to get back to the beach and climb the bank, and then another two or three for them to jog the trail to Pearson Cove. They don't pause where the trail forks up to Josh's house and head straight out the dilapidated gangplank and on to the dock. Sadie is pacing and barking out on the very end of the floating walkway. She doesn't quiet down until Sammie rubs her neck assuring her that it's ok. The three of them watch out in the water, only fifty feet from them hovers motionless a full size Killer Whale. *An orca.* Beside it is a juvenile orca, only one-third its length and a fraction the weight.

"Oh my god," says Sammie, "look at that," she rubs Sadie's neck more for her own reassurance than Sadie's. "Look at the black and white markings, look how clean and bright they are."

"This is absolutely fantastic, that's a momma and her baby," says Josh —"right?"

"Yeah, I think so," says Sammie, "they're supposed to stay together for several years, the babies are eight feet long at birth. That one looks close to ten feet."

"But they live in family pods and stay around here their entire lives, so that means there are more nearby."

"Maybe, but nearby may mean on the other side of the island, or. . ."

Without any warning, both whales spout, causing Josh to nearly jump off the dock, first the mom, lets out an explosive exhale, followed a second later by the little one. The juveniles little spout is over before the mom's giant exhale really gets going. A big cloud of moist momma killer whale breath shoots up and hangs in the air, and then dissipates into droplets that drift over the float and rains on them.

"Oh jeez," says Josh, "I just about jumped out of my skin, and—oh crap—we just got sneezed on—that's whale snot falling on us." Sadie barks her approval.

"Ewe," says Sammie, "stinky bad breath too, of course you like it, don't you Sadie." Sadie lays down on the dock, her head resting on her paws, she whimpers and whines, never taking her eyes off the orcas.

Up in the main house, Charley and Maggie have been watching from the big picture window in the old lodges great room. Sadie's arrival and barking caught their attention. They watched the whales spout and saw the spray drift over the kids. Maggie grabs her camera, she and Charley head out the door for the dock.

The big whale is resting, still and motionless on the surface, but the little one is in constant motion, swinging its long flipper fins like a swimmer treading water. It sinks below the surface and then with one stroke, it brings itself back up.

"Look," says Sammie pointing, "there's something hanging under the little one, look there," kneeling down, "see it? Oh my god, there's a rope wrapped over her back, its dug into her skin, see it? It's black like her back, but you can see it where it crosses the white on her side."

"I see it, I see it," says Josh, and then, "how do you know it's a her?"

"Cause Sadie says so," Sammie's weird glance at him suggests he has more to learn.

"That must be why she keeps swimming for the surface, she's all tangled up in some weighted net. If she quits swimming she will drown."

"Who will drown," says Charley, when he and Maggie reach the end of the float.

"The little one," says Sammie, it's wrapped in a net and has to swim just to breathe."

"I see it," says Charley, "that looks like part of a drift net, under water they are darn near invisible, poor baby just swam right into it. They outlawed them in our waters, but outside our territory anything goes. Dishonest or unscrupulous fisherman will cut loose damaged pieces they don't want, or entire nets to keep from getting caught. Then they drift around for years trapping and killing. That baby is lucky he's still alive, thousands of seals, dolphins, and porpoises die every year.

"Well not this one," says Josh matter-of-factly, "I'm going out there and cut it off." He abruptly turns and walks down the dock towards the gear shed.

"You can't go out there," says Maggie, "do something Charlie, do something right now."

"Wait a sec Josh, that's crazy talk," says Charley, catching up to Josh.

"The only thing crazy, is not helping her."

"Okay, think about it first, what are you going to do?" says Charlie.

"I don't know, just paddle out there and if she will let me get close, I'll just start cutting, and go from there."

"That's exactly what your crazy dad would say and do if he was here, and I would be helping him, just like I'm going to help you.

"Thanks Uncle Charlie, any ideas?"

"Yeah, we need life vests, sharp knives, some rope, and a long boat hook."

"What's the rope for?"

"Don't know yet, but you always need rope around water and boats, right?"

"Yeah, dumb question, I guess. Do you think this is safe, I mean really?"

"I think it's scary, I don't know if it's safe. You don't have to do this Josh."

"Yes I do." *Mom would want me to try.*

Maggie, Sammie and Sadie maintain their vigil at the end of the dock; the orcas slowly drift with the current inside the cove, the little one treading water, its mother a flipper fin width away. Josh and Charlie shove off in the aluminum skiff; Josh has tossed his hiking stick in with the new oars, ropes and a long pole with a bent blunt hook on the end. Josh rows, Charley looks at the orcas, and avoids Maggie's icy stare, but he still hears her voicing her displeasure.

"You were supposed to talk him out of it, are you crazy too?" says Maggie. "Turn around right now, you don't know what you're doing. You can call somebody; it's not your job."

"Just take a picture and relax, we'll be fine," says Charley quietly across fifty feet of cold killer whale filled water.

"Josh—" whispers Charley, "I think you should row over to their left so both of them can see us approach and go slow, we don't want to spook them."

The mother orca does scare Josh, extra deep concern too. Her all encompassing, yet calm relaxed presence fills the cove

ORCA BOY

The water is calm, the normal seagull racket has taken a break. Sammie sits cross-legged on the dock with Sadie's head in her lap. They watch in silence. The world outside Pearson Cove is on hold.

Chapter 8 – Orca hoist

present time

After cutting away the loose net and weights from Pepper, Josh is still faced with wire cable imbedded in her flesh.

"She's not sinking anymore," says Charley, "but that wire has to be cut. If Pepper and her mommy will let us move her over to the hoist slip, we can try to get at it with a cable cutter. That is—If they will let us."

"We have to do something; it's worth a try, any ideas how to get Pepper over there?"

"Use the rope," says Charley, "toss one end to Sammie and have her tie it fast to the floating dock."

Josh's intuition tells him to ask big momma for permission, but all he has at his disposal is a long skinny stick, two oars, a hunk of rope, and a little aluminum boat. So far, he has been touching, scratching and talking to the big orca occasionally, now he does it in earnest.

"Hey momma, please don't get upset, if you can read my mind, now would be a good time. Use your esp. you people have esp. right? How about a good rubbing on these barnacles here. You would rather not have them right?" Josh is sure that Pepper enjoyed being scratched in front of her dorsal fin but big momma is so big, he can't reach the middle of her back without shoving Pepper away or climbing out of the boat and standing on her. Still soaking wet, the thought causes him to shudder and then he shivers for the first time since falling in.

"I'm gonna give these barnacles some rough scraping, let me know if it hurts? You're listening right? You got your esp on?" He spends five minutes giving momma whale personal attention. Charley uses the boat hook, and holds them steady and strokes Pepper while

45

Josh reaches over her and scratches momma. Pepper continues soothing whistle sounds, but momma is quiet. Suddenly she lifts her tail out of the water causing them to freeze, no one moves or speaks. A small wave rocks them as it rolls across the cove. From deep inside momma orca , they feel and hear her exhale and sigh. She slowly lowers her tail leaving only a faint ripple. Josh and Charley breath again, Sadie whimpers.

The orcas deep breaths are regular and stink. Thankfully, there have not been any more explosive spouts. Josh is running on adrenalin, he trembles and his voice quivers, but his instinct to help overcomes his fear.

"Okay big momma, it's time to give it a try," and he raps her extra hard. "Wake up and pay attention, we don't want any sudden surprises, like you knocking me into the water again." Josh gently pulls on the rope Sammie tied to the dock, moving the boat. Using the boat hook pole Charley hangs onto a piece of net that's still attached to Pepper and holds tight. Pepper weighs nearly half a ton, but she is easy to pull slowly through the water. Josh keeps steady tension on the line, Charley hangs on to Pepper and they all move away from big momma.

"It's okay, momma, don't do anything crazy. Read my mind, use that esp. we're just moving over here a little bit. You can come too if you want, just keep calm, ok momma, chill. Do you use that term?"

Handling the rope and the stick together, Josh manages to give Pepper a few more dorsal fin scratches when they are about halfway to the dock, and is rewarded with an immediate drawn out whistle, a pleasure sound she has repeated many times. Hearing the whistle reassures Josh and Charlie but, as Charley was so thoughtful to point out earlier, *separating a mother from her child, whether it is a bear cub, or killer whale, goes against nature.*

"So far so good," says Charley, "I think we should turn her around and pull her tail first into the lift slip, she may panic if it looks like a cage, which it does. Your grandpa built this lift to raise rental boats for making easy bottom repairs; I'll bet he never figured an orca would use it one day."

Charley climbs out of the dinghy onto the floating dock and loosely ties the rope letting the boat with Josh in it, and Pepper, float free. Momma drifted or swam, no one noticed, but she is further away near the mouth of the cove. Josh looks over at the adult killer whale and notices she has turned around. Her other side is badly scarred. On her side, behind her white eye-patch, is a row of sharply curved scars, evidence of her being cut by a boats slashing propellers.

"Look at momma," says Josh, "she's all cut up." Maggie snaps some images, zooming in on the scars. As the rowboat, and Pepper come near them, Maggie, Sammie and Sadie movefurther down the dock keeping a comfortable distance so as not to alarm Pepper. Sadie's barking may be enough to cause her to suddenly thrash around, warned Charley. Sammie has her by the collar, but Sadie only whimpers her concern. Charley cranks the old winch handle lowering the cradle until it is about three feet below the surface.

"Okay Josh, it's up to you now." Charley stands back to watch.

It's been an amazing experience for everyone. Josh is making it up as he goes and so far, he's got it right. He is still wet from the earlier dunking so it's not surprising when he climbs out of the boat and stands waist deep on the submerged cradle. With his stick, he pushes Pepper, turning her around. The excess weight is gone so she floats like a space walking astronaut, except in her world, she breathes the air. Josh has poked, prodded, and scratched Pepper so much that she is ok with him pulling on her tail and dorsal fin. He very carefully guides her into the lift slip next to him. Pepper is facing out toward where momma was last seen, but her mother has slipped beneath the surface.

"Okay Charley, raise it up just a little bit at a time." Says Josh.

With each crank of the handle, the boat cradle rises a little, it pushes upward on Peppers belly lifting her partially out of the water; with each ratchet click her blubbery sides squeeze out a little more, until a section the wire cable is exposed in front of one fin.

"That's it, perfect—hold it right there," Says Josh, "hand me the cable cutter." He hooks the curved jaw and pulls the handles together. The sharp jaws, and long handles do the job perfectly, and he cuts the first of two cables encircling her body. He hesitates before pulling the handles for the last cut, she may violently react when the pressure is released, and he will be pinned, unable to jump clear.

"Are you thinking what I'm thinking Pepper? You need to hold still." He slowly squeezes until he feels the cable sever. "Got it Pepper girl, we're almost done." Next, he very slowly pulls the loose ends out of Peppers flesh. "I'm sorry Pepper, this must really hurt. You and your mom are being very brave. Where is momma anyway?" When the cable is halfway removed, he stops to get a better grip. He flexes his cold fingers forcing them to function and then strokes his bare hand along the white patch above her eye. Pepper whistles quietly, only it's a new sound, one she hasn't made until now. It's unmistakable, so quiet, like a purr, Josh feels a rumbling with his hands, and through his leg jammed against her side. *I guess you're telling me you're ok.*

He considers finishing the job with a sudden yank; the way people wax their legs, jerk out a baby tooth, or remove a band-aid, except no one really enjoys the process, why would an orca be any different. He continues talking to Pepper while he gently pulls the embedded wire rope from her flesh.

"That's it, young lady, your free; the rest is up to you and momma. You can lower the lift now," says Josh, "I think you should crank it down until Pepper is floating free on her own, but leave it up enough to support her on the surface, that way she can leave or rest. For all we know she may need to sleep for a month."

Sammie and Maggie have been creeping closer as Josh pulled off the last of the cable. When Josh climbs onto the float, they converge next to him. Sadie sniffs his dripping legs, then turns to Pepper, and gives her a couple welcome barks. Before Sammie can clamp her muzzle, she lies down with her paws hanging over the edge of the wood decking and stares eye to eye with Pepper. Sadie acts as if she wants to play with her new friend, but settles for watching, whining, and whimpering.

Josh has been preoccupied with helping Pepper, but now watches from the dock. Sammie throws her arms around him just like she did to her dad earlier, and plants a kiss on his cheek.

"You are an absolutely crazy hero," Says Sammie, while hugging him, "you saved her life—ewe, and you're all wet." and then she pushes away from him because water is soaking through her clothes. "How did you know what to do, weren't you afraid?"

"I don't know, I just did what seemed right, and talked to her, I think we connected somehow. Isn't that right Pepper, we speak the same language." All of a sudden, Josh shivers a huge uncontrollable whole body shake. "You're freezing." Says Maggie, "You should go put on some dry clothes."

"I guess all the excitement has kept me warm, but I'm sure shaking now, you guys keep Pepper and her mom company, I'll be right back."

As if on cue, momma lets loose with a big noisy spout, the spray hangs in the air, but fortunately drifts away from them. They all direct their attention to her, in time to see her lift a fin, and then ease it back under water. Sadie jumps to her feet, and barks once while giving a big tail wag. Sammie hushes her and she resumes her vigil, whining her concern. She lies on the dock only feet from Pepper, their eyes watching each other.

Chapter 9 - Friends

Josh bounds back down the trail from the house; he has traded wet shorts, wet tee shirt, numb toes and sandals for long pants, warm hiking boots, and a windbreaker. He half walks half sprints down the gangplank. Loose dock boards flop up and down announcing his return.

"Do you think they have some sort of friendship?" says Maggie.

"Maybe," says Sammie, "but I'm inclined to think they are more like little kids and are just interested in playing with each other."

"Does anyone see my stick?" is the first thing Josh says when he gets back to the slip. Has Pepper moved or done anything?"

"It's right there," says Sammie pointing behind a raised brace, Charley said you would want it when you get back." Josh retrieves his hiking staff and sits cross-legged next to Sadie; Sammie sits on the other side and leans into Josh.

"Hi Pepper", says Josh, picking up his one-way conversation. "Did you miss me? How's the back? Any new pain? Have you got to know Sadie? She led us to you and your mom." Josh raps the dock gently, hitting the stick where Pepper sees it. "I don't want to scare you." He bangs the stick hard two times, then bangs it two more times. Next, he reaches out, and gently rubs the end of the stick on her back in front of her dorsal fin. Then, he switches to hard scratching the area he knows she enjoys. Pepper whistles her new whistle. Sadie whimpers.

"Listen to her," exclaims Sammie, "this is so cool, she loves it."

"I hope she likes it, because if this bothers her, she should be about ready to flip out. Sorry Pepper, I didn't mean to make a flipper joke." Josh taps Pepper a few times, and then hands the stick to Sammie. When Sammie touches her, Pepper flinches and strokes her fin as if to swim away.

"Whoa there Pepper, I'm your friend too." Says Sammie, she lifts the stick and hands it back to Josh. "I guess she was watching, and only trusts you."

"Well I've got enough pictures," says Maggie, "I'm going to catch up with Charley and head for the house, this is enough excitement for today. See you later Sammie, say Hi to your folks for me."

"Ok, I will Maggie, and thanks for sending Josh with the s'mores, I know that was your idea."

Sammie turns to Josh, he has resumed rubbing and caressing Pepper, but then he lays the stick on the dock and fishes out of his pocket a package of graham crackers, and a Hershey bar, Sammie takes the bar, opens it and hands Josh a section of chocolate, she gives Sadie a cracker. They contemplate the killer whale in front of them; momma hasn't been seen since they moved Pepper over to the dock. Pepper has made no effort to leave the cradle, her breathing is slow, and calm, almost relaxing, as if she is catnapping. Her blue eye is open, her green eye is closed but neither indicates she's awake or asleep. Sadie yawns and half yelps aloud that she is bored. With her head on her paws, she dozes.

ORCA BOY

Chapter 10 - Winthorp the 3rd

Watching an orca sleep and listening to her breathe may seem exciting at first, but it gets old.

"It's getting dark, Sadie and I should go home," says Sammie.
"I'll walk down the path with you."
"You don't have to, I'm fine, and Sadie's with me. Let's do another campfire sometime; maybe you can rescue a bald eagle. Come on Sadie." Sammie walks down the dock heading for home with Sadie reluctantly following.

Noticing both eye are open and her watching, Josh says, "It's just me and you now Pepper." He lightly strokes her back with the stick. The sounds of the day have subsided, it's quiet in the cove. She responds to his touch with a barely audible purring whistle.

"That's my girl." *I don't have any problem saying the right words to a killer whale, an orca ,that may not even be a girl for all I know.* "It's okay Pepper, if you turn out to be a boy, I'll still be here for you. Speaking of support, where is your momma?"

Pepper has made no effort to leave the supporting lift cradle, and Josh has not considered abandoning his new friend, he sits with her in silence, their conversation decidedly still very one sided, although her occasional purring whistle is undoubtedly her communicating her appreciation of his comforting strokes.

"Do you think he's ok?" asks Maggie, watching from the great room window as the last fleeting light leaves the cove.
"Yes he's just fine, that orca and Sammie are just what he needs." Says Charley. "Josh has started his life over without his mom.

If you think about it, Pepper and Sammie are pretty much his whole world now, were just Aunt Maggie and Uncle Charley."

"It's getting cold out there, I'm taking him a blanket and something to eat." Says Maggie.

"How's your patient Josh?" says Maggie as she arrives out on the floating dock.

"I don't know, she hasn't made any attempt to swim away, and she keeps purring, I think she must be resting, or waiting for momma to come back."

"I brought you some snacks, and hot cocoa, a flashlight and a blanket."

"Thank you Aunt Maggie, I don't know how long I'm going to stay out here, but Pepper needs a friend right now, and momma whale isn't around.

"Ok, Charlie and I are up at the house if you need anything."

The Summer sun rises early, and at 5 am, finds a shivering Josh Pearson still on the dock. Wrapping up in the blanket and his coat helped make the night bearable, if he could stay awake. But each time he fell asleep he would topple over and curl up on the dock, dampness from the cold water only a foot below him permeated his clothing and his dreams making for an uncomfortable miserable night. When he warmed enough for his wits to return and brain function became normal he looked into the slip expecting to see Pepper, but the lift cradle is empty. Where the killer whale had been is a torn apart seal carcass. The only identifiable part is the mangled head and some ribbons of blubber trailing in the water. Josh uses his stick to push the mess off the cradle where it sinks to the bottom to become a crab buffet. He is thrilled that Pepper apparently was strong enough to swim away, but if she left behind a severed seal head as some kind of parting gift, then they weren't communicating yesterday as well as he thought. Maybe it's for Sadie, except Sammie won't be pleased with that ugly scenario either.

Josh gets to his feet keeping the blanket wrapped around him. He finishes off the last of Maggie's cheese and cracker snacks while peering out of the cove into the main channel beyond. No boats are out yet, it's still too early, for all but the most devoted fisherman. He finds himself scanning the water for spouts; he watches one area at a time, slowly extending his view across the open water to the island on the far side. All the time he is watching miles of offshore water, he is ignoring his own cove, and what has surfaced only ten feet behind him.

The spout catches him by surprise; again, he nearly jumps out of his skin, but manages to stay on the dock. He grabs at his chest and spins around in time to get sprayed.

"Jesus Christ Pepper, you nearly scared me to death, can't you at least let out a little warning whistle or something, maybe a click, to let me know you're sneaking up on me, or did you snot me on purpose? I'll figure it was an accident this time." Pepper swims forward until her belly is partly on the cradle, exactly where the seal head had been minutes earlier. "Look, I'm sorry for accusing you, if you want that gnarly head, it's on the bottom with the little fishes and crabs." Facing the other direction than when Josh removed the cable, Pepper is floating with the rear of her body under water, her dorsal fin, blow hole and eyes are all that are showing unless she arches, raising her head. Josh and the orca make eye-to-eye contact. Her green eye is open wide and conveys as much feeling to Josh as yesterdays purring chirps and whistles did.

"Well girl, do you remember yesterday, or have you blocked it out. Let's see if this stick does anything for you." He sits cross legged on the floating dock only feet from Peppers head. Their eyes watch each other. He reaches the stick to the base of her dorsal fin and scratches her back, she responds with the low purr sound that he hoped she would, but also lifts her tail clear of the water and arches her back forcing the creaky lift to support her. He can feel the vibration through the wood and see ripples surround her in the water.

"Oh man, you really do like this, don't you?" He scratches extra hard with two foot strokes like he is petting a really long dog with a garden rake that has only one tine.

While resting between scratches, Pepper whistles a short burst, but it's different this time, almost a trill like chirp, she raises her snout above the water as if she is looking or listening. Josh scratches some more but she doesn't purr. She chirps again.

"What is it Pepper?" says Josh. "Am I doing it wrong?" Then he hears it.

"Woof, woof," it's Sadie Barking, as she bounds from the woods. Sadie tears down the trail and turns onto the rickety dock boards, her claws keeping her from skidding over the edge. She sounds like ten people running on piles of loose lumber.

"Slow down Sadie," holding up his hand, "you're going to crash and burn and scare Pepper." Sadie comes to a halt before running off the dock, she's nose to nose with Pepper; she barks right in her face. Pepper returns the greeting with a string of clicks Josh has not heard before.

"Ok, I get it, you two have better hearing than humans, well I've got news for both of you, everyone knows dogs and whales have superior hearing, but what I didn't know, was that you two apparently understand each other, or do you, huh?" Pepper whistles once. "I don't believe you, and besides Pepper, you're not really a whale, like Moby dick or something, you're just a big dolphin. Oh that was mean, look, I'm sorry I said it that way, being a dolphin is not bad, that's good, dolphins are cool, remember Flipper? Everyone loved Flipper, and Kieko, and Tk, Shamu, them too. Right Sadie? orcas are cool.

Where 's Sammie, Sadie? Does she know you're here?" Sadie trots off, and then sprints when she spots her stick. She drops the stick next to Josh's hand, and then using her nose, shoves it onto his fingers. Josh dries the back of his slobber covered hand on his shorts, and then toss's the stick down the dock. Sadie's back with it in seconds for a repeat.

Josh's cell phone vibrates in his pocket, it's a text from Sammie. *Have you seen Sadie, she ran down the path, is Pepper ok."*

He texts back. *Sadie is here with me, and Pepper. What are you doing?*

I'll be there in a minute. Texts Sammie.

—Ten minutes later—

"Sadie, there you are," says Sammie from behind Josh, "I figured you would be here."

Sammie has silently arrived by kayak. She and a resort guest have paddled into the cove. "Is Pepper still here?" asks Sammie.

"There she is, right in her own bed, she was out swimming around while I was sleeping, but she swam back in by herself while I stood her watching. We have been chatting for an hour."

"You've been talking with a killer whale?" questions Sammie's guest.

"Josh," says Sammie, "This is Winthorp Chesterfield, he's staying at the resort."

"The 3rd," says Winthorp, "Winthorp Chesterfield the 3rd."

"How do you do." says Josh, "I'm glad to meet you,"

"I'm sure you are, I do quite well, thank you. So, pray tell, what does your whale say when it speaks to you?" says Winthorp.

"She whistles, chirps, clicks and purr's"

"Purrs huh—like a cat—Is that what you expect us to believe."

"No," says Josh "—she purrs like an orca ." *I don't care what you believe!*

"We should get going," says Sammie, making eye contact with Josh, for an instant, she tilts her head, sending an unspoken message. "Can Sadie stay with you and Pepper while we paddle to Rock Island?"

"Yeah Sadie is fine with me, but I can't speak for this killer whale, she'll have to do that herself." Josh looks at Winthorp as he says it, and then strokes Pepper in front of her dorsal fin, and above her eye patch, it's very quiet out on the float, Josh waits for Pepper's response. A thirty second pause is broken by Winthorp's snickering smile and subtle—I thought so—nod telling it all. Pepper remains silent for the first time. *Thanks Pepper, nice to know I can count on you.....not!*

"Ok, this way to Rock Island." Sammie digs in with a long pull, she hits the next stroke in stride and leaves the cove behind. Josh suspected she had been holding back when he paddled with her before; watching Sammie streak away leaves no doubt, he was right. A satisfied smile creeps across his face when he looks at Winthorp's keel-less rock-basher guest kayak, just like the slow boat he had been using two days earlier. *You'll never beat me in that kayak, had been Sammie's words.*

"You better get going Winthorp," says Josh, "she's fast, and you don't want to get left behind out there with the really big killer whales on the loose."

"Don't you worry yourself about me—*Orca Boy*. I'm captain of the WU rowing team and president of my frat, I know how to move fast and I always get what I want. Right now I have a Summer-fox to nail." With that, Winthrop spins the kayak, and a flurry of splashing strokes sends him on his way. *You'll have to do better than that Winnie.*

Sadie stands, and then barks once at Pepper while lowering her head over the edge of the dock, her tail wags pull her rear half back and forth. She pays no attention to the kayaks departure, she has another agenda that is more important. With her nose, she shoves her stick over the edge of the float into the water next to Pepper and excitedly barks several more times, her tail still wagging her. Using his hiking staff, Josh fishes the stick to the edge where he can reach it and then tosses it down the dock. Sadie is after it while it's still in the air. She brings it back and drops it over the edge to Pepper again.

"Hey Sadie, quit dropping it in the water if you expect me to throw it for you." Josh takes a running start and attempts to heave Sadie's stick across the water all the way to the gravel beach, but he comes up short as the stick plunks into the water fifteen feet from shore. Sadie hesitates, she saw the splash and sees ripples circle out in all directions, her inclination is to jump in and swim directly to her stick, but she holds back. She whines and lays her head on her paws. "Come on Sadie, I'll show you how, be back in a minute Pepper." Josh heads down the float towards shore, but Sadie has it figured out, and runs past him in a blur, she jumps to the beach, gravel flying from her feet. She runs into ankle deep water and stops. The bottom drops away, and she will be swimming, but the stick is bobbing only ten feet from her.

"Go get it Sadie, jump, jump." Yells Josh. Its' all the encouragement she needs, she launches herself straight out, and makes it halfway to the stick before splashing down, tail still wagging. She dog paddles the remaining feet, clomps down on the stick, and turns around. "Bring it here girl." Sadie drops the stick at Josh's feet, and as he stoops to pick it up she shakes. "Hey, stop that." But its' impossible for her to stop once she starts. First she head rotates, and then the rest of her follows until the shake ends with her right leg, her sopping tail slaps against Josh's leg and she's ready for Josh to toss the stick again.

"Here we go Sadie." He brings his arm back to toss the stick down the beach, and she anticipates the throw sprinting away before he lets go. This time, the stick lands a little further out than before, and Sadie hits the water running; in seconds she is paddling in deep water. When she still has ten feet to go a dorsal fin knifes through the water, Pepper has beat Sadie to the stick and flicks her snout under it, sending it spiraling through the air where it lands on the beach. "All right Pepper," yells Josh. The stick has sailed right over Sadie's head, she turns, still in hot pursuit and scrambles after it.

"Charley," says Maggie, after clicking another picture and pointing out the big picture window, "you should see this. Josh is down there throwing Sadie's stick. I just watched Pepper steal the stick and toss it on shore. They're all playing. Watch."

Josh throws the stick again, only this time he makes sure it lands on the beach. Sadie is a streak of sunshine dripping rain drops, she's racing a killer whale and turns on the afterburners. She nabs the stick while making her turn and is halfway back before slowing. Pepper watches. The next throw is out in the water towards Pepper, she strokes her powerful fins one time and has the tiny stick clamped in her huge mouth before Sadie gets past knee deep water. With her tail wagging yanking her back half sideways, she lowers her head and barks non-stop at Pepper.

Pepper swims with the stick poking from her mouth only feet from shore. Sadie runs alongside barking. After fifty feet of dog and whale chasing, Pepper spits out the stick and using her snout again flips it toward shore, only this time she muffs it and the stick ends up floating between them. Sadie dashes into the water and nabs the stick. In an instant she is sprinting back to Josh with the trophy.

Josh's next toss is meant for Sadie, he makes sure it lands on the beach where she can race to it. Pepper follows the action and creeps into water barely deep enough for her to float.

Looking around in the endless driftwood higher up on shore, Josh spots a four feet long orca size stick, of course, Sadie wants it for her own. Using both hands and spinning like a discus thrower, Josh heaves the mini log over Pepper's head. Pepper reacts like the youngster she is, and with total abandon launches after the stick. Her pec fins and tail splash water in all directions, her thrashing body sends a wave rolling onto the gravel beach.

She chomps on the the stick crosswise in her mouth as she lunges forward. Then using a trick copied from adult killer whales hunting seals, she rises straight up, half out of the water letting the stick go in the air, and catching it again before she circles back to shore. Finally, after whistling her excitement, she lets go of the stick in the shallows, and using her pec fin, bats it into the air. Ten gallons of salt water fly towards Josh, the stick lands on the gravel at his feet.

"Hey, watch it, you're as bad as Sadie," yells Josh as he jumps backwards avoiding another bathing.

"I got one with the stick in the air," says Maggie, still at the window, "Look at these Charley, you can see the sun rays, and there's Sadie barking, Josh is getting splashed. These are fantastic pictures, we can sell these."

"Get ready," says Charley, "Josh is about to heave that log again."

His next spinning throw sends the whale size stick down the beach into six inches of water, Pepper and Sadie race for it, but Pepper can't get to it, and stays in deep water, whistling and watching, while Sadie struggles barely able to drag the oversize stick. The next toss is straight out into deep water; Pepper swings around, watching the stick splash beyond her. Sadie runs and long jumps into the water, she makes it almost to Pepper and keeps on paddling after the orca . Pepper takes the stick by one end and turns around face to face with Sadie who instantly chomps onto the end of the stick. Both animals are going opposite directions but a dog, even a big dog is no match for a killer whale, and Sadie is pushed backwards towards shore.

"Get this, get this shot; yells Charley, an orca and a dog fighting over a stick,"

"They're playing," corrects Maggie.

"You know what I mean, keep shooting, Josh is going to love these pictures."

Pepper pushes Sadie and the stick, backward into shallow water where Sadie finds her footing, she let's go of the stick and barks non-stop for Pepper to throw the stick. Pepper also lets go, when she grounds out on the gravel. It's a -strange animal friends- stand off; the stick floats between them, each one expecting the other to pick it up and throw it.

"Sadie hush, you two are sad." Says Josh. Using his hiking stick, he fishes the big stick to shore and repeats his spinning track toss, heaving the dripping orca stick again as far as he can. Sadie can't wait, and anticipates the throw again, she is back in the water before Josh let's go. Pepper gets the stick and is back in a flash, forcing Sadie to turn around.

When Sadie walks out of the water this time, she is panting, gagging and barking so much she is choking.

"Time to quit Sadie," says Josh, "you're having more fun than you can handle, and throwing this log is killing me."

Josh leaves the two new best friends to stare at each other and disappears inside the gear shed for a minute. And then he heads back to the floating dock where he tosses his stick, a short rope and an old float into the aluminum skiff and shoves off. Soon he is rowing towards shore where Sadie is wading in a foot of water nosing the big stick out to Pepper. When the boat is twenty feet from Pepper, she strokes her pec fins pulling her away. She keeps a safe distance and eyes him.

"It's ok Pepper, It's just me in the boat." Josh rests the oars and using his stick, he bangs on an oar two times, pauses, and then two more bangs in rapid succession. "Remember this beat, two raps, pause and two raps, ok? That's our signal." He pauses and then repeats it a few times before resuming rowing towards shore. Sadie has moved down the beach staying near Pepper. Josh pulls the abandoned whale stick out of the water and lays it across the boat, and then paddles out into deeper water. He smacks the stick four times—clack clack – clack clack—mimicking the beat. Taking the short piece of rope, he ties it to one end of the stick and then fashions a loop on the other end, and then remembering that loops in a cable net are what got Pepper in trouble he unties the loop and in its place ties the foam crab pot float. The bright orange float is the size of a small soccer ball and built to be indestructible. Next he makes a show of splashing the log into the water and hooks the five foot rope and float to a cleat on the boat.

"What's he doing," says Maggie.

"Can't you tell," says Charley, "he's making a pull toy for an orca and a Lab. Now he's going to teach a Killer Whale how to play, our nephew is a whale trainer."

Josh slowly rows and glides closer to Pepper dragging the stick and float in the water, talking all the time, reassuring her. Sadie threatens to swim out to them, but stays in ankle deep water, whining and the occasional—*hey, what about me bark.* When he is within reach, Josh uses his stick and scratches in front of her dorsal fin. Soon he is floating alongside Pepper, much like they spent the night at the boat cradle. Her rumbling purr is special, only josh can hear and feel it through the water and the thin metal boat. The rowboat is several feet longer than Pepper, but with only a foot between them, if she decided to lift a pec fin, Josh would be in the water in a heartbeat. He strokes her eye patch, the orca   vibration intensifies.

"You know Pepper, you may have some sort of mental connection or esp with Sadie," says Josh, "but I don't have any idea what you're thinking. I know you and I are friends, I think that's pretty obvious. I wish we could talk." Josh smacks his stick lightly on her back- whap whap, - whap whap. He repeats the two thuds, pause, two thuds message a half dozen times.

"That's all I got to say." He puts the stick in the boat. Pepper responds with a whistle. "Yeah, right back atcha." Using his hand, Josh pushes away from Pepper, he floats about six feet to one side, and then dangles the whale stick with the float on a rope in front of her.

"See this Pepper, I made it for you to play with." He holds the rope by the float and twirls the stick over his head a few times and then lets it fly about twenty five feet. Sadie goes berserk on shore, barking and dashing back and forth, but they are way too far out in the bay for her to swim out. All she can do is bark and get excited. Pepper swims up to the floating line and plastic float, she rubs her snout on the floating bobber the same way a dog would sniff a strange new toy. She leaves it alone and circles, her dorsal fin is the only indication she is in the cove. Josh places the oars in the water, and pulls for the dock; he ties the rowboat in the slip next to the boat cradle where Pepper spent the night. Sadie races from the beach out on to the dock to be with her orca friend and Josh, but Pepper keeps her distance.

Voices out in the channel cause Josh to look up, just as Sammie and her resort guest, Winthorp come around the point, heading for the cove. They are resting side by side, talking and laughing, letting the current do the work.

"Look who's back," says Josh to Sadie, "It's Sammie and the disbeliever." As if on cue, Pepper submerges and she stays under, her dorsal fin no longer a giveaway. Sadie whines her concerned answer, but then settles down on the dock resting her head on her paws waiting for something to happen.

"I don't see Pepper," says Sammie when they get near enough so yelling is not required.

"She was here playing with Sadie, chasing that stick out there, until a minute ago, when I tied that float to it she quit, and went under water somewhere. You should have seen them. Sadie and Pepper both had the stick and Pepper pushed her backwards, but then Sadie swam right back out, as if she was going to take the stick away. It was awesome. They did it a bunch."

"Surely you don't mean that big chunk over there with the orange float," says Winthorp.

"Yeah, I tossed and she brought it back, except when Sadie got to it first in shallow water. I took it away because Sadie was too excited and kept gagging."

Sadie stands and crowds the edge of the float when she hears her name. She leans out like she's going to jump in the kayak on top of Sammie .

"Stay there Sadie, oh yuck, look at you?" says Sammie, "you're a wet mess." After getting a good look at her sopping fur parted down the middle, with sandy gravel and bits of seaweed clinging to her legs and underbelly. "You need to be washed."

"I'll do it," says Josh. "I'll clean her up and bring her home."

"You don't mind, really?

"Really."

"Ok, you can hose her off, but I'll bring a towel and come and get her in about an hour, I have some things to do for Sandy first."

"See ya orca boy," says Winthorp, "maybe you'll become known as the *whale whisperer* of the San Juans." Winthorp looks at Josh when Sammie's head is turned, he smirks, his comment is meant as a joke, but he's making fun of Josh.

"Yeah, sure, that sounds great," says Josh, smirking back, "maybe you will be able to brag to your frat friends over a beer that you met me and Pepper. You can tell them how cool and brave you were around a killer whale. " *Pompous jerk, is what you are Winthorp!*

"Oh, that reminds me," says Sammie. "We saw a large pod of orcas out in the strait. I'll bet Peppers mom is out there."

"Could be, I didn't tell you, there was a seal head in the boat cradle with Pepper when I woke up this morning."

"Maybe momma whale brought her food. Was Pepper still backed into the cradle?"

"Seal-a-meal," jokes Winthorp.

Josh ignores the semi-crude remark, "You're right, she couldn't back herself in. Momma had to deliver a dead seal."

"Meals-on-wheels, orca Style, you heard it here first, direct from the whale whisperer himself."

"You know, Wintwerp, you may not be an ass, but you certainly sound like one." Says Josh.

"You think you're the first to mess with my name, most people don't get a second chance, orca boy. If Sammie wasn't here I would teach you a lesson."

"You mean if you weren't fox hunting, and sitting in a kayak with ten feet of water protecting your wealthy stuck up butt, that's what you're really saying."

With two quick paddle strokes, Winthorp has banged the kayak into the wood plank and climbed onto the floating dock. The dock is eight feet wide and Josh stands in the middle, his hand on his stick like a shepherd holding a hooked staff in front of his flock. Winthorp walks toward him.

"You think that little housekeeper's broomstick is going to help you?"

Josh sets the stick on the dock. "Look, I didn't mean anything," he lifts his hands, " let's just forget it, ok." He looks across the water at Sammie, their eyes meet. Josh mouths, *I'm sorry.*

ORCA BOY

"You should have thought about being sorry before you dissed me, orca   Boy." Winthorp shoves Josh backwards almost knocking him off his feet, and keeps coming at him intent on shoving him again. When he reaches out, Josh grabs Winthorp's wrist in both hands and twists it while turning it behind his back. He raises his wrist and bends Winthorp's elbow between his shoulder blades, the pain forces Winthorp to the decking on his knees and then his face to the planks. He turns his head sideways to keep from hurting his nose .

Josh leans down to his ear and whispers, "Look Winthorp, I'm sorry I dissed you, but are you done being pissed, or..." he forces his arm a little more until Winthorp cry's out yes. Josh immediately lets go, and stands up. He retrieves his stick keeping a fair distance. Winthorp struggles to his feet nursing his sore arm and elbow.

"You're lucky this time." Is all Winthorp says, and gets in the kayak still floating against the dock. He says nothing and paddles out of the cove back towards the *Islander Resort.*

"How did you do that." Says Sammie

"Look I'm sorry, I egged him on, I know better.

"No—how did you do what you did to him, you tied him up like it was nothing, was that some sort of martial arts move, and what was that remark about fox hunting?"

"That was just a basic one-arm take-down; any first year judo student knows that move. Earlier he called you a *Summer-Fox to nail*, it pushed my buttons, so I said he was acting like an ass, you heard me. I'm sorry, he's probably going to get you in trouble with Sandy. I should have ignored him."

"No way, you were defending my honor." And, if Sandy says anything, she can find another kayak tour guide for her renters to make cracks about." After a pause, "Josh, what about you, do *you* think I'm foxy?"

"If that means, the prettiest girl on this island—*yes."*

Sammie doesn't try to hide her blush, or her wonder of the shy tongue tied boy she met on the ferry a few days earlier. But now, she is the one that is looking away.

"I gotta go—*Sadie, let's go, Sadie go home, go home."* Sammie shoots out of the cove like a girl just named queen of the ball.

"Bye Sammie," says Josh to himself. *I guess I won't clean her up after all.*

Chapter 11 - Big Momma

"Aunt Maggie these pictures are cool, you are a great photographer. This one, with Sadie and Pepper both, is great."

"Thanks Josh you're just being kind. I saw you and that guy, do you want to talk about what happened? It was over so fast, did you have a fight."

"Oh no, it was just a misunderstanding, I said he was acting like an ass, which he was, and he wanted to push me down so I did a one arm take down, he's ok, but his wrist is sore."

"Does Sammie know you competed in the national martial arts tournaments?"

"No, we haven't talked much about me, besides, I'm not going to just blurt out, *you better watch out— I know Karate, or I'm a mixed martial arts fighter,* and I haven't won any big tournaments, I just competed in the west coast finals, my team won the overall points standing."

"Your dad said you took first place."

"My team took first place."

"Don't you do Zen or something?" says Maggie.

"Yeah sometimes–Zen-Tradition teachings are part of eastern martial arts, so I practice it, it's a Buddhist teaching where you cleanse your mind, and focus your thoughts and body into one being. It involves meditation, It's helped me a lot since mom died."

"Oh, ok, I guess I just don't understand. Before I forget, look at this picture I found online."

"Yep, it's an adult orca ," says Josh.

"See the dock, and the scars, look familiar?"

"Oh my god, it's Peppers mom. Where'd these come from?"

"They're on file at the whale museum web site," says Uncle Charley, entering the room, but we got the originals around here somewhere.

"Your grandpa took them right here in the cove. Your dad and I were kids then, but I remember a whale hanging out in the cove for about a month. It was all cut up from propellers, like it had been run over by a big boat or maybe a ferry or something. Your grandpa didn't tell anyone, he said they would just make a spectacle of it, or kill it. He would sit out on the dock in his chair for hours reading his book. Said he was keeping his girl company. I hadn't thought about it until now, but you're doing the same thing."

"The museum blog says that a group of transient orcas has been spotted out in the straits." Says Maggie, "you should read it Josh, it says they are dangerous."

"I'll do it right now, how do I find their site?"

"Just search Friday Harbor Whale Museum, you'll see it," says Charley.

"I will e-mail all these pictures to you Josh," says Maggie, "and if you don't mind, some are going on Facebook and to your dad."

Other than a few pictures, the museum has very little information about his grandfather and the orca in his cove. Since he didn't tell anyone until after it had left the cove, there was no way to verify the story except the pictures.

Josh learns that the local orca pods, stay in the area year round, they don't mingle with transient orcas that travel up and down the coast, migrating with the seasons. The transient orcas kill juveniles and sometimes attack weak adults, killing them too. They try to mate with the females or steal them away. Eventually they move on, after wreaking havoc to local family pods. Several volunteer whale spotters on hills and headlands throughout the San Juan's have reported seeing transients, and some have seen attacks in the last week. All very scary news for Pepper.

Chapter 12 - Stick Toy

*C*ome on *Pepper, everyone is gone, you can come back now.* The stick and float are still tied together, and are floating in the middle of the cove, it seems odd to him that they had not drifted to the beach or out into the channel. With his hiking stick, he bangs the side of the rowboat, *bang bang - pause - bang bang,* he repeats the message, and then in a half minute or so, gives it a rest. So far Pepper has demonstrated a willingness to please, and follow instructions, she is no dummy and Josh gives her credit for being every bit as smart as he is, and certainly wanting to play as much as Sadie, only in an orca sort of way. He has no doubt if she hears the message beat; she will know it's him talking to her, which is why he quits banging. If she can't hear it, what's the point, and if she does, it's up to her.

He climbs into the rowboat and shoves himself towards the float and stick. He rows slowly, he has no plan except to retrieve it and leave it hanging from the dock where Pepper can reach it when she comes back. With only a few more strokes left, he is about to ship the oars, when a dorsal fin breaks the surface in the cove entrance. It was just an instant, hardly a ripple, but he saw enough to judge her direction and speed, *I saw you Pepper.*

When the rowboat is only ten feet from the whale toy, both the stick and float jerk together, and then disappear below the surface leaving a tell tale ring. No Pepper, no dorsal fin, and no stick or float, just Josh sitting in the middle of the cove in his uncles rowboat. For thirty seconds he looks around scanning the surface, he knows she has pulled them under. It's not exactly what he expected her to do, but no one expected an adult killer whale to bring her tangled up daughter to get help from a human either.

With hardly a ripple the stick and the tethered float, pop to the surface next to the rowboat, twenty seconds later Pepper comes up just beyond, she whistles at Josh when her eyes break the surface, as if to say, *you called, here I am!*

"Hey Pepper, I knew you understood, we don't talk the same language do we, but we don't need to, as long as we think alike, right?" Josh snags the rope with an oar and pulls the stick and float into the boat. Holding the float in both hands he spins the heavy stick around until he is just about thrown out of the boat before letting go. The stick sails off in the wrong direction landing on the other side of the boat. Pepper strokes her powerful pec fins and comes right at him.

Josh yells —"*no Pepper*," but she is already moving, her dorsal fin clears the boat by inches as she arches her back. Diving under the boat, her tail fluke slaps the water where she had been an instant before. "Oh criminy," says Josh startled, "don't do that."

It's totally unfair, he thinks how fast she can get to his throw when it was all he could do to toss it that far. Pepper has the rope in her mouth and spins in the water like Sadie spins on land, in a twisting motion with one fin in the air, she is back with the toy. Waves and swells radiate out in all directions as a thousand pounds of muscle and blubber churn the cove in fun. Again, he snags the rope with an oar and drags it into the boat while Pepper watches.

"We need to change this toy Pepper, I can't throw this heavy stick while sitting in the boat, hang on a second while I untie this knot." He holds up the float and stick so that she can see what he has done, and then drops the stick into the boat. He twirls the lightweight float one handed over his head, faster and faster until it is a whistling orange blur, and then lets it go in an arc that sends it easily over a hundred feet.

Pepper is off just like Sadie, she saw it go, she saw it land, it belongs to her. Her dorsal fin never drops below the surface, and the rest of her never breaks above water. Suddenly the float jerks under water as she grabs the rope in her mouth and dives. This time she slowly surfaces next to the boat just a couple feet from Josh.

"I know what you want." He reaches out to her eye patch, and pats her rapidly more times than he can count. Then without letting up, he switches to his stick and rubs her back in front of her dorsal fin. She responds with her special vibrating sound that can only be described as, purring.

"Where's your mom, Pepper girl, I'm worried about her, and you too. You and her and all your relatives need to stay out of the straits until some bad boys leave town."

Chapter 13 - Tide rip

Text: *Hey dad, it's been an incredible time here, Uncle Charley says you were just kids when an injured orca stayed in the cove for a month. Well that same orca came into the cove yesterday and brought it's ten-foot baby. The baby was all tangled up in a net and sinking, the mom had to hold it up to breath. Uncle Charley and I cut it loose. I was terrified, but even more scared that she was going to die without help, now we are friends. She has been playing fetch with the neighbor's dog. They both were tugging on the same stick at the same time in four feet of water. It's unreal. Maggie will send some pictures later. Joshua.*

Josh pushes send, and then his e-mail pops up he has a message. It's some of the pictures from Maggie. He looks at them laughing, and then forwards to his dad, the one with him falling between Pepper and big momma, and one showing the cable when he cut it in the boat cradle, and then he forwards a whole bunch of Sadie and Pepper chasing the stick. There is one of Sammie looking very pretty, *very foxy,* she looks concerned, and is holding Sadie back, and keeping her from barking. He and Pepper are in the same picture, he's waist deep next to Pepper on the boat cradle, big momma is in the background, it's a cool picture, he sends it too, and then he sends it to Sammie as well. He adds a caption for Sammie, *very foxy,* and pushes send. The one he sent to his dad pops up, *unable to send,* so he clicks on the one to Sammie and forwards it to his dad. Just as he pushes send, he remembers the foxy caption, and then what his mother told him.

Never send anything or post anything you don't want the whole world to someday see. He remembers his mother's exact words, and he's ok with it. *I wish you had met Samantha mom, you would've liked her too.*

Josh's phone chirps an incoming text message from his dad. He pushes message.

"Awesome picture Josh, the ones with the orca are pretty cool too, wish I was there.

Dad."

I'm glad you agree dad, I wish you were here too.

"Well Pepper, you're famous now," says Josh. Once you get your picture in cyberspace there's no turning back. I'll throw the float a little bit more and then I'm going for a kayak ride. You're welcome to tag along."

Ten minutes and five throws later, Josh hangs the float by its rope on a loose plank hanging over the water, if Pepper wants, she can snag it off easy enough, putting it back may be a bit more creative. In the gear shed, he straps on a life vest, and then pushes his grandpa's old beater rock basher kayak into the water. His second time kayaking, and he feels at ease like it's old news. For an instant, he balances over the seat and then drops inside, his double ended paddle steadying him. He digs in, the paddle flex's, and the boat move forward and turns sideways, his next two strokes are spent fixing his first strokes mistakes.

Following Sammie's instructions, he angles his paddle straight down next to the boat making sure not to pull in an arc. It works—he doesn't rocket into warp drive like Sammie in her Ultralight, but with practice he masters a decent power stroke.

You're right Sammie, I'll never catch you in this kayak, and that's ok, I have nothing to prove. He clears the coves narrow entrance; he can turn left towards Sandy's *Grand Resort Bed and Breakfast,* or turn right towards *Rock Island.* He chooses neither, instead of hugging the shore he paddles straight out into the channel. The cross current drags him to the left anyway. Josh paddles hard and steady, experimenting with his form and learning the most efficient strokes. He borrows from his martial arts teachings, and applies to kayaking the principle— *master of himself, peace, and respect of all things.* In no time, he is but a distant speck as seen from shore.

Aunt Maggie and Uncle Chuck watch from the picture window as their nephew strikes out on his own, looking for his future, or perhaps just escaping from a shattered past. They watch Pepper follow Josh, she's trailing behind but definitely following.

"I wonder if he knows Pepper is following him," says Maggie.

"He probably sees her, that dorsal fin is hard to miss when she is on the surface," says Charley. Look over there, that big boat is going fast, Josh is way out, he's going to get a big wake in a minute."

"He needs a light, if he's going to paddle in the evening, it will be dark soon," says Maggie.

Pepper is keeping a safe distance behind Josh; the kayak is not the aluminum rowboat she knows. She watched her friend paddle out of the cove in front of her, but the kayak is new, she lags far behind. Less than 100 yards from Josh, the powerboat blasts by. Josh waves at the people, but they stare straight ahead. No one waves or even notices the boy in the low kayak with the orca following him. Josh keeps the kayak headed into the waves thrown off by the passing boat.

When the water calms he turns the kayak around and heads toward shore spotting Pepper's dorsal fin. *There you are girl, you've been following me, I wondered if you would.* He thumps his paddle on the boat, whap whap—whap whap—whap whap. It's the signal Pepper has been waiting for, her fin cuts a straight line leaving its own mini wake. She sprints to his side, and comes to rest five feet away announcing her arrival with a couple little double clicks.

"Hi Pepper, I guess you needed an invite, you don't need to keep your distance, I should have realized this boat may spook you." He scratches her back once with the kayak paddle. "Come on, let's go for a spin." He dips his paddle and turns toward shore. The current has dragged him way past the point, the lights of the *Grand Resort* are a half mile away and receding fast. He settles into a pattern of rhythmic stroking, soon his arms and hands warm to the task, but the distant point is not getting any closer. Twenty minutes of good hard paddling against the strong current has not gotten him any closer to shore. Pepper is coasting alongside like she's taking a walk in the park. Josh made a beginners mistake letting the current carry him away, now he makes another mistake when he doubles down and pulls long fast strokes trying to overcome his first mistake. Hot spots form on his palms warning of blisters soon to come. The point gets closer, but he cannot keep the pace needed to bring him to safety.

Pepper effortlessly strokes her long pectoral fins one time for every ten strokes Josh makes. Her broad tail steers serenely, its turbo boost not needed. Adult killer whales achieve thirty mile per hour bursts of speed when hunting, but Pepper is not in a hurry, or hunting. With the *Grand Lodge* lights guiding him, Josh slowly regains lost ground, the setting sun drops behind far off Vancouver Island casting long shadows, the channel and surrounding islands blend together into darkness.

This isn't working Pepper, even if I can keep up this pace, and I can't, I'm running the risk of getting run down in the dark by a powerboat. We need to forget getting home and concentrate on getting out of the main channel and near shore, while there is still some light.

Josh changes course, and paddles at right angles to the current, just like a swimmer caught in a riptide that is impossible to swim against. The current whisks him and Pepper further away from home but they rapidly move across the current. The new direction and distant shore are a long ways off, but they make good progress, and Josh maintains a steady stroke. The point, thrusting out into the channel, accelerates the current and forces it away from shore, it also causes a back eddy in it's lee. Josh and Pepper ride the eddy all the way until only a hundred feet from shore, the reverse current carry's them back toward the point. Pepper floats along hardly moving a muscle, Josh dips a paddle just to keep pointed ahead. The two of them are almost invisible silhouettes in the descending darkness.

"Hi Maggie, this is Josh, I should have called earlier, but I was too busy paddling,"

"Where are you, are you ok, it's dark?"

"Yeah, we're fine, I let the current sweep me past the point, now I have a long haul hugging the shore to get back, everything is under control, I just didn't want you to get concerned. Pepper followed me, she's keeping me company, I'll see you later."

"Okay, bye," says Maggie. She wants to send Charley with a boat and outboard, but resists saying anything. As hard as it is to be an aunt, it's even harder to be an aunt and surrogate mother to a boy with a kayak that has adopted a killer whale.

"It's just me and you now girl." Says Josh, to Pepper. "Me and you.

Resting and riding the back eddy, he makes his way toward the lights on the point. Close to shore, the gentle current is easy to deal with but the dinged up old kayak bumps rocks every once in awhile.

In another hour the rising tide will cover the same rocks and darkness will be complete.

"Watch it Pepper, it's shallow here, we need to go further out, don't get yourself high grounded."

With Pepper for company, and time and darkness not an issue, he makes his way around the point. The lights of the *Grand Resort* make a great navigation landmark, but don't give off much light. Josh and his kayak are invisible from shore, as he ghosts along in silence. As soon as he clears the point, the current ceases to be an issue, so he moves further off shore into the darkness. Voices from the resort trail off the terrace, and drift over the water to where he and Pepper are paddling. They paddle along without splashing—keeping quiet. Some of the voices are Sammie and Winthorp's, talking and sitting around the *Grand Resort's* fire ring. The fires soft glow and the resorts flood lights softly light up four people.

Josh suddenly feels out of place and dreads being discovered. He stealthily paddles deeper into the darkness risking being caught in the current and swept away again. The resorts spotlight or even a powerful flashlight could easily betray his presence, and then Winthorp will accuse him of spying.

He and Pepper are straight off shore and at their most visible point when he hears Sadie bark, the sound is muffled as if she is watching at a window, but can't get out. Josh holds his breath and keeps paddling, he's sure that at any second a beam of light will shoot out from shore searching for the source of Sadie's alarm barks. Pepper chirps one long low sound that Josh barely hears, and then Sadie becomes quiet. *Pepper, did you just tell her to quit barking? Are you two able to talk that well? I don't believe it, even if you can communicate somehow, Sadie does not mind me or Sammie, why would she mind an orca, it's got to be a coincidence.*

The light beam never comes, and the oddball conspirator mission of boy and orca slip safely past the *Grand Resort* into the darkness. Their secret remains safe, unless Sadie talks.

Chapter 14 - Buddy system

*T*hirty minutes later, back at the old Pearson Cove Lodge.

"Here's a light you can use next time. I'll set it up here on the mantle," says Uncle Charley. "We could barely see you out there, but it sure looked like that powerboat came awfully close to you. He may not have seen you."

"Yeah, I was wishing I had something to flash at them, they never looked at me."

"You have to be careful out there off the point Josh," says Charley, "boaters are forced to go out around the point, so they cut it close, it's the shortest route between two places."

"We saw Pepper following you, did she ever get catch up?" Says Maggie.

"After I called her, I think the kayak bothered her. Until then, she had only seen me in the rowboat. She kept her distance, but when I called, she came close enough for me to scratch and pat her a few times. After that, she stayed with me; it was like having a buddy on a hike. I left her in the cove."

"Help yourself to nachos in the kitchen if you want.

"Great, I'm starving."

"Were off to bed, turn off the lights."

Chapter 15 - Exposed

*T*he sound of crunching gravel, and squeaky brakes, wakes Maggie from the remainder of a light slumber. The sun is up, and outside in the turnaround, a deputy sheriff gently closes his car door trying not to bother anyone, unless he's just being sneaky. What may have been, good intentions have the opposite effect, she's up and peering out the window from around closed curtains.

"Get up Charley," says Maggie, "the Sheriff's car is in the driveway, and there's two green *forestry dept.* or something pickups pulling in behind it."

"Something's going on," says Charley, parting a curtain, and looking out the same window, "there's at least six of them, and they're all looking down at the cove, ones pointing. I need to get out there."

The deputy sheriff, makes sure everyone is awake when he uses the old lodges big iron door knocker. Predating modern doorbells, the ornate knocker is a heavy foot long sculpture of an orca . It's mounted horizontally as if the arching orca is caught in mid-breach before landing with a big splash. The cast iron work of art is hinged on the back and welded to a striker plate designed to look like waves. He lifts and drops the orca three times. Once is enough to rattle the door, the second time shakes the house. The third isn't needed, but he drops it anyway. Who knocks only twice?

"Hey Danny," says Charley when he opens the door, "What's going on, I haven't seen you in awhile, something wrong."

"Hi Charley, no, no, listen, I hate coming over here getting you and Maggie worried and all, but these guys," motioning towards the fish and game people, "they called the office saying they need police help out here."

"I don't understand, what's happening?"

"They say, you got a killer whale penned up, that someone here netted it and they're keeping it in the cove. That don't make sense, but they're in an uproar like it's their prize orca from L pod or someone's bar-b-cueing bald eagles. Do you know anything about what I'm saying Charley?" Danny looks him in the eye, and waits for Charley's response.

"Hey Sheriff," Josh steps from behind Charley out onto the covered porch. "I'm Joshua Pearson, Charley's nephew, I found an orca tangled in a net and cable, I cut it loose and set it free, is there something wrong with that.?"

"Your darn right there is," says a heavy set red faced fish and game warden as he struggles up the steps. "Let me get my breath, it's a long ways from around back."

"You can't go around back, this is private property, right Danny?" says Charley getting his hackles up.

"Now hold on here a minute, Charley you got nothing to hide, right?—Right Charley?" says the Deputy Sheriff.

"Yeah sure," says Charley, "but he can't go snooping around without my permission or a search warrant, can he?"

"Yes I can," says the fish and game warden between catching breaths, "I'm a federal officer enforcing the Federal Marine Mammals Act, I can go where ever I want to protect our marine mammals. I have a report that an injured orca is being held trapped here and I aim to investigate so you best not hinder me."

"Excuse me Rich, err Warden Rogers," says Deputy Danny, let's put a lid on this, why don't you and your boys go take a look around, and we can all go back to work. That is, if it's ok with Charley here,

"*This **is** my work*, Pearson are you going to cooperate or not." Spits Rogers.

"No—It's not ok. This is dumb, you didn't need to come out her with a swat team, the only captive orca here is right there on the door," says Charley, pointing over his shoulder.

"Were not swat, were federal compliance officers, and you're interfering."

"No I'm not, I was asleep, and you roared in here. You and your guys can all leave. Danny, sometime when you're not on official business come over for a cup of coffee." With a head jerk Charley motions Josh inside, and then closes the big carved oak door leaving Rogers fuming on the porch.

Josh, Maggie, and Charley all face each other in the entry, and then walk through to look out the big picture window, each searches the cove for any sign of Pepper.

"I don't see her," says Maggie.

"More importantly, what's going on," says Josh. "Why did you say no."

"That's precisely why I said no, what is going on? Plus, Danny winked at me and shook his head. We go way back, he wouldn't steer us wrong, that fish and game guy is up to something, and I'm afraid Pepper is in the middle of it."

Light knocking at the door takes them away from the window and they all walk back to the front entry. Maggie goes to a side window.

"Oh my god," says Maggie, "there's a news van out there, its channel 12. It looks like the reporter is interviewing that game warden guy, what should we do?"

"For starters I'm opening the door." Charley swings open the door he closed five minutes earlier. In front of him is a smiling man in his twenties or thirties. He has on a channel 12 baseball cap, and is carrying a notepad. A digital camera is slung from his neck. Behind him milling around in the parking area are the Fish and Game people and the deputy sheriff. The heavy set Game warden is still out of breath, and animatedly gesturing, pointing at the house, and at the cove. He's talking to another man wearing a Channel 12 cap.

"Hello, I'm Chad, and I work for Channel 12, can we talk?"

"Sure Chad, If you're not with them, I'm Charley, come on in." Charley opens the door wide gesturing Chad through and then looks outside before closing and locking it behind them. "This is Josh and Maggie, come on into the great room where we can enjoy the view."

"Thanks Charley, good to meet all of you, Josh I feel like I know you, your orca video is awesome."

"What orca video," says Josh.

"You don't know?"

"No—we don't know why the sheriff is here, or Channel 12, or the fish and Game people."

"Well, allow me to fill you in. Someone put a video of you on u-tube, and all the social media sites are buzzing. Here, you can watch it on my phone." Chad pushes a few keys and turns his screen towards the three Pearson's. It shows Charley falling over in the rowboat and Josh falling over Pepper and landing on big momma, the recording continues until Josh climbs over Pepper and gets back in the boat. *The caption reads, Local Boy Nets Big Catch.* Everyone looks at Maggie.

" I didn't write that, I didn't say anything like that, But I think it's cute."

"It is cute, everyone loves orcas, you guys are heroes." Says Chad.

"Well then, why are the cops here," says Josh. And how did they find out, and how did you find out who we are?"

"That's easy, Channel 12 is here because Fish and Game led us here, and Fish and Game got a tip you were netting and holding an orca captive.

"Where did the tip come from," says Josh and Charley together.

"Don't know, and I don't think Fish and Game know either, but they won't tell anyway."

"Winth,"—says Josh, and then he stops.

"What, who did you say," asks Chad.

"Nothing," Josh ignores Chad's question and asks his own, "Explain to us Chad, are you interviewing us, will you report what you see or learn here. How do your rules work?"

"I won't report or tell anything except what you approve, you have my word."

"Ok, if everyone agrees, let's talk. You first Chad," says Charley.

"Where's the orca ?" —everyone looks at Josh.

Shrugging, Josh says, "I don't know, she's a killer whale, they go and do whatever they want."

Laughing, "Ok, that makes sense. When did you see her last, and how do you know it's a she?"

"She—Pepper, was hanging in the cove last night, Sadie, the neighbor's dog led us to her and her momma originally, and they seemed to all get along well, so I figured they were all girls." *Better than saying Sadie said so.*

"Why Pepper, and where is the adult whale."

"Pepper is not a whale," says Josh, "she's an orca. Orcas are big dolphins, not whales, Killer Whale is a nickname."

"Ok, I got it, strike whale or add *killer*, but why Pepper?"

"Because her black and white markings reminded me of salt and pepper, and salt seemed like a dumb name but Pepper sounded right, and I had to say something to keep the conversation flowing, I called her mother, Big Momma and we haven't seen her since."

The four of them stand at the window gazing past the cove and across the main channel towards the other San Juan Islands. Josh and Charley replay for Chad how they helped Pepper, Maggie fills in details and shows off her pictures.

"Off in that direction is Haro Strait," says Charley, "That's where the resident orca pods hang out."

"I see her," says Maggie, pointing midway out in the channel, "see?"

Josh and Charley spot her too, but Chad is unsure he sees the small dorsal fin and spouting they are looking at.

"How do you know that's Pepper out there," says Chad.

"It looks like her spout and her dorsal, the adults are a lot bigger, I've been watching Pepper for days, that's her," says Maggie.

"Is she coming here, what do you think she is doing?"

"Well she is probably chasing seals and salmon," says Charley.

Deputy Danny lightly knocks on the door, thoughtfully sparing everyone from being startled by the doorknocker. Charley excuses himself and goes to the front door leaving the other three watching out the window.

"How about that coffee right now, Charley." Says the deputy sheriff, all smiles.

Charley looks around outside, the fish and game vehicles are gone, the only ones left are the single news van and Danny's cruiser. "They've left, my job is done."

"Thank god, sure, sure Danny come on in." Charley leads the way to the kitchen where they huddle up to the island counter with some high stools. The coffee pot is full after being set and auto programmed the night before. "What's up Danny, you haven't normally hung out here since we were kids?"

"I know, and we should change that, but you're right. Look, I want to give you a heads up. That warden, his name is *Rich Rogers,* has left for now, but he has some kind of ax to grind or chip on his shoulder, maybe he's climbing the ladder and wants to make a name. If he thinks a federal crime has been committed, then he's the one to get to the bottom of it."

"Have we done something wrong or illegal untangling that poor baby orca ?"

"I don't know, but it's not up to me, *Rogers* was going on about interference with a protected mammal in violation of the *Marine Mammal act.* He says no one is allowed within 200 feet of an orca . Injured or not, period!

"Well we all know that, that rule is for power boaters, so they don't run into them. He can't possibly apply that to people on shore on a dock. What were we supposed to do, let her drown after her mother brought her to us?"

"No argument from me Charley—save the whales—I say.

"She's an orca." Says Charley snickering, catching Danny in the standing local joke.

"I know, I know, look—I just wanted to let you know, he's not happy. Anyway, I gotta get going Charley, thanks for the coffee. I should go meet Josh properly and say hello to Maggie.

Danny passes the Channel 12 reporter as he is going out the door.

"Hey Chad, I suppose you'll be calling me later."

"Count on it Danny."

"So you are Joshua Pearson," says Deputy Danny, vigorously shaking Josh's hand, "I know your dad well, Ray and I played right here in this house when we were little. I learned to paddle and row in the cove. Your uncle Charley was our best friend and we were his greatest tormentors. Those were great times. I never knew your mom, I wish

I had. You can call me, if you ever need anything Josh, I think I still owe your dad some favors." Danny grins as he drifts into a memory. "I need to get back to work."

Things have calmed down at Pearson Cove, everyone is gone except for the news team that is hanging around outside hoping to get some footage.

"Can we go down on the dock Charley," asks Chad, "maybe Pepper will come in and see what were up to."

"I don't see why not, but it's your call Josh, do you want Pepper on the news. We haven't heard the last of that Rogers guy from Fish and Game."

"It's fine with me, let's go."

"Listen," says Charley, "I don't think at this time we want to allow any pictures of us with Pepper. We don't want to violate any laws, or give Rogers some ammunition, so we must stay back 200 feet. You guys run ahead, Maggie and I will come down later, we have some things to do here." Josh gives Charley a puzzled look, and in return, gets a nod to go. On the way to the float Josh grabs his hiking stick he left leaning against the railing the night before. Partway out the dock he stops at the slip with the old aluminum rowboat, and explains how he stood on his knees cutting off the net before falling in. He uses his stick as a pointer showing how he helped Pepper, twice he thumps the stick on the boat like a drum, wham wham—wham wham. Ten seconds later, wham wham—wham wham. They end up standing in front of the submerged boat cradle, Pepper's float and rope are hanging from the plank on the end.

"Weren't you afraid she would swat you like a fly if you hurt her?" says Chad while they scan the cove.

"Oh yeah—I was terrified, I was scared to death, that's why I talked to her—to calm myself."

"So why did you do it."

"I couldn't not do it, they came to us needing help, they looked me in the eye, it was like I could feel their need, and I was able to do it."

"On Facebook, Maggie said you spent the entire night sitting with her, is that correct?"

"I guess, I kept dozing off, but we talked, or I talked, she kind of purred, clicked, and whistled, but that was mostly when I rubbed her back."

While answering questions Josh spots Pepper in the cove, she's keeping her distance, and staying almost invisible.

"You gave her a back rub? Can I quote you on that."

"I guess so, what's the big deal."

"Big deal? Josh—orcas are the top predators in the world, not since dinosaurs ruled the earth has any animal been more at the top of the food chain. You don't just give them a back scratch, and a tummy rub."

Josh picks the float toy off the plank hanger and gently twirls it around making sure Pepper sees it, but the two men are watching him.

"Oh, I didn't know that," says Josh joking, "well then I probably shouldn't have stood on her mommas flipper when I fell between them."

"Watch your heads; I'm going to toss this float out in the middle." He knows where Pepper is, and spins like before. Pepper watches, and when he lets fly, she's off. The float arcs through the air trailing the rope, it's intended landing spot, some 100 feet in front of Pepper. The two television men follow its flight and are staring right at Pepper when she explodes from the water so unexpectedly they are caught off guard and only yell holy ### expletives while grabbing cameras. Pepper hits the knotted rope on a dive and disappears below the surface taking everything with her, leaving only rolling waves and frothy bubbles behind. In three seconds she has said hello, let's play, and guess where I am.

"You guys might want to watch out, she normally plays with a big dog and doesn't spare the water." About thirty long speculative seconds drags by while the flabbergasted TV guys scan the cove. If they could see under water they would see Pepper circling the cove at high speed, her float trailing bubbles behind her. Fifteen feet in front of them, the float pops to the surface like an oversize fishing bobber on a rope.

Where the heck is she, nervously whispers one man, but Pepper is not showing herself, not yet. Beyond her float, tantalizing bubbles come up first, and then her snout and eye show without creating a ripple in the still water. Lastly her dorsal fin rises out of the water. Cameras click and they get terrific shots as she lifts one pectoral fin clear of the water. Josh see's it coming, and takes a couple steps back as she launches the float and a wall of water toward the dock. The float lands at their feet. The TV people get one of a kind orca action shots and splashed.

"Meet Pepper—by the way, I didn't teach her to do that, she taught me."

Josh sits cross-legged on the dock in a dry spot next to the cradle where he sat the first night with Pepper, the float toy sits next to him. With his stick, he double taps the boat lift cradle, the two wet TV crew are in disbelief as Pepper slides onto the cradle and Josh scratches her back, and then rubs her eye patch. Both men lift their cameras again, but Josh recoils.

"No Pictures of me with Pepper, we agreed, you promised." He jumps up, spooking Pepper, she backstrokes and sinks below the surface.

"Sorry, its reflex, but we never took any pictures." Says Chad, but Josh doesn't believe him.

"Well, she's gone, I guess, if you have more questions, I'll be up at the house, or you can stay here and see if she surfaces." Josh doesn't wait for an answer, he simply walks away leaving the wet TV crew behind.

"We watched Pepper chase the float," Says Maggie, still at the window.

"That was so cool," says Josh, "the way she splashed it up on the dock, she is really smart, and accurate. She's done that before on the beach, but not the dock. I saw what she was up to and stepped back. Charley, why did you say to not be in any pictures with Pepper. Was it something Danny said?"

"Yeah, it was, he warned me that that federal warden guy, Rogers was plenty steamed, and not done throwing his fat ass around. Technically we aren't supposed to be anywhere near Pepper, so getting a picture taken with her is proof of a violation, and that may be what he wants to come down on us. I just think it's better we stay out of it until things blow over."

"You mean, what I posted is what caused him to come out here?" says Maggie

"No, no, someone made a false claim that we netted her, that's what started it."

"I think Charley is right," says Chad, the two of them walking in through the open door. "Steve says, Rogers was making threats, this is Steve, my partner, tell them what you heard."

"Hi I'm Steve like Chad says, I heard warden Rogers talking about getting a search warrant and even arresting someone. He was going to talk to someone at the State Department, he was pretty vehement. He also said any injured orca is his responsibility, and not some kids feel good project. He said no one here knows the first thing about fixing up injuries. He said they may have to move the whale to a facility."

"He said whale?" asks Josh, "what an ignoramus, what facility?"

"Well she sure looked in good spirits and plenty active to me," adds Steve, holding his hands out showing his wet front half. I notice you didn't get wet Josh, care to explain."

"Easy, she telegraphs her moves, weren't you watching her left pectoral flipper when she cranked it back?"

Laughing, "I guess I missed it,"

"It's like a catapult, she got me on the beach the first time chasing a small log with Sadie.

"Sadie is the dog that led you to her. Is she the neighbors dog, at the *Grand Resort Bed and Breakfast,* How did that come about?"

"I think they both hear, and make sounds above and below the human range, I also think they communicate."

"What—do you mean like talking or something?"

"No, but I know they understand each other better than we understand them. Last night we were..." and then Josh trails off when he thinks about Sammie and Winthorp together around the campfire, "Never mind."

The TV crew sticks around another hour, they record some interview footage, and hint around, trying to get him to run his mouth, but Josh doesn't bite. Instead, he asks his own baited questions digging out what the reporters know. Charley and Maggie mostly listen, sometimes smiling, their nephew is not the brain-dead teenager kid often portrayed in the news. Before leaving, Chad asks if they can come back sometime.

"I don't know says Charley, let's see what you write."

Chapter 15 - U tube

"I'm sorry I brought this down on you," says Josh to Maggie, and Charley. "If I hadn't insisted on cutting her loose, and called someone instead, none of this would have happened."

"Don't feel that way for one second Josh, you did the right thing, everyone is proud of you, hell the whole world is behind you thanks to Maggie and u-tube or Facebook. That Rogers guy is just hot air, you'll see."

"What if he's not?"

"Charley, someone's on the phone for you, it sounds like a reporter." Says Maggie.

The Seattle times, says they have a tip that an orca is trapped in the cove. Because the tip was relayed from an amateur whale watch blog they think the story is a farce. They want to know if there is any truth to it. Charley sets them straight and asks where the tip came from, as expected they don't know the source, or in any case, wont share. After hearing Charlie's story they ask if a reporter may come by for an interview. While on the phone with the Seattle Times another call flashes through, Charley hangs up one to answer another.

It's the University of Washington Whale Research center. The research scientist on the phone knows all about Pepper and her mother. They have identified big momma by her scars showing in Maggie's pictures. Big momma is really L21, and Pepper was born about eighteen months ago according to the researcher. She wants to know if Pepper and L21 are in the cove right now.

Charley takes pause over the urgency and the _right now_ part of the question, and then says he has not seen either orca in awhile and he does not know anything else. He agrees to call and let them know of any sightings he has of L21 and her baby or any other orcas. She also mentions transient Killer Whales have been seen in Haro Strait.

After her phone call to Charley, the researcher reports to _Rogers_ as he requested. Charley tells Josh about the peculiar _right now_ question and gives him the phone number when he asks for it.

Chapter 16 - Protestors

"**W**ow, this is really breaking loose," says Charley when he gets free of the phone, "we may be deluged with media and who knows what else."

"You can say that again, someone's coming in the drive right now." Says Maggie coming back from a look out the front window. Outside an old VW van sporting save the whales stickers has parked to one side where they can see the cove. The van is stuffed full of people, arms and hands pointing as they scope out the cove.

"Oh geez ," says Charley, "look out back,"

Eight kayaks are entering the cove, with Sammie leading the flotilla. She has switched kayaks from her normal lightweight speedster to a two man cruiser, Sadie looks like a little child sitting bolt upright in the front seat. Seven more rock bashers follow behind, each one slightly askew but upright as they try to keep pace with Sammie.

"What should we do," asks Maggie.

"For now, nothing," offers Josh, "If someone comes knocking and they are pleasant, I think we should be pleasant back. But I've got a job to do, and Uncle Charley, I'd like your advice."

"Ok Josh, but I thought we were gonna dispense with the uncle stuff, what have you got in mind?"

"I'll try Charley, anyway, I think I should collect all that netting and cable, we cut off of Pepper and store it properly after taking some pictures. I would not be surprised if that Rogers dude wants to take a look at it when he calms down."

"That may be a problem, most of it's on the bottom."

"I saw some heavy wire in the gear shed, maybe we could bend it up into a grappling hook and snag it."

"It's worth a try, you know some of those people out there will think we are trying to snag an orca ."

"You are probably right, at least the idiots, but it needs to be done."

Sammie and her group tour the cove and not seeing Pepper or anything worth sticking around for, leave as quickly and suddenly as they appeared. Josh and Charley working together rig up a reasonable grappling hook in no time, and head out to where they did the net cutting. The first two tosses bring up nothing, so they throw the hook further and on the third throw they score pay dirt, or more like nylon web, and lots of it. Plus as a bonus, the save the whale group is watching, and decides they need to find out what's going on so all of them traipse out to see what Charley and Josh are up to.

Charley and Josh pull fifty feet of slashed slimy net onto the dock. After a dozen throws they move over to the boat-lift cradle and hook the remainder of the dropped cable

The apparent leader of the save the whale group is a cherub faced fifteen to twenty something followed by a stunning blond girl with hair to her waist, both sport tie dyed tee shirts with breaching orcas. Their dress code must call for expensive sandals, because every one of them is wearing Teva's; half of them have their faces permanently buried in an I-phone.

The Cherub speaks first, "Is that the net you used, it looks like our Island orcas really tore it apart, ha, ha." The blond, and all the minions join in laughing. Someone in the group adds, "Yeah man really ripped it to shreds, ha, ha." The I-phone chorus joins in.

Josh and Charley look at each other, and share a knowing look, Josh puts his finger to his lips signaling he would talk. Maggie is coming down the path with her camera.

"Hi guys, my name is Joshua Pearson, would you guys like to help out here? We need to photograph this net as evidence for the investigation. We're going to find out where it came from and who is responsible. First we have to stretch it out, and then were going to weigh it in that gear shed down there."

Nothing more needs to be said, the Cherub changes his tune from annoying protester activist with no original ideas of his own, to a helpful team player. Josh's team.

"My names Chet, short for Chester."

"Hey Chet, call me Josh, and he's Charley. You boys, and the pretty lady", smiling and nodding at the blond girl, "look like your home on summer break." Josh glances at Charley and gets a mission-accomplished nod and wink back.

Chet straightens up, and stands a little taller at Josh's assumption, "No, well actually I'm planning to go to community school after I finish high school here."

"Eastsound Orcas right,"

"Yeah, I'll be a senior," says Chet.

"Glad to meet you, I'll be a senior there too. I just moved here from Portland." They do a modified flying high five fist bump cementing their alliance.

Five converted protester recruits pitch in and stretch the old seaweed encrusted net to be photographed, Josh offers a few directions but they get it done. While the group is working Josh smacks the unneeded grappling hook on the loose plank next to Peppers float. *Wham wham – wham wham,* is all he does. The sound the grappling hook makes is a dull thud, not at all like the clear bang when he hits the aluminum boat. He wonders if she will hear it, or even recognize and respond to the single double tap call message. They continue arranging, and Maggie gets the pictures Josh asks for.

"That's it Chet, now we need to get all this mess down the dock to that shed, that is if you want to help some more.

"Sure Joshua, let's go boys" says Chet, after they pile it in a heap, he says, "Anything else we can do."

"You can meet Pepper," and he points out in the cove.

Pepper chooses this moment to spout, and follows it with a whistle, anyone watching would think she is calling attention to herself. All eyes turn toward her as they hurry back out the dock for a better view.

"Holy crap" yells one of the I-phone minions, who switches from game playing—to taking video. Chester is silent, none of them has ever been this close to a real killer whale, even a little juvenile one like Pepper is impressive, all her adult markings are complete, she's just smaller.

The blonde, crowds close behind Josh and says, "Is it safe, it's coming closer," she latches onto Josh's arm for security and ducks down making sure Pepper can't see her.

"Yes, her name is Pepper, and she like blondes, lots more than she likes, boys or reporters.

"Really, are you sure, warming to Josh and his assurance, my name is Christy, Chester's my brother."

"Am I sure it's safe, or that she likes blondes?" Talking over his shoulder.

"Both," says Christy, relaxing her grip on his arm.

"She likes what I like." Josh turns to sneak a look at her, their eyes meet, and for an instant, they connect, and then both turn back to Pepper. *Alright—I said the right thing.*

"Let's see if she will show off." Josh abandons Christy and walks to the end of the wobbly slip, all his new helpers stay back on the main dock, he picks the *float-on-a-rope* off its plank and walks back to the group dangling the float over the water and splashing it up and down. Pepper takes the hint and anticipating what's coming swims forward causing all of them to gasp and back up.

"See if you can get some pictures of everyone with Pepper," says Josh to Maggie. Then he drops the float right on her nose, it's too close for her to get a swing at it with a pectoral fin so she does what any playful orca would do. She twists here body back and forth looping her head and snout under the float, Josh steps back and nudges Christy saying watch out, then with a quick flick, Pepper sends it, and several buckets of water onto the dock.

The thrilled minions yell their approval. "She likes you guys," says Josh.

Next he picks up the rope and gives the float two quick spins before lofting it over Peppers head into the cove. She spins and tears after it at full throttle, her tail fluke clears the water and then slams back down. The boat slip erupts in cheers as a geyser shoots twenty feet into the air. Pepper dives under and nails the float as she breaches.

The energy in the cove is enormous, cheers are spontaneous, including from Sammie's kayak entourage that has quietly made their way back to the cove. Sadie is in her front seat, and barks getting Peppers attention. Pepper detours, and swims right by the kayaks and Sadie, as if to say, I got the toy and you don't.

After sassing Sadie, she turns a one-eighty using a single long pec stroke, and then cranks up the speed back to the slip. She has the rope knot in her mouth, the float trails skipping across the water, and bouncing off her back as she races back for another toss. Sadie is out of her mind wanting to jump in the water to play. Sammie keeps yelling, *no Sadie, stay in the boat.*

Pepper deposits the float toy in front of the group and backs up. Josh grabs it with his stick before she can wind up and splash it onto the dock. His new cheering group takes turns throwing and Pepper entertains everyone for another hour. She does a medley of wet returns splashing the dock and thrilling all of them.

When the action calms, Sammie's group leaves and Josh sits on a dry spot out by the cradle and asks Chet and Christy to sit with him. He hangs up the float, Pepper gets the message and drifts in close enough to be touched with the stick. Soon she is resting against the dock at Josh's feet and he is stroking her back.

"It's ok Christy," says Josh, "you can pet her, she likes being rubbed on that white spot above her eye."

"How do you know what to do," says Christy, while she nervously touches Pepper.

"What do you mean."

"I mean, how did you learn to train a killer whale. This isn't taught in high school."

"She and her mom came to me for help, so I helped her, and now were friends. There's no training, she's just really smart and wants to play, that's all."

Chapter 17 - Nap Time

Chet's protest group is totally on Pepper and Josh's team, they all worship Pepper and are in awe of Josh, but catching the ferry back to Friday Harbor trumps their rally and they reluctantly pile into the van.

Later, when everyone is gone and the cove is empty of kayaks, Josh sits on the planks next to the cradle talking to Pepper. He strokes her eye patch and scratches her back in front of her dorsal fin. She is purring and clicking with an occasional whistle. The two unlikely friends commune for a long time. Josh stretches out and lays on the dock, only a couple feet separates them. Their eyes watch each other, but mostly they doze.

Chapter 18 - Warning

"Pepper, turn on your esp, you know I'm your friend, so please understand, I'm only trying to help you. It is a mistake to be so trusting; you have to learn to be on your guard."

Josh takes his stick and rapidly smacks it on the dock six times, causing Pepper to flinch, but she stays next to him.

"That means danger, when you hear that message, it means danger and to run away."

He smacks the stick as fast as he can, six more times, pauses, and then smacks six again.

"Run away, run away—got it?"

With tears welling up in his eyes, he says, "I'm sorry girl," and hits her once, right on top of her head behind her snout. Not very hard, but harder than a normal rubbing. Then he reaches out and kicks her with his foot at the base of her dorsal fin. "Run away, run away." He hits the dock six more times. "bam bam bam bam bam bam."

Pepper reacts slowly, she is not hurting, she is confused, her friend has never acted mean to her, and she doesn't get it or know what to do. She watches Josh stand, tears streaming down his face. And then, using his stick he shoves her out of the slip. Without looking back, he walks up the dock and goes into the gear shed and closes the door. *I'm sorry Pepper, that Rogers guy may be right.*

Chapter 19 - Escape

Crunching gravel gives away the early morning visitors again. Maggie peeks around the curtain just like before. Pulling into the parking area are the same fisheries pickups as before, plus a black interagency car. Game Warden Rogers climbs out of the passenger side, the driver and a man in the back seat exit at the same time, the newcomers have badges showing on their belts, they all walk straight to the front door.

"Charley, they're back." Says Maggie.

Rogers lifts the heavy orca door Knocker, and then for emphasis, he slams it down, he does it four times, and then impatiently waits. *I'm coming, I'm coming*, mutters Charley to himself while he walks down the stairs pulling up his pants, but instead of going to the door, he heads for the kitchen, where Maggie hands him a cup of coffee. *He can wait, if he's going to be an ass.* The coffee is hot, while sipping and walking to the door, Charley resolves not to extend any hospitality to Rogers.

Rogers lifts the knocker and slams it down four more times as fast as he can.

Wham wham wham wham.

"Open the door Pearson," says Rogers, "I've got a warrant to search the premises, we will break open the door if you don't cooperate."

"What the heck," says Charlie, "does he think we have a killer whale in our house?"

"What's going on," says Josh, from the top of the stairs.

"It's that Rogers guy," says Charley, "and he says he has a search warrant, I think you should stay out of sight."

Charley swings the door open, "Ok, the doors open, what the hell do you want?"

"Are you Charles Pearson," say one of the new people while holding up his US Marshall badge.

"He knows who I am," pointing at Rogers.

"Just answer the question," says Rogers.

"Got, to hell," says Charley, "Now get off my property." He tries to shove the door shut, but the new guy blocks the door, and steps inside.

"I'm Federal Marshal Jones, and I'm placing you under arrest for violation of the federal marine animals act, put your cup down, and put your hands behind you." Charley does not resist, but he does tell them they are making a mistake and it will cost them their jobs.

Text Compose: *I'm sorry dad, but when Charley and I rescued the orca, I guess we violated the marine mammals act, federal marshals just arrested Charley, he's in handcuffs and they said they're taking him to Seattle.* Send:

Text Compose: *On a lighter note, I met some locals from the high school and introduced them to Pepper. Oh and Maggie has called an attorney. Charley's not having any fun, but it is kind of exciting right now.* Send:

"I want you to call the orca ," says Rogers to Josh.

"No—I can't,"

"You're lying; I saw some video where you call it tapping with a stick. Now let's head down to the dock, and you will call it." Rogers shoves Josh ahead of him

"No I wont, but if you let Charley go I might try."

"Move," says Roger, as he nods to an agent that then shoves Josh ahead of him. "And find that stick he uses."

Rogers leads them out to the slip with the boat lift.

"What's that." Pointing to the cradle.

"It's a drydock, for boats, I'm surprised you don't know that."

"I think you built it for the orca."

"You're insane, that's looks a hundred years old, my grandfather built it."

"Call the whale smart ass. Or you will be charged with hindering an investigation" Says Rogers. "Give him the stick."

"She's an orca, and I told you I can't."

"You mean you won't."

The less than tranquil cove is disturbed by two fish and game boats moving off the channel, and turning toward the entrance. One big aluminum boat stays outside as if on guard, the other enters the cove, its wake rolling onto the beach. Rogers says something into his walkie talkie and the boat immediately takes up position blocking the entrance. The boats are equipped with davit cranes and winches, three men are visible on each boat. One boat has a large net on a reel mounted on the stern.

"Last chance Pearson, either call the whale or those boys will drag the cove and snag her.

"You can't capture her, why are you doing this?"

"It's your fault, if you hadn't turned it into a pet…"

"She's not a pet."

"The researchers say she is likely to get injured or killed because she has lost her natural fear. You did that, she needs to be protected. Now call her with that stick."

Josh walks over to his aluminum rowboat and beats the stick as hard and as rapidly as he can six times. Then he looks over at Rogers,

"There—satisfied?" Then Josh repeats the code again, and again, until Rogers face turns bright red, and he grabs the stick.

"That's not what I saw in the video. You're warning it, you son of a bitch, take him into custody, I'm charging you with hindering. Put him in the car with his wise ass uncle." Rogers is panting like he just ran a marathon, except he has hardly moved ten feet in the last twenty minutes. Maggie is at the window taking pictures.

"Come on, you heard him." says the driver of the black agency car. "You are under arrest for hindering the investigation, let's go." He holds Josh by the arm and they walk towards shore. Part way up the ramp where he has a good view, Josh stops and turns to look for Pepper.

"Why are those boats here?" The agent releases his grip on his arm when he turns to look himself. The agent is young, possibly only a few years older than Josh and barely out of school. "What are the boats for," Josh asks again.

"They're going to capture the baby killer whale and take it to the university for protection."

"So there is no investigation, you guys are simply capturing an orca , and claiming it for research, right?"

"Look, I'm just a new game warden doing what I'm told. Rogers calls the shots."

"Do you have law enforcement training," asks Josh, "what if Rogers is violating the law and ordering you to do something illegal? Are you supposed to blindly follow orders, or go to a superior? Well—you're hesitating, what if he ordered you to drive me into the woods and leave me chained to a tree, would you do it?"

"Look you're talking crazy, Rogers is following the law, he's doing what is best for the animal, we all are."

"Are you helping and abetting him, are you sure you're not participating in a crime, maybe your putting your career on the line, by not doing something? Look, think about it logically, Pepper is in perfect shape, living out there with her pod and her mother. She doesn't need protection, so ask yourself, why is Rogers so dead set on capturing a young wild orca?"

"Lets go." The young Game warden reaches for Josh, but he turns and walks up the gangplank without further coaxing. Josh glances up at the big picture window and smiles at Maggie. His calm demeanor sets her at ease. She has her phone in one hand, camera in the other. Her home has been invaded, her family under arrest, and yet she is very worried.

"Stand here." Orders the game warden. Josh does as he's told, and stands beside the black cars back door.

"Have you thought about what I have said," asks Josh.

"Yes I have, and you may be on to something, but it doesn't change anything, at least not today."

"So does that mean you will, look into his motive and check into the legality?"

"Yes."

"Good, what's your name, and how can I contact you."

"You don't need my name where you're going, but it's Ted."

"Come on Ted, humor me just this once, what's your number," says Josh.

Ted opens the front door and retrieves spare handcuffs from the glove box. Then he opens the back door with the empty seat next to Charley.

"Hold your hands out." Josh places his wrists together palms up in front of Ted, his fingers loose, his arms limber. The next move is lightning fast. When Ted reaches for his wrist to snap the cuffs on, Josh takes the cuff and pops it over Ted's wrist, the bale rotates in a blur and clicks home. "What the, hey, ow, ow, ow," is all Ted manages to get out, as Josh turns Ted's thumb in towards his palm pushing hard and causing excruciating pain.

"Don't resist Ted, this wont hurt much unless you fight me. Now, you get in the car." Josh steers Ted by his thumb into the back seat.

"Josh don't do this," says Charley.

"It's too late Uncle Charley, I have to save Pepper, they're trying to catch her and I just assaulted a game warden. Ted, I want you to lean forward and wrap the cuff around that bar, and hook your other wrist, that is what that bar is for isn't it? He guides Ted forward by the thumb, as soon as the cuff clicks closed he lets go. "I'm sorry Ted, but I have to do this, I hope when they let you go that you will help. Rogers is not what he pretends to be." Josh and Charley lock eyes. I can't not help Pepper Uncle Charley, her momma brought her to us for a reason, I won't let her down." Josh carefully closes the car door, looks around, and sees they are still alone. He confidently walks to the house and through the front door.

"Josh, thank god they let you go," says Maggie, "what about Charley, where is he?" She hugs Josh.

"I'm sorry Aunt Maggie, but I handcuffed the warden in the car, I only have a minute. I want you to watch the front and the back for me while I grab a few things."

"No Josh, you can't do this, you have to stop right now."

"Please Aunt Maggie, this is important, and I need your help, now watch outside, please." Josh races upstairs to his room and grabs his daypack and a few things.

In a few short minutes, Josh has committed felony assault, and probably a whole host of crimes. Now he is poised to go on the lam, all on a mission to keep Pepper out of the clutches of Fish and Game warden Rich Rogers.

"Anything change Aunt Maggie," yells Josh as he bounds down the stairs heading for the kitchen." He grabs Maggie's big floppy sun hat as he goes by the coat rack, and pauses at the side door.

"No, nothing, everyone's down on the dock."

"Ok, I want you to tell everyone that will listen that Rich Rogers is trying to illegally capture Pepper and take her away, call Chad at channel 12, tell em all."

"Josh are you sure, this is what you want to do."

"Yes, more sure than anything in my life." He dons the hat and steps out the side door; the woods trail is only one hundred feet away. He is invisible to the dock, but Ted, cuffed in the car can see him. Both Charley and Ted notice him immediately, the floppy hat hides his face, but does nothing to disguise his height or walk. In seconds, the thick spruce forest swallows him and he sprints for the *Islander Grand Resort*. He stops while still hidden in the trees at the edge of the forest. There are six cars in the parking lot. Inside the dining hall guests are having their wake up coffee's, croissants and OJ's.

Text compose: Fish and Game boats are in the cove trying to catch Pepper, Charley's in custody, I escaped. Meet me in woods right now, don't tell anyone.

Come on Sammie, look at your message. Josh watches the dining terrace door open, and then out steps Sammie, she eases the door shut behind her not letting it slam, and takes the steps down to the fire pit area, she crosses over the bricks and follows the gravel path into the woods. Where the gravel ends and trees begin, she quietly calls his name.

"Over here."

"What's going on?"

"Pepper is in trouble, they say they want to take her to a research place for her own protection, the whole thing is bogus. Charley and I got arrested, but I handcuffed the warden in his own car and ran over here. They're going to be coming down the trail any minute, I need to lead Pepper away, I want to borrow a kayak—please, I need your help, we have to hurry before she gets caught in their net?"

"What should I do?"

"Sneak a kayak down to the water, and leave it, but don't let anyone see you, I don't want you in trouble too, I'll say I stole it. Then tell everyone you know, that Rich Rogers from Fish and Game is poaching an orca named Pepper, call the news and get word to the whale museum."

"Ok, I'll do it." Sammie reaches out and throws her arms around him, for a moment they embrace, cheeks touching, and everything is at it should be. She pulls back and kisses him square on the lips.

"Who are you?" says Sammie looking into his eyes.

"Go—we only have minutes." Sammie turns and runs back to the lodge. "Say you were out jogging." Yells Josh. *Oh wow –she kissed me!*

From his phone contacts he scrolls names until he finds Chet-Chester-save the whale-people. He pushes call. Three rings and then a sleepy Chester answers.

"Hey Chet wake up, this is Josh Pearson, we have an orca situation, and need your help." Chet has heard enough to snap him wide-awake.

"At your service Josh, what do you need?"

"The fish and game people are trying to catch Pepper; they want to take her to a research facility for her own protection. It doesn't sound right, I think the whole thing is bogus, and they are up to something. They have boats and nets and are in the cove right now. I want you to rally the troops and get the news out. You don't by any chance know where their main office in the islands is?"

"It's at Friday Harbor, Josh, right next door to the marina office, the same building as Customs and Homeland Security why?"

"What do you think Chet—would a protest rally would draw much media attention in front of their big fancy sign?" Sammie comes back into view; she is carrying a kayak and paddle on her head using a life vest for padding. "I have to go Chet, my ride just arrived, keep your phone on, I might need help." Sammie sets the kayak near the bank where it is hard to see and heads back up the stairs to the guests having breakfast. Josh hurries through the woods to the beach trail, and is kneeling next to the kayak in minutes. *Oh my god, she's giving me her own kayak.*

He scrolls his phone looking for the university researcher that called Charley. *There you are!*

"Hello, whale research."

"Ahem—This is Winthorp the 3rd, someone at this number asked us to let you know if we spotted L21 and her baby. I just saw the baby spouting and heading toward West Sound, around the point past the *Islander Grand Resort,* if you know where that is?"

"Oh yes, we know the point, you say you just saw it?"

"I'm watching it right now as we speak."

"Okay, thank you Mr Winthorp, I'll pass it on."

"You heard, they spotted the baby, what do we do." Says the research assistant.

"Call Rogers, this may be just the chance we've been waiting for."

Josh puts his phone in a waterproof white water bag, and zips it all into his backpack.

He looks up to a scampering on the steps, its Sammie coming down carrying a plastic bag full of donuts and sealed OJ bottles.

"You may get hungry; I packed you some feel good energy food." Instead of taking the bag he takes her by the shoulders and holds her in front of him.

"I can't believe your giving me your own kayak, that means a lot to me." He pulls her to him and kisses her like she had kissed him earlier, only he holds and hugs her afterwards."

"I'll get you ten more," she says, her arms draped around his neck. They begin another kiss, but a high-speed motor whine breaks the silence ending the tender moment. The first Fish and game boat clears the cove entrance. Josh turns, and pulls Sammie down to kneel beside him as the second boat heads out. In a minute the boats are gone around the point.

"That's my cue, I gotta go find Pepper and get her to safety."

"Where?"

"Rock Island." Josh picks up Sammie's special lightweight boat and carries it to the water's edge. *I kissed her, I kissed her twice, and now I'm leaving, still dumb as a rock.* She watches as he stows his backpack, and then the donuts where he can reach them. He gets in like an expert, like she taught him to do in his own boat. Once situated and floating free he takes the double ended paddle and raps it on the boats hard storage lid, thump thump—thump thump.

"Sorry," he says to Sammie, "It's all we understand." Thump thump—thump thump.

"I don't mind, get going."

Josh pulls gentle slow strokes at first, as his speed and confidence builds, so does his picture perfect strokes. *This boat is awesome, and so is Sammie.* When he approaches Pearson Cove he quits paddling, and signals Pepper again, but she has been waiting to see who was in the approaching kayak. She clicks a long string, saying hello.

"Hello girl, let's go, we need to disappear before they wise up and come back." He doubles down before the kayak comes to a stop, and quickly rebuilds his momentum. Then he adds more effort. *We are not going to lose this race because of one weak stroke.* The shoreline flies by as Josh digs in, Pepper glides along effortlessly a little further offshore, Josh hugs the beach keeping his silhouette blended with the background he can dash for shore should the Warden's boats return.

By now Rogers undoubtedly knows he locked Ted in his own handcuffs. What Josh does not know is that Ted never mentioned he saw him take off on the woods trail. Josh never expected his escape route to be a secret, all he wanted was enough time to get Pepper away. He assumes they will catch him, throw the book at him, and he will go to jail. When Rock Island first comes into view Rogers still doesn't know, how or where he has made off to.

They don't enter the cove at Rock Island. Pepper has most likely explored the cove but never with Josh. He paddles away from the cove, circling the Island instead. On the far side facing Haro strait, is a volcanic shelf extending out from shore, the shelf has a broad crack that runs from the cliff face out into the ocean underwater for five hundred feet. The crack is easily fifty feet wide and fifty feet deep. Big Momma could rest there and take a nap, and she may have. There is no beach except for a tiny spot of gravel, any bigger boats floating along the shelf are likely to sustain damage if they get too near shore. Josh brings Sammie's kayak next to the gravel and turns sideways, being careful not to damage its thin membrane skin. Pepper discovers the crack and floats in deep water only a few feet from where Josh sits down.

"That's it Pepper, I haven't planned anything beyond this point, I'm all ears and open for suggestions—Nothing to say?" *What's that, hide the kayak you say, that's an excellent idea.*

"Share a donut?"

Chapter 20 - Seattle

The ferry and car ride to Seattle is four hours. An hour waiting for Rogers to give up looking for Josh, and Pepper, one hour on the ferry, one hour on the freeway, and one hour in heavy stop and go traffic. Charley has gone from pissed to bemused to aggravated, and back to pissed. Rogers chewed his agent Ted a new one, and in the process tossed some nasty vulgarism's and threats Charley's way, plus some nasty's targeting Josh. Pepper is reduced to being called a whale again. Upon arriving at the Fish and Game home office in Seattle, Charley is still in handcuffs and led up the sidewalk past three tie died long haired demonstrators, chanting and carrying signs saying save the whales.

"See," says Rogers, "these people don't want you keeping that whale in your cove."

"Arrest Roger's, arrest Roger's—free Pepper, free Pepper," is what they are chanting.

"What the, I'm not the one in cuffs," says Rogers to field agent Ted, as they push past the sign holding demonstrators shoving Charley ahead of them. Before they enter the building, a reporter followed by a TV cameraman runs up and sticks a microphone in Rogers face and ask him why he has arrested an innocent man. Rogers face darkens five shades of red.

Once inside, he is met with orders from his superiors to release Charley and immediately deliver him back to Orcas Island. It seems that while in transit an attorney's office served notice of their intention to bring suit on behalf of Mr. Pearson for unlawful search and seizure, unlawful arrest and detention, trespassing, harassment, and a host of other misconduct charges. They were also petitioning to have Rogers arrested for violation of the marine mammals act.

"What about my nephew, agent Rogers," says Charley smugly.

"What about him?"

"Is he free to come back?"

"Hell yes, he can do whatever he wants, and when we catch him he'll be charged with assaulting a federal agent, and fleeing arrest."

"He didn't actually hurt me," says Ted while rubbing his thumb, "he just snapped the cuffs on me, he's really fast."

"Doesn't matter, he can't do that and get away with it. Now turn around and take this asshole back to his hole. I'll see you tomorrow for your written report explaining how a kid put cuffs on a trained agent." Rogers is fit to be tied, and he just walks away, leaving Ted and Charley in the main lobby of the Fish and Game department building.

Holding his arms up, Charley says, "Do you think we can dispense with these." Ted produces a key and takes the cuffs off.

"Sorry Charley." Says Ted snickering at his old joke.

"I've heard that one."

"Mr. Pearson?" a young man asks that has been standing to one side. He comes forward holding out his business card.

"Yeah, I'm Charley Pearson," massaging the red marks on his wrists, and taking the card.

"I'm an attorney for the law office of Chesterfield & Chesterfield; I filed the petitions this morning that led to freeing you."

"Oh, well thank you, much appreciated, Maggie must have called you, but what about my nephew, he's hiding out somewhere, and probably afraid to come back."

"I'm sorry to say it, but Agent Rogers is right, he assaulted a federal officer, he will probably be charged in federal court with felony assault."

"But all he was doing is protecting an orca from being captured by these guys."

"Of course there are mitigating circumstances that need to be played out, but right now your nephew needs to give himself up. This is not a game."

"Let's go, we have a long ride," Ted reaches for Charley's arm, but Charley yanks it away.

"You can keep your hands to yourself agent, if Josh is right about Rogers; you're on the wrong team."

"Call us, if you hear from Josh, but we will be in touch regardless," says the attorney, "these things tend to be involved."

Outside, a TV crew is waiting for them. "Mr. Pearson, is it true your nephew Josh speaks to whales."

"No, no, that's not true, he speaks to an orca ." Says Charley, all friendly, smiley and not too sarcastic.

"How does he do it, what does he say?"

"He talks to her with respect, much like we talk to each other. He said to her to be brave, and not afraid. He told her he would not hurt her."

"And what did the orca say to that." Says the reporter, trying not to snicker.

"Pepper said nothing, she's an orca . The best she can come up with is clicks, chirps and whistles. The real story here is that Rich Rogers's person, the fish and game agent in charge. He has been trying to capture Pepper for research. He claims it is for her protection, he wants to take her from her mother and family, and lock her up in an aquarium. She's just a baby, that's the story."

"Where is Pepper now?"

"I don't know."

"Where is Josh?"

"I don't know."

"What are you going to do now?"

"Go home and have dinner."

Ted and Charley climb back into the black Crown Victoria agency car they arrived in an hour earlier. Ted is driving of course, but Charley is riding shotgun instead of being cuffed in the back.

"I'm sorry," says Ted, "I think Rogers may have over stepped his authority, but I'm unable to do anything, I'm liable to be brought up for reprimand as it is for letting Josh get the drop on me."

"You couldn't have stopped him, Josh is a champion martial arts fighter, it's fortunate you were an easy take down. He could have easily hurt you. He is also very smart, maybe genius smart. He sees thing others miss, my money is on him being right about Rogers."

"While I was escorting him up the dock, he stopped several times, I sensed he was playing me, calculating what to do."

"I'm sure he was, he can't help who he is. Listen Ted, we can both get home at a decent time, and save your department some money if you drop me at the *Victoria Clipper* passenger ferry dock, instead of driving all the way back to Anacortes. Just put my ticket to Friday Harbor on your government credit card, and I will pick up the tab and the shuttle over to Orcas Landing. Everyone wins, and I'll be sure to keep quiet about your not saying anything about the person with the floppy hat walking off into the woods."

"It's a deal," says Ted.

Chapter 21 - The Feds

Maggie and Chet have been busy all day. After calling their local Orcas Island Attorney and being assured he would look into getting Charley released, Maggie logged on to Facebook and posted pictures of Pepper and Josh and a plea for help. She did what Josh asked and at every opportunity said the Fish and Game people were capturing baby orcas.

Chet contacted his *Save-the-whale* friends in Seattle who were responsible for the news people showing up. What Chet and the Seattle people started, was just the beginning, by the time Charley and Ted left, more protesters had shown up, and they kept coming.

On San Juan Island, Chet and Christy met up with their local entourage of dedicated young people and formed a line twenty people long in front of the local Fish and Game office. The building fronts on the waterfront promenade overlooking the marina, and also houses Customs and Immigration and Homeland Security. Reporters with cameras have converged on Friday Harbor and images with the government building in the background are flooding the Internet. With each incoming ferry, a new batch of tourists and reporters join the growing throng outside the Rogers office.

"Save Pepper—arrest Rogers," is the mantra chanted.

Just as Josh anticipated, the truth is nearby but not necessarily in line with facts. One blog has game wardens selling orca aphrodisiac parts overseas. Another has Rogers smuggling illegal aliens in through Canada. The actual images that Maggie has posted are being hijacked and reposted with new text, some claiming horrendous acts perpetrated against baby orcas.

Every new ferry arrival from the mainland brings reporters looking to scoop a story. Each group of foot passengers disembarking down the gangway includes more tie-dyed, wild haired young people eager to get involved with saving whales—or just a good protest. The phone at the *Islander Grand Resort Bed and Breakfast* is ringing non-stop, Sandy is booking all her rooms, everyday, and has agreed for a fee, to let news crews set up in her parking area. She has consented for interviews where she is quick to insert, *Islander Grand Resort Bed and Breakfast,* at every opportunity. During one interview, the reporter asked her if the disruption was good or bad for business, and she quickly replied how great it was; only she felt bad that Josh and Charley had gotten in trouble, and for that, she was sorry.

The fish and game boat crews gave up early, they were there to net a juvenile orca , not chase down a teenage runaway, accused of handcuffing a warden in the back seat of his own car. After their early wild goose chase and subsequent sightings and reports phoned in by many of Chet's allies, they give up and report back to their marina slips in front of the county building in Friday Harbor. They are met With protesters, and reporters accusing them of stealing orca babies. It's a bad day to be wearing a uniform in San Juan County.

Charley looks like any of the hundred or so tourists boarding the Victoria Clipper at Seattle's waterfront terminal on Elliott Bay. All the hubbub at Fish and Game and in the San Juans has not filtered down to them yet. For the first hour, Charley walks around the decks like any tourist enjoying the view and marveling at the power of the high-speed catamaran passenger ferry. Soon the wind and sea chill send him indoors where he finds a window seat and falls fast asleep. He wakes for a moment when the captain announces they are transiting the renowned Deception Pass first explored by Captain Vancouver. Leaping onto the swells of Juan De Fuca Strait quickly lulls him back to sleep until the boat slows and enters Friday Harbor. Walking up the gangway, Charley has no idea, all the commotion over in front of Customs is about Pepper, he hardly gives it a second look and turns toward the inter island shuttle on the next wharf over.

"Hey Charley, haven't seen you in awhile, what you been up to," says the shuttle skipper.

"Nothing much, went to Seattle today, lots of people there, you know. Ok if I sit up front here?"

"That's for sure—about two more minutes," yells the shuttle skipper to the other commuters heading for home around the islands.

"Is this the boat going to Orcas Landing," asks a pretty girl dressed in a blazer, baseball cap, and sneakers.

"Yes Ma'am, it's our second stop."

"Ok—this is it Pete, over here." Pete arrives momentarily, loaded down with back packs and video gear, they both climb in the back.

"I'll get the lines for you," offers Charley, he steps onto the dock, and throws off two ropes.

More boats have pulled into Pearson Cove today than perhaps any day in the last century. Sammie has led groups of up to twelve Kayaks from the *Grand Resort*. Whale watching tour boats with thirty passengers each, came through all day. One small cruiser with two people on board is anchored off to the side. Several times boats have tied up to the lodges old dock and people have come up to the house to ask Maggie if she knows where to see the orca . The driveway has been blocked by Fish and Game trucks all morning while agents beat the woods looking for Josh.

ORCA BOY

"Do you have a ride picking you up Charley?" Says the shuttle skipper.

"Naw, I'm early, Maggie doesn't know I'm coming, I'll get the taxi."

"Why don't I drop you at the cove, we're going right by, and you can surprise Maggie."

"That would be great, Skip, I owe you one."

"Think nothing about it Charley, we all owe each other sooner or later."

Skip brings the water taxi all the way in, gliding past the anchored boat and the boat lift. He noses up to the dock right next to shore. Charley is already standing and steps off as Skip brings the bow around. The entire diversion takes thirty seconds, the boat is back on plane at thirty knots before it clears the cove entrance.

The good looking lady in the blazer, clinging seat by seat works her way, up to the helm.

"Excuse me driver, what was that place called where you just dropped off that man?"

"That's Pearson Cove, once upon a time it was called orca Bay."

"Is that where all the orca controversy today originated?"

"Beats me lady, I been driving the boat all day; I don't know anything about any orca business, But that's Orcas Landing up ahead there and end of the road unless you're going back to Friday Harbor."

Maggie is watching out the window. The day has been hectic to say the least. When she sees the boat with TAXI blazoned across the roof in big white letters, she groans. *Not more,* but then she waves and yells, *"Charley,"* when she sees him step onto the dock. Looking up at the house, he sees Maggie at the window and waves back. Maggie is out the door before the water taxi clears the cove.

Sammie is finished taking care of the last of guests needs and her chores. Sandy is at her keyboard tweaking her web sites and promotions. She has been raking in the rents and extra fees she charges for kayak excursions and news people in her parking lot. She is earning a lot of notoriety that she hopes will convert to more profit. Reporters have interviewed her, asking about Josh and

Charley. She has freely offered tidbits of information gleaned from Sammie, but promoting the *Islander Grand Resort Bed and Breakfast* is her primary agenda

Chapter 22 - Fugitive

Sammie slides the two passenger Kayak into the water, Sadie is already sitting in front wedged in with a backpack.

"Be quiet Sadie," she whispers, "lay down." Sadie minds, she senses they are being stealthy and rests her chin on the smooth fiberglass. Sammie follows close to shore staying in the long afternoon shadows and out of sight of prying eyes.

"She's acting sneaky," says the federal agent, "she took a backpack, and she's up to something and doesn't want to be followed, so let's follow her." The two agents drive their unmarked car up the road but they can't see her, they nose into the drive at Pearson Cove in time to see her paddle by the entrance. "She's still going west, let's keep on it." Another quarter mile up the road they pull into a driveway leading to a vacation cabin, the place is well lit indicating someone is home, they park and dash around back. The view out over the channel is narrow. They keep their eyes on the water.

"Hey—what are you doing out here?" says the owner coming out the door of the house.

"Keep watching," says one agent to the other. "Sir we're federal agents investigating an assault case. For your own safety, go back inside. She should have been here by now, we must have missed her. Come on hurry." They race back to the road and turn down a lane leading to six more cabins; the first two have no water access or view. "Were screwed," says one of the agents, "I don't know if we are ahead or behind her, and past here the road turns inland and goes over the ridge. According to the map, there's nothing but uninhabited land for miles. Let's go back and watch, or find a boat."

Sammie hugs the shore, she blends in with the darkening background so well she is almost invisible. It's slack tide, there is no current, she is working for every mile, and the heavy two-person kayak and Sadie are not helping. Approaching Rock Island, she texts Josh one word, *"dinner."* Josh is not expecting her, but the message is clear. He jogs quietly, staying on his toes, avoiding pounding along the trail.

The island is small enough that he can get to any point quickly, but it is large enough that an unwanted federal agent could easily arrive without his knowledge. When he comes to an open area he spots Sammie in the cove, he also spots a small cruiser ghosting along the shore about a mile back. He hustles down to the beach making sure he is out of sight of any binoculars on the lurking vessel.

" Hi Sadie, did you come to visit the dangerous felon? I think you may be followed; I saw a boat way back, let's get this kayak hidden." Sadie jumps out barking.

"Wait," says Sammie, "if I was followed, then I need to paddle back out. And lead them away from the island."

"You are probably right, but if they saw you come in here, then it's too late," says Josh, "If they saw you paddle out of sight around the Island, same thing. Besides, this island is such a logical choice anyone really trying to find me would have been here ten minutes after I arrived. The person in that boat either doesn't know, or doesn't care, or they want something else."

"Where's Pepper?"

"Exactly, they want Pepper, not me. Hopefully she's around the other side, or better yet, out in the strait. There's a deep natural crack leading right up to the cliff base, that's where I came ashore, I don't want her coming into this cove, and then getting trapped and caught.

"What happened after Pepper and I left."

"Everything—It's been a police and news feeding frenzy. I've been working my butt off. Sandy has rented or sold out the next month, there are protesters roaming around, and news people have set up in our parking lot. The news is showing protestors at Friday Harbor and Seattle. They took Charley away, that Rogers's guy was on the news saying he was here to protect the baby orca from people like him. Sandy is thrilled with all the news mentioning Orcas Island and the *Islander Resort,* and she keeps saying it's too bad about Charley and you getting caught up in all this."

"Charley's ok," says Josh, "he came home in the water taxi a couple hours ago."

"He did, how do you know that, I saw the taxi go around the point. That explains why he was so close to shore. He must have just dropped him off minutes before, but how did you know."

"Maggie texted me, she also told me that the anchored boat had left the cove right after you and Sadie went by."

"You knew I was on my way, boy, you're not missing a thing."

After lugging the kayak into the woods they keep hiking to the clearing at the summit and then sit in front of *Proposal Rock*. Sammie empties her pack, dumping out hot dogs, buns, a blanket and a backpacker's sleeping bag. Josh scurries around scrounging tinder and firewood from the underbrush.

"I brought some paper to kneel on," she smirks, "but you look dirty already." He readies a ring of stones and sets a fire using the same shaved stick technique as before, only this time he squeezes a juicy hot dog and rubs an oily smear onto a thin strip of torn paper.

Looking at Sammie, he says. "Don't try this with marshmallows, it gets really sticky." Then he tucks the greasy paper into his tinder and throws a spark directly onto the exposed tip. The flames take and the fire grows. "We want to keep this raging infernal small and hot so there is little smoke." Sammie skewers two hot dogs on a fork and sits cross-legged in front of their tiny cooking fire. Soon the sizzle and smell fills the clearing.

Sadie barks a warning, someone is coming up the trail but it is too late for Josh and Sammie to melt away into the woods.

"It's ok, It's just the people that followed you, whispers Josh, don't volunteer anything about us or Pepper." A man and woman trudge into the open, they both have the look of a couple out on an outing much like Josh and Sammie. He looks to be about Forty or older, she is somewhere between eighteen and forty. She carries a water bottle by the strap and sports a WU baseball cap with her ponytail pulled out the back. He wears a fanny pack, jeans and a button down long sleeve shirt.

"Sorry to interrupt your dinner," says the man, "we didn't expect anyone to be up here."

"Yeah," says the woman, "there's no boat at the dock so we thought the park was deserted."

"Oh, that's ok, you're not interrupting, enjoy the rest of your hike." Says Josh.

"Nice day," says the man not making any effort to walk away, "getting dark soon, doncha think?"

"Boy," says the lady, "that's a big rock,"

Sammie and Josh eye each other, grinning. The couple is obviously trying to make conversation.

"It is a nice day," says Josh, speaking to the man first, and then Sammie, "What do think, will it get dark soon?"

Sammie joins in the fun, mocking the newcomers to their face. "It seems to me it might get dark soon, but one never knows for sure." With the last remark they all uneasily stare at each other and the rock, they know they are all being insincere jokers, withholding their true thoughts, but Josh and Sammie are enjoying making the couple squirm.

"Ok, the getting dark question was lame. I'm Dave and this is Kirstin."

"Glad to meet you, Dave and Kirsten," says Josh, "now tell us why you have been anchored in Pearson Cove all day and then decided to follow us here?" Dave and Kirsten trade glances, apparently their activities in the cove had been watched and they are not considered discreet boating tourists like they have hoped.

"First—you tell us who you are." Says Dave in a weak attempt to take charge.

"Maybe later Dave," Josh suddenly stands and takes a step toward the couple, "I asked why you are following us." Dave's neck muscles flex and he involuntarily swallows looking up at Josh. Kirsten moves slightly closer and behind him. The intimidation maneuver establishes Josh's dominant status.

"We're from WU whale research lab, we heard that a juvenile orca was trapped and we are going to learn what we can and record the event." Josh watches Dave and Kirsten's faces for telltale signs of deception.

"You are Dave Johnson and Kirstin Jacobs." Says Josh. They don't need to acknowledge his identifying them, their wide eyed astonished faces show he has nailed them. "Why are you following us." He moves ever so slightly toward them while flexing his fists. He tilts his head sideways as if he is trying to pop a vertebrae like some people crack knuckles, but gets nothing.

Sammie quits cooking the hot dogs, leaning the carved sticks on a rock. She has visions of Josh forcing Winthorp to the ground, and the news report of him overpowering the game warden is dancing in her head. She anticipates trouble; the dicey encounter at the rock is quickly coming to a head. Sadie senses the growing tension and is growling her plan to follow Josh's lead. Sammie strains holding her back by the collar.

"Wait a sec." Dave raises his hand as if to halt an impending attack. "We just thought you would lead us to the orca. How do you know our names?"

"Never mind how I know who you are, what's your connection to Rogers." Sammie is as nervous as the two strangers are. Josh is forceful and intimidating and when bringing up Rogers he increases his intensity to the point of losing control. *Oh jeez this is easy, but Sammie's getting scared, I have to stop.*

"Nothing, we hardly know him, our department head deals with fish and game."

"You wrote a paper about the high mortality rate of new born and juvenile orcas."

"Yeah, that's true." Says Dave. "but it was never published though, how do you know about it?"

"I read a lot? It was a good paper, why didn't it get out?"

Sammie is dumbstruck, she's proud and excited to be with Josh, but he's scary. He keeps revealing amazing aspects of himself. The shy geeky kid with modest possibilities that she met on the ferry is unpeeling layers like a chameleon changes colors. He lights fire from nothing, he effortlessly takes down an older boy, then handcuffs a game warden, befriends and goes on the run with a rescue orca and single handedly starts a statewide protest; now he is passing judgment on lost research publications from a WU PhD.

"The program supervisor...."

"Peters?" says Josh.

"That's right, Nasal Peters, he said it was unsubstantiated poppycock and not worthy of a research scientist. That was years ago, and deleted, how did you read it?"

"If you want something deleted, you need to burn it, but once it is shared on a net, it's too late."

The tension in the clearing has reduced, Sammie catches Josh's wink. She can't wait to throw her arms around his neck and ask him again, who he is.

"But the university uses a secure encrypted network." Says Dave.

"Security is only as good as a password is strong." Says Josh, "Do Peters and Rogers have a working relationship, you know, share information and do each other favors."

"Well sure, that's how we learned about you, or I mean the orca . It's happened quite a few times."

"Excuse me Dave, can you be more clear, what has happened quite a few times?"

"You know, like with you, where a juvenile or a baby orca or dolphin gets trapped in a net and lost or separated from its mother and pod."

"Do they know where you are right now?" asks Josh.

"No," says Dave and he looks at Kristen.

"No," says Kristen, "I took a call from someone this morning reporting a sighting and wait a second, it was you that called," pointing at Josh, "I recognize your voice."

"Then what did you do?" prompts Josh, staying focused.

"So then I passed it on to Nasal, and called Dave. It was your idea to get a boat." says Kirstin.

"And then we looked around for an available boat and borrowed Ed's old cruiser" adds Dave, "and came over to Pearson Cove. Now we've answered all your questions."

"Did you tell Ed where you were going?."

"No, we have a standing offer to use his boat or a couple others whenever we want, he probably thinks it's still in the slip."

"One more question," says Josh, "why did you follow Sammie out to this island?"

"The dog, I saw the dog and you in some video on utube. It was obvious. So now we all know who everyone is, except what explains your intimate knowledge of orcas and my work at WU."

"I told you, I read a lot, and have a memory for details." Says Josh.

"And you," says Kirsten, asking Sammie, "what's your role."

"I play Josh's good friend and deliver hot dogs, and what do you do?" At that, she hands Josh a dog on a fork. "Hold this; I'll get you a bun." Then she bends over and reaches into the sack, the other three watch. "Stop that, you know what I mean." Says Sammie.

Josh and Sammie share the fire and hotdog's; they also share information about the University research program and Rich Rogers. It seems Rogers and Peters and Kirstin have known each other from long before Dave had come to the program. Jacobs tells Josh she has lived on San Juan Island her entire life. She says her mother was active in whale research before her, but dementia forced her into a home. Jacobs says she works in Peter's office doing much of her mother's old job. Josh learns from them some missing pieces to a large puzzle.

When the long shadows merge and chills in the breeze cause shivering, Dave and Kirsten head for their boat. But not before exchanging e-mails and phone numbers. Josh has volunteered precious little, about his plans, Sammie even less, but he does ask them about locating a tenacious and well connected reporter in case they need to break a big story when he turns himself in. He also asks Dave to e-mail him stats for every juvenile orca death at WU, or orca that was transferred to another facility.

"That was an interesting picnic crashing." Says Josh grinning, when they are alone again.

Bursting at not knowing, Sammie blurts out, "Who are you Joshua Pearson! You scared me to death, I thought you had snapped, you terrified them by simply standing up. That thing you did tweaking your neck convinced *me,* you were ready to kill someone. After that they would have told you anything you asked. And how do you know who they are, and their names, and what was that about unpublished papers, you can't know all that, can you?"

"Slow down Sammie, have a tic-tac." He holds her hand as she taught him and shakes two tic-tacs into her palm, he picks one up and pushes it against her lips, when she cracks a grin he pops it in her mouth, then she places the other one against his lips and does the same. Next he takes her in his arms and she is sure he is about to kiss her, but he pulls her to him and wraps his arms around her.

"Listen Sammie, I'm not scary—I'm scared of you. I'm pretty good at martial arts, my mother made sure of that, and I have a good understanding of computers."

"You're really smart aren't you," still in a warm hug.

"What would you like me to be." Asks Josh, fearing her answer.

"Just be who you are and my friend." They both pull their heads back and plant a short kiss square on each other's lips. Pulling back again, she says, "What kind of grades do you get in school—A's?" says Sammie.

"Yes"

"AP classes?"

"Yes"

"Have you ever not got A's?"

"No"

"Really?"

"Really, I can't help it. I have a good memory."

"How did you know what to do when those two came up here."

"I didn't, but I intimidated Dave using aggression techniques that are part of martial arts, it's their vivid imagination that scared them. I'm sorry I scared you too, anyway, they may be on our side, you heard him say his professor, that Nasal Peters dude quashed his paper. That was five years ago and Dave was suspicious then. I wasn't sure this morning, but I am now, and I have an idea what to do.

"What?"

"Money, look for the money trail, people don't do what they do unless they get money for doing it. When I find the money, I can follow it and then everything will be revealed."

"How can you do that, you sound like a detective, but you're a kid hiding on an island."

"I know a little about computers and I have some friends, I need to spend some time on a public terminal, preferably a newer fast one. Any ideas?"

"There's a library in *Eastsound,* and I read about a computer summer camp at the middle school."

"One of those might work, but schools and library's set up all sorts of anti porn and violence filtering software that will have to be worked around. They even have alarms sometimes."

"Why can't you use yours or... I know, Sandy has a brand new PC she runs the resort with."

"I will if I have to, but it would be best to stay hidden, and keep our IP addresses out of it." Sammie's face is blank, "I don't know where this is going. I've been using my phone all day running off a solar charger, but now its dead and the sun is gone. Can I use your phone?"

"Sure, but not to call any girls, so that's how you knew all about the WU research program."

"You think?" laughs Josh, " I said I read a lot."

"Save the whales, this is Chet."

"Hey dude, You've done a great job rallying the troops, the news coverage is awesome, the net is exploding, I'm calling you Orca-man

"Josh my man," says Chet, "don't tell me where you are, we might be tapped."

"Good idea, listen I need some Internet time on an open public terminal, it needs to be unrestricted and fast. Any Ideas."

"Absolutely—mine."

"Sorry Orca-man, *public,* we need to save your butt for bigger things, not sacrifice it."

"Okay, I certainly appreciate not getting sacrificed, how about the *Whale Museum* at *Friday Harbor,* they have a free Internet room, and they know us there."

"That's perfect, and they're expected to be sympathetic to our cause. What are their hours?"

"Ten to five everyday."

"Thanks, I gotta run."

"Whoever that was, you were playing him like a fiddle?" says Sammie. "Are you playing everyone?"

"That was Chester, he's involved in the local *save the whales bunch.* You mean, am I playing you? Of course not, but If I say you are foxy, and you are, and you like to hear it, what's wrong with saying it to you."

"Nothing, I guess."

"Good, I think you're hot."

"Just shut up."

Later they hear the old cruiser leave the cove and then see it heading for San Juan Island. Sammie assumes Dave and Kirsten are both onboard, Josh assumes nothing. Logic escapes some people, but not Josh. Ever since he was a precocious tyke, just learning to ask questions, people commented that nothing got by him without a thorough examination or proper explanation. His early teachers enjoyed explaining to him things like, why chalk worked on the board but not on the window.

Josh has formed a scenario that fits everything he knows about Rich Rogers and orcas, including likely explanations for, why Rogers hasn't aggressively pursued him, and yet goes after Pepper with a vengeance, and why he is chummy with Nasal Peters. Tomorrow he will fill in enough holes to prove his suspicion.

Sammie reluctantly catches the incoming flood tide, whisking her home in record time. She and Sadie arrive back at the *Islander Resort* in total darkness, still eluding prying eyes.

Chapter 23 - Friday Harbor

As usual, the dark eastern sky gives up the night, but first it does a last brilliant starlight dance before finally relinquishing to the sun rising behind Mt Baker. Twilight was working over the last of the darkness much earlier when Josh pushed off. To make sure Pepper didn't follow him, he carried the kayak across the island and left from the cove. He has to travel about seven miles as the seagull fly's but dodging small islands and staying away from the main waterways forces him to cover more miles. Sammie's kayak is all she touted it to be. He skims the surface leaving only a hint of a wake. His measured strokes maintain momentum, and he steers the boat like an arrow homing in on a distant bulls eye.

Partway across the channel, the same two fish and game boats race out of a small side channel straight for the kayak. Josh coolly tilts the floppy hat hiding his face and paddles on; secure knowing that no one, not even Sammie knows where he is, his plans, or where he is headed. The boats go right by him; they are not concerned with a kayaker getting in some early exercise. It's more likely they are looking for Pepper. The thought riles him as he paddles, now more energized than ever.

Approaching Friday Harbor, he slows to a relaxing pace. His destination is in sight, and dangerous ferryboat encounters are no longer an issue. The difficult channel crossings are over so he hugs the shore paddling in water only a foot deep. He has some time to kill before the *Whale Museum* opens so he takes it easy and casually makes his way among the many boats crowding the free anchorage area.

Morning activities are in full force, dinghies and kayaks scurry about, Josh blends invisibly in plain sight. He paddles around the matrix of floating docks working his way closer to the gangway leading up to the bustling city.

Near the main walkway is a special low dock reserved for kayaks, he lifts Sammie's boat up onto the float and slips the paddle inside. Walking up the ramp with his backpack slung over one shoulder, he spots cameras sprouting from the first building. Lowering his face, hiding under his hat, he passes in front of the first floor *US Customs office,* and the secretive *Homeland Security* behind darkened windows.

The second floor houses Agent Roger's Department of Fish and Game. No protesters are in sight, not yet at least, it's still early for young people accustomed to island time and partying until all hours. The few eager media types milling around hoping to scoop a story don't know Joshua Pearson has walked right past them.

The empty promenade receives its first surge of people as the early ferry disgorges a batch of foot passengers. The regulars with somewhere important to be, briskly step around gawking tourists with cameras swinging from straps. Josh blends in with all the other kids.

Where the promenade meets Main Street there is a turn-around with a tiny park in the middle. He claims a freshly painted white bench and sets up his solar charger facing the morning sun. Then he stretches out laying his head on his pack, his floppy hat covering his face. Sleep overtakes his exhausted body in minutes.

Chapter 24 - Freedom

Game Warden Rich Rogers had been at his desk only minutes when Josh slipped into the marina right under his nose. The Fish and Game office has a commanding view of the marina but with thousands of boats and a busy ferry terminal, the agents don't even try to keep track of events. Same thing for Homeland security, they have boats and airplanes to track down bad guys, but right outside their doors are thousands of tourists, protestors, and people going to work. They all look the same to the agents, everyone is under suspicion, no one smiles in their office, not one person outside their doors is to be trusted. No one comes in their door to turn themselves in, saying arrest me, *I'm a bad guy terrorist, take me away*, so they have no customers.

In the Customs and Immigration office, they have lots of customers. They do the country's business making sure American tourists have the proper credentials to re-enter the country after spending a day in Canada. With all the tourists coming and going, it's bustling, and right now the *save the whale protesters* are showing up with their signs, so the promenade has become one big pedestrian bottleneck.

Rogers is perplexed, the little backwoods kingdom that he has run for over a decade is suddenly in the spotlight. Higher ups in the department that normally ignore him are weighing in on his decisions, and dirty hippie protesters are materializing along with reporters and cameras.

"This is Rogers, any leads on that juvenile orca ."
"No, nothing Rich," says Nasal," I'm surprised, it seems like this one is charmed."

"It's that Pearson bunch. They taught it to fetch sticks, and hide, it's a real shame, the only safe place for it now is somewhere like Sea World. If I don't pick it up soon we'll have a tragedy on our hands."

"What about setting up a net at the cove entrance and just wait." Says Nasal

"Good idea, but I'll go one better and withdraw assault charges against the kid. With no reason to be on the run he may show himself, and call the whale back."

"Now you're thinking Rich"

"All right then." Rogers hangs up.

Chapter 25 - Hacking is illegal

A tired person can sleep through almost anything, that is except being cooked alive. After three hours Josh is covered in sweat, the morning sun has risen high and is beating relentlessly down on him. The little park is across from an ice cream shop and draws crowds of melting ice cream lickers to its benches. Josh wakes hearing people saying things like, *for a homeless person, he sure has a nice solar charger.* He tries to doze back off, he's relieved thinking that no one has stolen his phone or charger, and sleeps for another five minutes.

Finally thoughts of Pepper and what needs to be done today ease him fully awake. Without getting up, he surveys the crowd, and checks his phone. Its 10:15, and he has 65%. Sitting up with his head hanging, he slouches on his pack, his floppy hat hides him. Looking around he see others like him, each with their own personal look and bench. He logs on. Peppers new Hotmail account has some messages. He checks the senders and subject lines.

YES!

Walking the promenade toward the Whale Museum, the crowd thickens near the Fish and Game building. Media are interviewing protesters and tourists flock to the show. His inclination is to mix with the crowd melding in, hiding in plain sight. Maybe when some video is aired Rogers will spot his face looking right at him, and know he just got poked in the eye right in front of his own building. *Dumb idea,*

Peppers life depends on him. He turns and walks away. The side street is busy, but there are no cameras. The Nouveau riche touristy people are in a hurry and move along as if their stressful lives will catch them if they slow down. The young people slinging packs move in their own non-deliberate way. Josh is on an important mission, but he takes it easy, he can't help Pepper if he is caught. The Whale museum is back from the waterfront with a minimal view in the low rent area. He watches from across the street. The building has seen better days, but the front entry was updated forty years ago with rockwork and small tile murals depicting breaching orcas, flat plank chainsaw carvings adorn one side. On the door is a neatly lettered sign, "Free Admission, donations accepted"

Well, here goes. He walks in, head down, hat down, he doesn't look for cameras, if he sees a camera then the camera sees his face. To his left are the restrooms; ahead is a desk for taking donations and answering questions, a young girl his age watches him from behind the desk. He returns her smile. *A friend, I bet she knows Chet and Christy.* Beyond the desk is a large room filled with displays. To the right of the desk is a hallway with a sign saying Orca Theater, below that is a smaller sign reading *Free Internet room.*

"Hi, my names Joshua," he waits for her to answer.

"Hi, I'm Carly

"Is the computer open Carly." He barely lifts his head for an instant to make eye contact.

"It sure is, help yourself." Smiling she tilts her head and ducks down to see under his hat, he's smiling back at her, and then she motions him down the hall as if he's an eccentric old friend that comes in all the time but still needs to be told it's ok to be there. With a surge of confidence, he turns and opens the only door. Inside is a darkened room with rows of folding chairs facing the screen. The fifteen-minute show is playing; suspenseful base reverberates through the museum theater room. Three people are sitting in the middle, eyes glued to the screen.

Josh lets his eyes adjust to the dimness and spots a row of three empty computer stations along one wall. He plans to choose the fastest newest PC but they are all the same, he goes to the last one and turns it on. Then he reaches over and punches the on button on the empty one next to him and sets his pack on its chair. As an afterthought, he turns on the first one too and then plugs his phone charger into the power strip. While he waits for the computers to boot he pulls out of his pocket some bathroom paper towels and lays a folded one across the top of each monitor blocking its camera. His monitor lights up.

"Welcome to the Whale Museum." He clicks on control panel, then settings. The message box asks for an administrator password. He types, orca , then Whale, Museum, Guest, 1234, abcd, and then hits it with, -*password*-. *Got it, twenty seconds, is better and faster than taking it apart and pulling a jumper.* He goes into settings and resets to factory defaults, at the start up menu, he disables all the ads and promo software. Next, he looks at Internet options. Satisfied the computer will function as it was meant to, he clicks restart.

He types in Hotmail and goes to savingpepper911 at Hotmail. Already there is a full screen of e-mails, he opens one marked query results code and copies the thirteen-digit number and letters to the clipboard. Next he pastes the number into a blank document and shrinks the screen. Going back to Peppers e-mail account he opens an e-mail titled DataMaster24 and clicks on the hot link. The whale museums fast new computer instantly opens the web site. The instructions are clear, "enter launch code" you will have twenty four seconds before the connection is broken. Josh types in the string of numbers and clicks enter, word document pages populate the screen.

His fingers blur as they fly over the keyboard short cut keys. *Five seconds is all I need, but thanks anyway.* Next his favorite part—he watches the remaining countdown until the DataMaster24 web site explodes in a shower of fireworks and the message -unable to make connection- appears. *Pepper thanks you guys, put it on my tab.*

Josh goes back to the blank doc. and saves it as –saving Peppers money trail.doc. He e-mails to Pepper at Hotmail an attachment plus he inserts the info in the e-mail body, and then clicks send. *Remember Pepper, you don't know how you got this information, it just appeared.*

Now that the important step of saving information to e-mail is complete, he reads the info supplied. Subject: Nasal Peters: age 46, WA State employee credit union - user name, Nslptsn – password, 362436TltS. All of Peters and the other individuals requested financial accounts with activity in the last ten years are listed, including account numbers and most recent passwords. Manhattan Bank, Wells Fargo Visa, First National Visa,   wife Naomi Peters: age 46, WA State Employee credit union, Chase Master card, Key Bank. Child: Preston Wells age 9 Chase, ECU online. Child: Arthur Peters age 3. David

Johnson: age 40, First National Montana, Chase Visa. Kirsten Jacobs: WU Employees Credit union, Edward Jones investments. And of course Richard Rogers, and the WU Whale Research dept.

Much of the financial data was readily available using simple searching software, but some of the encrypted information required hacking by a human data geek, and thus the need for secrecy and datamaster24. The loose community of worldwide computer enthusiasts Josh belongs to created datamaster24 offshore for their own protection and privacy.

They have no interest in anything but overcoming challenges and beating the system at its own game. Many of them see themselves as modern day Robin Hoods and techno-superhero's. Each member has their own expertise. Josh's memory for details helps him debug software. Members anonymously post what they want, and another member posts the answer or results. There is a friendly point system, Peppers query cost only 150 points, Josh's handle, ninjawhizkid13 has 3750 points remaining. Thirteen was Josh's age when he chose his user name.

Let's get started. He looks around, the Whale Museum Theater is empty, the three watching the video have left, eerie soft humpback whale sounds fill the theater. He types in WU Credit Union and accesses Nasal Peters's accounts. He takes only a minute to set filters for the reams of useless data and graph ready garbage that bank programmers seem to love. The numbers and dates pile up fast, some numbers are large forcing wider columns increasing pages. At first, he scrutinizes anomaly's only to find an explanation and ultimately wasting time. He can study later, his fingers fly, he saves page after page.

Knowing that Rogers or Deputy Sheriff Danny could walk through the door at any moment, he creates files for each person and e-mails them to Pepper for safe keeping. Josh is focused on collecting and transferring data, he doesn't notice the sliver of light or brushing sound as someone enters the theater. A large person approaches Josh from behind and watches, and then quietly whispers.

"I thought you might be here." Josh's entire body tenses, he is caught totally off guard, his reflex is to dive under the counter and come up kicking and punching. Luckily his first instinct is not to fight, but to preserve data, he hits send one more time, and at the same time he recognizes Chet's voice.

"Oh crap, you scared me to death, I'm going to get you back."

Sorry, what was I suppose to do, Knock.

"Yes—knocking works."

"What have you got here," Chet plunks himself down in front of the middle terminal, "this looks like a bank statement, who is this Jacobs person," he lowers his voice to a whisper. *"are you hacking?"*

"No—hacking is illegal, I have passwords and user names, I'm simply looking around. This one is done." His fingers fly over the keyboard short cuts and types Washington University Credit Union again, and then clicks member sign in. Then he types Dave Johnson's user name and password. Chet watches in astonishment, he can't begin to follow the rapid keyboarding, and he can't be quiet.

"Who is this Johnson guy, how did you get his password."

"He's a scientist at the WU Whale Research department." He ignores the part about how he got the account password.

"What's his credit union got to do with this?"

"Probably nothing, unless he's a crook, and then he will leave a money trail. I'm looking for clues, you know—follow the money."

"How do you know how to do this, I thought you just mind melded with orcas."

"That's funny, but you're the Orca Man. I have a knack for computers and something doesn't feel right about the fish and game people trying to catch Pepper, give me five minutes to finish copying deposits, and then we can analyze and look for connections.

"You got it Josh, I'll go get us some water."

Text message: *Sorry I'm not there helping, but from what I see on the Internet, you're having lots of fun. With us being half a day off, I don't know if you know that Charley was released and never booked, and they withdrew felony assault charges against you today. That will look better on your resume for sure. Watch your back, if you are correct, someone is getting plenty worried right now. Attorneys Chesterfield and Chesterfield in Seattle sprung Charley and are at your disposal. You met Chesterfield the 3rd – Winthorp. His dad is in your gratitude, apparently you taught Winthorp a lesson in humility, more importantly what did <u>you</u> learn from the exchange? How's Pepper doing?*

Dad

Text reply: *"Thanks for the update, I started out in the dark today and paddled from Orcas Island to Friday Harbor, my phone was dead, I knew Charley was home but not that I'm no longer a wanted man. Things are exciting but there are many ways to have fun. I've met some kids from Eastsound High School. Pepper is fine but, I'm wondering why she hangs around and wants to be friends, I hope she's not a whack job."*

Joshua

"Ok Josh, what can I do to help." Says Chet as he sits back down and sets two water bottles on the table.

"You can help me spot transactions that seem abnormal." Says Josh.

Both of them sit in front of monitors, Josh accesses Peppers E-mail and opens several windows with Rich Rogers banking information.

"See look here, he deposits the same amount each month," says Josh. "Probably his paycheck, that's normal, what were looking for is something that doesn't fit, look at the names look for anything."

"Right here," says Chet, "eight years ago, he made a 51K deposit, that's not normal."

"Let's bring that up and take a closer look at it. Ok, it says here the payer was American Title, that's probably from selling a house."

For hours, they sit in the darkened theater room, painstakingly scouring financial histories. They go through years of the WU Whale Research Department records, and don't spot any smoking guns. Rich Rogers has divorced and remarried three times, and has four children he pays to support. Nasal has been married twice, and has four children. Dave Johnson and Kristin lead simple uncomplicated lives. The WU Whale research dept is one convoluted dead end after another, the WU program receives grants and donations from all over the world and has complimentary sister programs with hundreds of research facilities. The whale department helps fund projects from one-person listening posts in the Antarctic, to expeditions in the Indian Ocean. Josh is sure that whatever Peters and Rogers are up to is buried somewhere in international dealings with organizations outside the country.

Text message from Maggie: *We see Pepper, but not you, are you Ok?*

Text reply: *Yes, I'm fine, I'm in Friday Harbor, Dad says the arrest warrant for me has been lifted so I can show my face again.*

Text: *That attorney, Winthorp Chesterfield called asking for you, he said they dropped charges, but you should stay out of their sights because there are bound to be bad feelings.*

Text reply: *OK*

It's the 3rd, Winthorp the 3rd, that's what he said, where's the 2nd? Is there a 2nd? Rogers has four children, is one Rich the 4th!

"We need to look at the kids!"

"What do you mean?" says Chet.

"Rogers and Peters, we need to verify the children exist and look for financial dealings in their names. Look for anything that has to do with children, you know like, school, sports, doctors, insurance."

"You got it Josh."

Josh types in the datamaster24 URL, and then opens a new query window. Subject: Nasal Peters, WU Professor, Whale research Lab, Orcas Island. Must verify four children exist and financial accounts are within normal bounds. Subject: Rich Rogers, Washington Fish and Game, same info, four children. Subjects: Dave Johnson, Kirstin Jacobs WU whale department researchers. Verify zero children and financial if children are found. Josh clicks enter and is assigned a number, he logs out. *Now we wait.*

Text message: *Hey Josh, I have some figures for orca deaths going back years, where can we meet? Dave J.*

Josh: *I'm off island, can you send it in an e-mail.*

Dave: *it's a hard copy.*

Josh: *can't you scan it?*

Dave: *I need to explain what some of it means, I'll bring it to you.*

Josh: *Ok, meet me at the FH Whale museum at 3 p.m.*

What is he up to, insisting we meet?

Chet and Josh continue to pour over the financial numbers, but Josh's pretty sure they aren't going to find anything, he likens what they are doing to peeling an onion or stripping toilet paper from a roll. When your all done, it's just like you knew all along, nothing, but you still do it.

"I'm starving," says Josh, "any suggestions?"

"There's a bunch of carts and stands down by the ferry landing, one place has huge burrito's, lets go, I'll show you."

"Ok, I'll e-mail you these files, you can look at them at home, maybe you will see something later."

Chapter 26 - Peppers Revenge

Josh and Chet head down the public stairs beside the Whale Museum, they come out on the waterfront promenade overlooking the Friday Harbor Marina.

Protestors are chanting, "Save the whales, save the whales," as they walk back and forth in front of the fish and game office. From his second story office, Rich Rogers stands back from the window, he has a good view of the crowds and can see every boat in the marina.

Unsmiling homeland security agents downstairs watch the crowd expecting terrorists to appear from every nook and cranny.

Chet knows most of the protesters, he nods to some, high fives others. A big person with long hair and a beard and carrying an earth first banner stops them.

"Hey Chet, this is a great protest, lots of news and media are here. That Rogers guy keeps looking out his window, you can tell he's not happy. Every time I see him look down here, I give him the fist and wave the flag at him. I know he sees it because he backs up out of view."

"Come on, let's go" says Josh, "I don't want any trouble."

"That's what this is all about dude, causing trouble and making waves, it's the only way anything gets done." Says the bearded one.

"Excuse me, aren't you Josh Pearson?" says a female reporter with a cameraman taping her every move . She sticks a microphone up to Josh, "Are you Josh Pearson?" she asks again.

"Yes," says Josh, He stops walking, Chet moves to one side, Josh faces the reporter, the cameraman elbows the bearded one out of his way to get the right angle, and then gives a thumbs up to the reporter.

"Why are you doing this?"

"I'm sorry, but you will have to be specific, why am I doing what?"

"This protest, why are you protesting?" says the reporter.

"I'm not, but I support everyone's right to protest, right now, I'm simply walking through, perhaps you should be asking your questions of Chet here." And then, he motions Chet in front of the camera and, dashes out of view. Chet cozy's up to the reporter and begins a practiced save the whales speech. When the reporter indicates her impatience with Josh leaving, Chet holds the microphone to make sure he gets in his two cents worth. Josh quickly places some distance between himself and the reporter and loses himself in the crowd.

"That's him, that's that little Pearson punk that started all this, you should be in jail you little twerp," yells Rich Rogers to nobody in his empty office. When I get my hands on you again, you won't be getting away like last time." Rogers continues his unheard threats and challenges to Josh and the whole Pearson family, including any distant or unborn relatives.

Josh slows after placing a good hundred feet between him and the reporter. He nonchalantly strolls, blending with another ferry load of tourists. He walks by the circular park where he slept earlier and makes his way to the wide sidewalk with the food carts and booths. According to Chet, the Burrito Bandit sells his burritos out of a converted trailer, and Josh has no problem spotting the brightly painted one man Mexican sidewalk eatery.

"What will it be Hombre, you want the Bandit to fix you up with the works with extra cayenne?"

"Yes," says Josh, "put it all on like you are making it for yourself, give me double refried pinto beans and hot sauce, and use two tortillas, not just one, with lots of hot enchilada sauce between them. Once it is created, wrap it up, cut it exactly in half on the diagonal, and then, wrap each half again, take your time, make it good."

"You got it Hombre, I like your style, and what shall we call it."

"Call it Pepper's Revenge, and if it's really good, I predict you will sell all you can make."

"Hey dude, you dumped me back there with that clueless reporter." Says Chet.

"I told you I would get even, but I don't know if we are yet. Anyway, you acted like you enjoyed it. I saw you grabbing the mike."

"Here's your *Peppers Revenge* Hombre, double wrapped and cut in half just like you asked, but who's Pepper?

"Pepper is that orca we're demonstrating about," says Chet, elbows on the window ledge, "where have you been?"

"I'll share the burrito with you Chet," says Josh, "the Bandit just created it, it's called *Pepper's Revenge.*" Josh unwraps the outer layer and holds the two halves up to Chet. "Pick the half you want."

"Why, what did you order, is this how you get even?"

"I Just told you, it's Peppers Revenge, choose one or I'll eat all of it myself."

Chapter 27 - Deceit

Josh and Chet cut through side streets and back alleys making their way back to the Whale Museum. They sit across the street in the shade. Tourists on foot from the ferry, steadily arrive at the museum, the nondescript double front doors don't do anything for the building. The sign on the wall is old. The little murals looks like a class project.

"Hey Chet" says Josh, "Friday Harbor is full of starving artists, I'll bet you could get someone to paint a big mural right there," pointing across the street at the museum front wall.

"Yeah why?"

"You want to help the killer whales right? Then you need to attract attention and give people something to identify with. See all those tourists coming and going, not a single one is taking a picture of themselves standing in front of the Whale Museum. They would if there was cool mural."

"Ok, I'm listening."

"I guess I have to paint you a picture. Hold a contest and offer a prize for the best design, plus offer a sponsorship plaque for individuals and businesses that contribute money. You could actually raise a lot of money for your group this way. Sell tee shirts and all sorts of orca stuff. Someone has to be in charge; you can pay yourself a salary and cover your expenses, even rent an office."

"I like your thinking Josh."

ORCA BOY

While Chet and Josh finish their Pepper's Revenge burrito and contemplate the future, a cherry red Lexus coupe drives up the street and slows in front of the museum. The car exudes perfection and performance. The flawless paint finish is a mile deep and reflects the day's few clouds, understated chrome wheels and low profile tires set the car in its own class of ownership. Dave Johnson is alone behind the wheel; he accelerates up the block looking for a place to park. Two minutes later, he walks down the sidewalk for his meeting with Josh.

"Do you know that guy," says Josh, motioning towards Johnson, "he was driving that Lexus that just went by."

"I've seen him and the car around; usually he has a hot babe with him. Why, is he someone special?"

"Could be, he's Dave Johnson, come on, let's go talk to him. Oh, and don't mention you looked at his bank accounts." Josh darts across the street as the door to the museum shuts behind Johnson. They catch up to him in front of the information desk.

Hi Dave," Says Josh from behind, "Hi Carly, I went to get a burrito, is the computer station still open, I hope?"

"I think so," says Carly, when she hears Josh's voice she turns toward him and straightens up in her chair arranging her hair on her shoulder, "I didn't recognize you without your big hat, go ahead." she beams at him. Josh holds her gaze, causing her to look down coyly. *She's nice and cute and I'm not saying dumb things.* Chet follows them back into the darkened room they had left an hour earlier. He pokes Josh in the back and whispers you're the man dude, but she's got a big mean boyfriend. The theater seats are empty; the video is ready to play again. They move three folding chairs together forming an impromptu huddle.

"We watched you pull up," says Josh while they arrange chairs, "That's a pretty impressive sports car you're driving."

"Boy, I'll say," jumps in Chet," I wish I could afford just the wheels on your car, I'll bet they cost more than my van."

"Yeah, they probably did, it's my pride and joy," says Dave, "it's cost me some bucks alright, but I've been lucky investing in the market, so it's like my reward to myself."

"It's an awesome ride, aren't you afraid the salt air will do some damage?"

"A little, speaking of rides," says Dave, "how'd you get here Josh? Did you paddle all the way, from where we met on Rock Island? That was only last night."

"I paddled over early this morning, my kayaks at the dinghy dock, right under Rogers' window. I'll head back the same way before dark. Anyway guys, we can talk cars and kayaks later. Dave what have you got?" Dave hesitates, glancing at Chet.

"He's ok, Chet meet Dave." Dave shakes his head yes, and pulls out a yellow pad turning it toward Josh.

"These dates are reported orca deaths," says Dave, "these dates are birth sightings, and these are orca shipments to other research labs."

"What's it mean," says Chet.

"Well first, a lot of this is guess work, sometimes we don't learn of a birth for months or perhaps years, and then we don't know for sure which adult is the mother. Some of these older orcas may have lots of offspring we don't know about, which reminds me, your girl Pepper has an older sibling born to L21 ten years ago, this one right here." Tapping an entry line.

"Really," Says Josh, "where is it now?"

Don't know, the sightings simply quit after two years, and L21 was never seen with another juvenile until Pepper was first spotted last year."

"According to what I have read online," says Josh, "right now, there are three pods totaling 135 individuals, but when I add up the numbers of births and deaths and orcas sent to other places, there should be around 175 Orcas here in the San Juan's. The numbers should be increasing, but they are barely sustaining a viable population. Up until about ten years ago the numbers were steadily rising, what happened ten years ago?" Josh looks at Dave Johnson and waits.

The meeting ends with Johnson abruptly announcing he will keep digging, but right now, he has to get going. He briskly exits the Whale Museum waving slightly to a cheerful Carly as he walks out.

"Well Chet, what have we learned?" asks Josh.

"That maybe some Killer whales are missing, and that guy considers my van a piece of crap."

"And?"

"And nothing, he doesn't know what I drive, how does he know his wheels are *probably* worth more than my van."

"You suggested it, and maybe he has seen your van."

"Doesn't matter, you don't diss a mans wheels or his mother."

"Or his sister or best girl, plus he's not telling the whole truth, we looked at his finances, there's nothing about investing or the stock market. He's hiding something, but you can't convict someone for what you don't know, you convict them for what you do know, and we know nothing."

"What do we do next Josh?"

"We keep looking at what we know and find a connection, but first I'm going home and get some sleep."

"Excuse me," says Carly from the open door, her hair and shoulders silhouetted in the bright hallway. Josh immediately stands and sets his theater chair straight.

"Is that better? Oh no let me guess, it's closing time and your throwing us out onto the cold hard street."

"Your funny, I'm afraid so, it's five o'clock and time to lock up." Carly lets the door swing shut, she has already gone through the museum display rooms turning off lights and making sure the last of the patrons have left. Lastly, she turns off the main lights leaving just the dim security lights for Chet and Josh to make their way to the front door. The three of them walk out together; Carly locks the door and drops the orca key bob into her pocket.

They exchange small talk, laughing about Josh's hat disguise. Josh thanks her for letting them use the computers. She asks them if they will be back tomorrow.

Josh says. "I don't think so, it's a long paddle from Orcas Island but is that an invite?" Carly's smile says yes. Chet punches him on the arm, and the two head down the stairs toward the promenade. Carly walks down the sidewalk toward a parked car in the loading zone. Her ex-boyfriend is sitting at the wheel.

ORCA BOY

Chapter 28- Fight

"I told you, I don't want to see you, now go away." Says Carly, through the open car window. He jumps out begging her to reconsider and blocks her way, forcing her to stop walking. She tries to go around him, but he grabs her wrists, holding her. When she resists and tries to pull away he squeezes harder, but she fights back and kicks him in the shins. He jumps back to avoid her kicks, but he doesn't let go.

"Stop it," she screams, "—Your hurting me—let me go." Hoping to shock him into leaving her alone, she screams help repeatedly as loud as she can. It works, he loosens his grip enough for her to pull free, and then she runs back toward the museum, fumbling for her key while running. She gets the key by the fob as he chases her up the sidewalk, and at the corner of the building by the top of the stairway, he grabs her wrist again.

"—Let me go—*help*," she screams while clubbing her fists at his face. The swinging key narrowly catches the corner of his eye inflicting a stinging pain, in retaliation he twists her arm and snatches the key from her. Josh and Chet are almost to the bottom of the one hundred foot long flight of concrete steps when they hear the commotion.

"Oh crap," yells Josh, "C'mon." he sprints, taking two steps at a time. He glimpses two people; one is Carly the other is a man holding her arms fending off blows and kicks.

"Hey, stop it, leave her alone," he yells, but the two figures move out of sight. He is halfway back up the stairs and not slowing down, for an instant, he remembers endurance training and the hundreds of bleacher runs he has sprinted. Chet is plodding back up the steps taking one at a time, slowing and resting often. Brad—Carly's ex has heard Josh yell and saw him running up the stairs, he forces her back to the museum, key in hand. At the door, he spins her around and holds her by the waist while he fumbles the key into the deadbolt lock. Carly stomps at his feet and ankles but he pulls her over backwards keeping her off balance. A loud thunk signals the heavy deadbolt has slid open; he turns the key back upright and pulls it out at the same time pulling the door open.

Josh clears the top step and seeing her being dragged in the door yells again to stop. He is only twenty feet from the door when Brad pulls it shut from inside, her screams are muffled by the heavy door. Still holding her around the waist, her ex tries to lock them inside, he has the key up to the lock but her struggles are keeping him from getting it in the deadbolt. Josh reaches for the door handle at the same instant her ex gets the key in the lock. With finality, he turns the key locking them inside. Josh yanks the handle repeatedly trying to force it open, he switches from banging with his fist to yanking, all the while yelling *open up, let her go.*

Her ex relaxes his grip when he gets the door locked and Carly seizes the opportunity. She yells let go of me, and drops to the floor, Brad reaches for her but she rolls over into a crouch and manages to elude his grasp, she gets up running. He is one-step behind her, his arms about to encircle her again when she reverses direction and drops to the ground ducking under him. He gets a hand on her shoulder but her squirming, twisting and kicking at him, keeps her out of his grasp. She jumps up and reaches the deadbolt only an instant before he has her, but that's all it takes for her turn the key and pull it from the lock. He reaches for the key but she pulls her arm back and heaves it over the reception desk. Josh heard the deadbolt slide open, but he doesn't hear anything else, he halfway expects the door to suddenly burst open, smashing into anyone standing just outside. Carly's ex has his hand over her mouth.

"Call the cops," Josh whispers to Chet, when he clears the steps. He waves his hand motioning for Chet to move away. Chet is okay with moving far away, and not being directly involved, he knows Carly's boyfriend has a reputation of being a hothead and brawler, things and people he avoids. Carly bites the hand over her mouth and viciously stomps Brad's toes. He doesn't cry out but he does lose his grip on her, trying not be bit again.

"Let me go," says Carly. From the sounds and urgency Josh can tell her ex is preoccupied controlling her. He pulls the door open keeping it in front of him to ward off any blows that may be flying his way.

"Let her go," he demands, as he steps inside and centers up in front of them.

"Or you will what?" counters her ex, "From what I see, you don't have much to bargain with."

"Are you ok Carly?" asks Josh.

"I'm fine Josh, I just want Brad to let go and leave me alone." She squirms again but he has his arm locked around her neck.

"Josh!—you must be that orca hugger all the news people are going on about, you're nothing but trouble, and all your stupid protected whales are eating my salmon."

"Let her go Brad, or are you afraid I might make you let her go." Josh takes two steps forward, baiting and goading Brad, and he succeeds. Brad releases Carly literally throwing her to one side while charging at Josh. He lets out a growling attack yell as he winds back his arm planning a smashing fist into Josh.

Eleven years earlier Josh faced his first opponent in a local martial arts competition. Parents and coaches eagerly watched as their favorite sons and daughters faced off. That was the first time Josh had been hit. He had seen it coming, but failed to recognize his opponent telegraphing the forthcoming blow. The results were quick and hurt a little and Josh was hooked. Brad is bigger than Josh, both taller and heavier, he has a longer reach and is undoubtedly stronger, but he clumsily positions himself and may as well be sending Josh snail mail updates.

"Run Carly, get out of here." He steps quickly away from Carly, and Brad follows him giving Carly an open escape route to the front door. Josh pulls up and faces Brads charge; it may as well be in slow motion. He feints to one side enough to misdirect Brad. The smashing blow has all Brads weight and momentum behind it, and Josh adds to it by pulling and steering his arm forward and down while sweeping his leg. Brad goes down headfirst, guided into the bathroom doorjamb. The thud is unmistakable, The top of Brads head is gouged and stinging, his shoulder smarts, his pride is damaged, and he has blood on his mind—Josh's blood. Josh has bought himself a few seconds and dashes for the door. Carly is running across the sidewalk and heading for Chet across the street. Chet has his cell phone to his head.

"Get out of here, both of you," yells Josh when he runs out the door with Brad in pursuit.

Like all of his many matches, this first short skirmish has revealed much about his opponent. Josh knows how strong Brad is, he has an idea of his reach and weight, but most importantly, he has judged his speed and reaction time. He now knows he can beat him on points alone, if there were judges. Josh has never been in a real fight; he has never intentionally hurt someone or disabled an opponent. All his championship matches were to score points, not draw blood or render someone unconscious or worse. His training has been to pull his punches, his masters have always cautioned against using excessive force, especially when employing the most devastating moves.

Always thinking, he has analyzed Brad's motives and what makes him tick. He figures Brad's a bully and used to getting his way, and right now he is incensed to the point of blinding rage. Rage towards Josh, but he still wants to control Carly. Brad is right behind him and coming fast, Josh lets him catch up: he has no intention of running away in an easily winnable footrace, but he dodges away to buy some time and define where the next fight will be. The two face off on the wide sidewalk in front of the Museum; the heavy self-closing door has shut. Chet and Cary are across the street a half block away.

"Look Brad," Say Josh, his hand up in truce, "why don't we just go home, call it a day. I'll paddle back to Orcas, maybe tomorrow Carly will talk to you. What do you say, friends?"

"Screw you half pint, your dead meat."

Brad is sealing his own fate, Josh will try once more, but he has doubts Brad will see things differently in the next thirty seconds. As expected he rushes at him, and again it may as well be in slow motion for Josh has no problem reacting swiftly. He decisively moves in close, only this time he slips his arm inside Brads and using both of their momentums forces the arm backwards while twisting his wrist and thumb. Brad finds himself unceremoniously thrown face down to the sidewalk. He has a split second to turn his face away from the up rushing concrete trading a broken bloody nose for a severe case of road rash. Josh straddles him, his knee on his neck, his hand forcing Brads thumb and arm upward. The pain is excruciating, and so is the rage.

"Last chance to change your mind."

"You've made a big mistake dickhead," barely able to speak with his jaw shoved onto the sidewalk. "My brother and father will see to you. You better go back to wherever you came from if you want to stay alive."

Josh's impulse is to grind Brad's face into the concrete, but his dad's words after a particularly well fought tournament come back to him. *You have gifts,* he said, *use them wisely, and you will not ever regret life's many choices.* As fast as he took Brad down he releases him, jumping up and moving back a respectable distance. Brad is slow to get up, his cheek is raw, multiple scratches are oozing blood, his ear is beginning to swell and throb. He nurses his thumb, flexing it and holding it with his other hand. Deputy Danny's car pulls to the curb; Chet and Carly inch closer, but stay on the other side of the street.

"What's going on here," says Danny, as he straightens his hat and slides his little two-foot crowd control baton into place on his utility belt.

"Nothing," says Josh, "just a friendly debate over women's rights."

"Is that right, Chester called and said there was a fight here?"

"I asked him to call Deputy," even though they are friends, Josh gives Danny the respect his badge deserves. "We heard Carly calling for help, I thought things might get out of hand, so I asked Chet to call the police, were fine now."

"You two stay right where you are." Danny walks across the street. "Hi Chet, Carly, what's going on?"

"Brad won't leave me alone, I told him, I want nothing to do with him, but he grabbed me and hurt my wrists, he had me by the neck until Josh fought with him. I'm scared of him, I want him to stay away from me,"

"I can arrest him for assault. Is that what you want?"

"Whoa, wait a sec," says Chet, "I'm scared of him too, I don't want to be a witness in court."

"It's not your choice Chet," says Danny, "if you are called into court to tell what you saw."

"Can't you just tell him to stay away from me," begs Carly.

"If that's what you want, stay here." Deputy Danny crosses the street. Brad is nursing his wounds, Josh is calculating tides and currents that will affect his paddle home, plus he is thinking about Brads comment about orcas eating *his salmon, rather* than, *our salmon.*

"Josh, I need to talk to Brad alone, would you go over there." Pointing over to Chet and Carly.

"You're lucky this time Brad, aggravated assault will put you away for ten years. I should lock you up simply for being older and stupid, you ought to know better than chasing after high school girls. You had already dropped out when she was still in grade school. If I see or hear one word about you coming around Carly or the Pearson boy included, just one word, then I will come and get you. And that goes for your punk brother and father too. All of you better keep your noses on fishing and leave these kids alone. Am I clear?"

"Yeah, I hear ya."

"Is that your car in the loading zone?" Brad nods. "Get in it and go home." Danny walks across the street a second time. "Josh, you're not doing too good staying out of trouble, I know your getting maligned and Bradley is everyone's nightmare, but my gosh, what's it been, three days since you walked off the ferry? You got the feds after you, I figure you're behind the protestors, and now you rough up one of our local thugs, what's next? Don't answer that, I don't want to know. Carly, I told him to stay away from you; this is a small town you need to keep clear too. Call the department, or me if he comes around." Brad pulls away in his car—he looks straight ahead. Deputy Danny hurries over to his patrol car intent on following Brad.

"You were awesome dude," exclaims Chet, "he didn't have a chance. You took him apart like a puzzle you had done a hundred times before. It's true isn't it, I'm right aren't I?" Josh looks at Carly, she is waiting for Chet's question to be answered or declarations confirmed.

"Look you guys, you're getting the wrong impression of me, I'm not a fighter or tough guy like that Brad moron, I've done a little martial arts, it's a sport where you have competitions, you know like a game. I've been doing it since I was little, and I've been in contests competing against champions.

"Hah, the truth comes out," says Chet, "champions only fight other champions, right, right?" Josh looks over at Carly again, Chet's probing is embarrassing.

"It wouldn't be fair for the more accomplished fighters to compete against intermediate levels, so we have classifications according to size ability, weight, and experience.

"And what level are you?"

"It doesn't matter. How come when we ran up the steps it took you so long to get up here?" Chet shuts up.

"I need to go find my keys," says Carly, "will you guys help me." They walk across to the darkened museum. Carly finds her keys behind the desk where she tossed them.

"Do you want a ride home." Asks Josh.

"Yes, oh please, it's only a half mile."

"Chet and I would be pleased to drop you at home, wouldn't we Chet?" Chet leads them walking down the sidewalk to his van parked in the free city parking lot about halfway to Carly's house. They drive the remaining quarter mile and then walk Carly to her door. They don't leave until she says it's ok. Chet swings the van back down to the marina, the whole time grilling Josh about martial arts and fighting.

Chapter 29 - Heading Out

It's still a few hours before sunset when Josh settles into Sammie's kayak. Before he pushes off, his thoughts drift to Sammie, then to Chet's sister, Christy. Then Carly, then back to Sammie.

If he hurries, maybe they can watch the sun set while sitting around a fire.

He texts Sammie, *your kayak is awesome—so are you! Leaving FH now.*

He texts Maggie, *I'm leaving Friday Harbor, see you in a few hours.* He leans against his backpack shoehorned into the compact cockpit, exhausted; he closes his eyes and nods off for a second, and the he snaps back awake. He knows he should turn around and go back, but sleeping on a park bench again holds no appeal, besides, he has paddled in the dark before. Long slow strokes and sore muscles immediately remind him of the early mornings crossing, adrenalin flows into his body, his heart rate increases.

Directly above him homeland security agents in darkened windows watch him leave Friday Harbor. The top floor Fish and game offices are closed, but the customs doors below are open. The Ferry Captain blows one long warning whistle that the engines are in reverse. Josh quickens his strokes.

Seven miles with a favorable current won't be too bad, with opposing currents, I may be paddling the last miles in darkness, maybe I should turn around.

Chapter 30 - Heavy Water Crossing

Waves slam into the kayak. Every fourth stroke is a defensive move keeping the kayak from broaching. Josh is learning the meaning of trial by fire. His chosen course was around Shaw Island to the right, but the current and evening thermals have conspired to build scary waves and set him to the left. High waves hide the kayak, burying it in deep troughs, and then promptly set it free to surf the frothing crests. Josh involuntarily yells his approval; he masters and then conquers one wave after another.

The first channel crossing offshore from Friday Harbor is only two miles. Ferries come from both directions, and Friday Harbor is the busiest port in the San Juan's. From the time a ferry becomes visible around a far point until it is on top of him is only ten minutes. The kayak is virtually invisible in the swells and wind borne spray. He can't risk getting caught in the middle of the channel and puts everything he has into sprinting to the safety of the far shore. When he started across, his planned course was the shortest route to home, but with the current and ferries his course has quickly become whatever it takes to get to safety. Powerful arm strokes nearly lift the boat clear of the water as it breaks over crest after crest. Sammie's kayak is a sleek racing machine. The far shore quickly looms closer. Josh's hyper sprint at over ten miles an hour is not sustainable, but he keeps up the effort until the swells diminish closer to shore. He slacks the blistering pace once he no longer fears being run over.

When he arrived in Friday Harbor early this morning he had come from the east, now strong currents are forcing him to the west, into waters he knows nothing about. Still fresh in his mind is the other night off the point from the *Islander Grand Lodge* when he was forced to paddle in the dark, far offshore to overcome a powerful eddy generated by the outgoing tide ricocheting off the point.

I guess we're going to the left after all. The ebbing tide has dragged him sideways along Shaw Island. Orcas Island is still two more major crossings and five miles away. First, he must follow the shoreline around Shaw and thread the treacherous whirlpools and rip currents at Wasp Passage. Second, he must cross another busy ferry and commercial boating channel. Josh must find his way strictly from memory; his phone with gps and maps is tucked safely away in a dry bag. Up ahead he sees a choice coming up, It's a small group of islets called Wasp Rocks. If he makes the correct choice he will stay in the recommended boaters channel, the wrong choice and he will be swept along, potentially into boiling rapids around shallow rocks.

Josh keeps to the middle avoiding making a decision until the last moment. He scans the shoreline and looks ahead for clues. A slight calm area forms where the water splits direction, the view is obscured in both directions by headlands, he is about to take the passage closest to Shaw Island when he sees a power boat come into view from around the farthest corner. *That's it, that's the main channel, it's a good thing I hesitated.* He paddles back into the current and heads for the far passage away from Shaw.

The current accelerates through the passage and shoots the lightweight kayak out the other end. A few minutes later he looks back up the other passage and sees white water rapids. *That would've been fun, some other time, and in a rock basher, not in Sammie's kayak.*

Somewhere amongst the islands, islets, passages, and seaweed-covered rocks nearby is a high horsepower engine screaming in protest. The barely muffled exhaust echoes off the rock cliffs, its extreme decibels flow freely blanketing the water with raw power. Josh looks around for the roaring boat motor, it's somewhere up ahead.

Then, three miles in front of him, he sees the rooster tail. A go-fast boat flashes by in the far pass, its fifty-foot high wall of water and mist hangs in the air long after the sleek thirty-six foot Stiletto Racer is out of sight beyond the next point. The noise softens when the driver slows to make a one eighty for another pass. Then the decibels increase as the driver puts the throttle on the floor.

Fifteen hundred horsepower connected to a single stainless steel screw propels the craft well over one hundred miles an hour. Again, the sound calms, as the driver slows to turn. Again, he makes a hi-speed pass, finally after one last fly-by, he re ignites his rocketing ship and roars out the channel onto Haro Strait. A glistening rooster tail dropping mini rainbows is all that is left behind. Watching the boat, outrun gravity at almost two miles a minute gives him goose bumps and makes his body quiver. The thundering noise is gone as fast as it arrived, but the excitement has reinvigorated him, he bends forward, digs deep and ignites his own fire.

Across San Juan Channel in the distance, he can make out Turtleback Mountain high above the point marking the *Islander Grand Resort*. Three miles separates Josh from Pearson Cove, and a well deserved rest. It's too far to see any detail, but he imagines Sammie lighting a campfire for her guests, and Pepper in the cove waiting for a back scratch. Maybe Sadie is keeping her company, barking for Pepper to flip a log on shore. He visualizes Charley and Maggie at the picture window making videos of a dog and her unlikely best friend, a killer whale.

Josh pulls hard on the double ended paddle, first one side then the other, his rhythm is steady, his pace comfortable and sustainable for as long as it takes. Looking ahead, he tries to keep Turtleback Mountain in front of him, but this section of the San Juan Channel is the meeting point of multiple passages draining vast island seas. The currents and counter currents coupled with the weather form treacherous tidal rips and swirling short lived eddies. For every foot he paddles forward, he is carried backward six inches, for every foot he manages to gain, he must except an equal sideways drift. For thousands of year natives plying these waters have used the tides to their advantage. The earliest mariners using skin kayaks and bark canoes passed their intimate local knowledge from generation to generation. Newcomers, slow learners, and the unlucky often perished.

Josh's view of Turtleback Mountain constantly shifts to the right, an indication he is being dragged to the left toward menacing ten mile wide Haro Strait. A slight breeze blows over him, at the same time the sky darkens causing him to look westward over Vancouver Island. The sun is dropping into low clouds warning him daylight is short-lived. The gentle rolling swell continues all the way to his destination but to his left it is interrupted by a far off wall of whitecaps riding the incoming tide rip.

Josh quickens his pace, he doesn't want any part of Haro Strait or big waves. His wild ride out of Friday Harbor taught him respect, and instilled in him a healthy dose of fear. He questions his decision to leave so late in the day, he furtively watches the sun drop lower. Josh is miles from shore in all directions, his decision to let the current carry him past the far side of Shaw Island has left him vulnerable to the wrath of windblown waves, and now he is in a lonely race against darkness.

His thoughts drift to Pepper, *I wonder if she can hear this far and just how good an orca 's echo location really is.* He pauses for a moment and taps the kayaks rigid frame with his paddle – *bam bam – bam bam,* his pace and his heart rate follows suit. He is breathing heavy, but not labored. After fifteen minutes, Turtleback Mountain is definitely closer, it's also ninety degrees to the right of where it was when he first started lining up with it, proving to him the current is forcing him to paddle harder and further. Shaw Island started out a comforting nearby island on his right side, when he looks for it he is surprised to see it only a distant shore. The rocks and islets lost in the distance.

Seeing Turtleback Mountain loom closer and higher reassures Josh. He knows he will make it. He takes a ten-second break to signal Pepper again. Bam bam—bam bam, this time the kayak hardly slows by the time he resumes paddling.

Chapter 31 - Attack

"Charley, I've been watching for Josh," says Maggie, "its been about three hours since he said he was leaving Friday Harbor, he should be getting close. A little while ago Pepper was dozing in the middle of the cove, now she's swimming back and forth in the entrance like she is expecting him."

"Or" says Charley, "it's dinner time and there's a school of salmon out there."

"Maybe" says Maggie, "wait—look, she's taking off."

"I see her, she's sure after something, look at her go," pointing, "she breached, she's excited and going after something, she's heading into the sun, what a sight, it's no wonder everyone loves orcas."

The roar of the go-fast boat breaks the tranquil evening ambience again. It's driver and passenger fueled by pure adrenalin, and possibly spiked with high proof alcohol. The boat blasts down the coast of Shaw Island. Just like before, it makes several high-speed passes before moving on between the islets and rocks Josh had transited thirty minutes earlier. The terrifying and annoying noise resembles something out of a low budget rum-runners smuggling movie, that is if it were filmed at an international jet airport. Except the setting isn't the lawless Caribbean, it's the peaceful San Juans, cozily nestled next to Canada. The noise penetrates the old lodge, Charley stands at the expansive picture window scanning the horizon, the rooster tail caught in the setting sun is his first visual indication where to look for the hundred mile an hour boat. Looking a thousand feet ahead of the erupting tail, he spots the low sleek craft skipping from crest to crest barely in the water, out running sound and water, attempting to take flight, but not quite able to stay airborne. Josh hears and sees the raw power display in the distance. *I'm sure glad he's not over here, I hope Pepper is staying under water.* Turtleback Mountain is dead ahead, he's not correcting for drift anymore, a sure indication that the current has taken the kayak completely past his shortest approach and is being dragged directly away from the cove. Fighting the current has taken him from paddling due north to southeast, from three hours to four and he is still miles away. Behind him is Haro strait and the approaching rip current signaling the incoming tide. If the riptide overtakes him, he will get a free ride and be whisked toward the point where Sammie is tending the campfire outside the *Islander Grand Lodge.* But along with the riptide and favorable current comes big swells, and dangerous waves if the wind kicks up. He can take it easy and let the turning tide eventually help him, but that comes with the risk of capsizing, and it is getting dark.

He digs deep, drawing upon his reserves. Long distance runners call it getting their second wind. *I know I can outrun this current, and I can beat the setting sun, is that Pepper? it is! She is showing her stuff, breaching for me.* For three miles Pepper has zeroed in on a straight line for Josh and the kayak. She has been following her original signal and breaching occasionally looking for a visual contact. Josh quickly taps out the signal, letting Pepper know she has found him. Now that she can see him, she breaches more often. She excitedly shows off, letting her body belly flop and splashing for effect.

Josh forgets all about being tired or the fact that he is miles from land, he paddles with renewed vigor. As Pepper closes in on him, he clears his mind and takes deep cleansing breaths. The last thousand feet or so she stays under water. *Where are you girl, I know your right under me.* Josh stops paddling and rests for a moment and on cue Pepper surfaces headfirst pointing straight up. Her smiling mouth is agape showing her teeth. She lets out a loud chirp followed by a string of clicks. Josh replies by slapping the water with his paddle.

"Hey Pepper girl, I missed you today." Pepper swims over to the kayak and Josh reaches out with the paddle to her favorite scratching spot behind her dorsal fin. She swims in close, her powerful pectoral fin under the kayak.

"Keep that big fin under water Pepper girl, you could flip me without even trying." He reaches over and rubs his hand on her eye patch while telling her that it's getting late and he needs to keep paddling, then he gives her a little shove sideways. With a small gentle stroke Pepper swims clear and Josh digs deep once again. Soon they develop a system, he paddles hard and steady keeping Turtleback Mountain in front of him, and she goofs off, swimming ahead for a while, then to one side and breaching every so often for good measure.

"Don't you dare land on top of me or next to me; you better read my mind if you can't understand me."

Josh and Pepper have cut the distance in half. The point at the *Islander Grand Lodge and Resort* has become visible. It's still much too far to make out any details, but the buildings are becoming visible. He can't see Pearson Cove yet but they are closing in. Also closing in is the go-fast boat that has been stalking the straits and circling Shaw Island. The fifteen hundred horsepower roar is unacceptable near shore or in any marina, but out in the San Juan channels and the wide-open straits, there is no one to complain or even witness the boat driver's antics. Younger people and adventurous boating enthusiasts are in awe, the displays of raw power and speed thrill them. Josh is no exception, he is thrilled watching the awesome go-fast boat approach, and loves seeing its rooster tail shimmer in the setting sun.

With each swell the careening boat bounces from side to side, its highflying tail swishes a short lived memory composed of glowing water droplets hanging in the sky. The driver steers a course to Josh's left, and then after a quarter mile changes course steering to his right. For an instant, he is pointed directly at the insignificant kayak and its lone passenger.

From more than a half mile distance Josh registers his first shudder of fear. With each pass the driver makes, Josh's imagination, or perhaps his logical thinking considers that maybe he is in danger. Is the drivers apparent multiple passes actually a search pattern. He remembers his dads last text, *watch your back.* Could this driver be Carly's ex., Brad, could he be so pissed off that he is hunting him down offshore. What about Rogers and his band of government agents, they are known to confiscate go-fast boats from drug smugglers. Dave Johnson knew he was paddling home to Orcas Island, maybe he's been putting his secret investment money into more than fast cars.

The boat changes course onto its next pass and adjusts its blazing speed for the new swell. The driver lowers the rpm accordingly. Josh is convinced the driver is not out for a joy ride at all, but following a methodical search pattern covering the most territory at the fastest speeds possible. With each pass the go-fast boat gets closer, zeroing in on him and Pepper.

Pepper fears the intruder. Her mother bears the scars of an encounter years earlier. She well remembers tangling with a boat deployed net and almost drowning last week. The boat closes on them she warily watches and cautiously swims away. The noise above water hurts her sensitive hearing, but under water it vibrates her to the bone. She doesn't understand why, but she senses danger.

The next turn lines up the go-fast boat with Josh. Not directly, but slightly to one side, Josh breathes a sigh of relief, the boat will miss him and Pepper. *Unless the driver is looking for him, and then he will spot him for sure.* Josh lowers his paddle and rests it across the kayak, no sense attracting the drivers attention if he is a search target. The sun is not behind him, the seas are relatively flat, he is pretty darn visible, the boat passes a quarter mile from him.

Thirty minutes later—

A new driver adjusts his course and heads straight at the resting lone kayaker. Josh digs deep and shoots forward, in three powerful strokes he propels Sammie's superlight kayak out of harms way, this boat will pass behind him too, except the driver adjusts and brings the kayak back in front of him. *Oh crap—get out of here Pepper, this isn't going to end well!* Josh pours on the power, but the driver keeps steering at him. He hears the engine whine increase when the driver shoves the throttle levers forward and accelerates pushing the rpm's to the max limit.

He back paddles hard, desperately trying to get away, but the last thing Josh sees is the big lap strake hull and pointed bow blocking out Turtleback Mountain. The homicidal driver slices through Sammie's kayak. The shearing force separates kevlar like scissors cutting fine fabric. The driver never looks back, he just throttles down to a comfortable cruising speed and slowly turns toward Wasp Passage and the anonymity that the many rocky islets bring.

Pepper listens and watches the perpetrator drive away. She surfaces near her friend, her clicks and chirps go unanswered. Pieces of Sammie's broken high tech kevlar kayak drift away. The debris field spreads from fifty feet, seconds after impact to one hundred feet in the first minute. The broken and severed front portion of the kayak stays afloat with the help of some foam matting; a light breeze blows it toward Haro Strait. Josh's torn up unconscious body is tangled with shards of ripped kevlar. His life vest and buoyant backpack containing his dry bag are keeping him afloat. Unseeing eyes stare uselessly into the water, his brain no longer receives signals. The concussion leaving him more dead than alive keeps him from feeling the pain wracking his body. The high speed propeller has chewed its way through the kayak and across his legs. His lacerated thighs bleed freely, his blood oozes through torn pants.

Pepper swims close and surfaces near her friend. With her snout, she lifts a limp arm, and then lays it back in the water. Her chirps still unanswered; they drift with the current, the sun drops below the horizon. Sammies scratched paddle floats fifty feet away. For another hour Pepper stays next to Josh, the tide changes from ebb to flood, the current reverses, twilight becomes darkness and Turtleback Mountain is the last landmark to fade away.

Chapter 32 - Investigation

"He should have been here by now," says Maggie.

"I know," says Charley, "but he may have left late or had adverse currents, he's never paddled around out there before, he could even be lost,"

Text message: *"Where are you?"*

Text message*: "Hi Sammie, its"Maggie, have you heard from Josh?"*

Reply from Sammie: *"not since he said he was leaving FH"*

"Thanks"

"I'm going to take the boat out," says Charley, "maybe I'll spot something."

Charley heads out from the cove. He has with him a portable radio and two flashlights, one with a big battery and powerful beam capable of lighting up an object five hundred feet away, but darkness consumes the light and he sees nothing. The aluminum skiff with its small outboard is lost in the vast emptiness of the channel between Orcas and Shaw Islands. Charley uses the point and the lights of the *Islander Grand Lodge,* behind him as a reference point, and then he heads across the five open miles towards the Shaw Island Rocks where he steers toward a flashing red navigation light. After twenty minutes he is two thirds of the way across. Charley swings the light beam on both sides of the boat and plows ahead.

Maggie is watching from the window but loses Charley's flickering light after the first mile. He makes a sweeping one eighty turn before the rocks endanger him and points the bow at the red light marking the point at the *Islander Grand Lodge.* Maggie is relieved to see the flickering light once again, putting to rest for the time being the nagging horror of losing both her men in one night.

"Charley Pearson calling the Coast Guard, Charley Pearson calling the Coast Guard." The small hand held radio resembles a child's walkie talkie, but it has full range capacity. Static spits from the speaker when he releases the call button on channel 22, the coast guard haling channel. He adjusts the squelch and knocks out the static leaving clear reception.

"Coast Guard, Charley Pearson, what's your vessel name."

"No name Coast Guard, I'm in a skiff in San Juan Channel west of Shaw Island light buoy number 6. My nephew is in a kayak and overdue coming from Friday Harbor. His destination is Pearson Cove on Orcas, he should have arrived before dark. I'm searching for him."

"Coast Guard—Pearson, do you have a phone available?"

"Maggie, are you here?" Asks Charley over the air.

"This is Maggie Pearson Coast Guard, I have a phone."

"Ok, copy this phone number and call me right back." The coast guard radio operator stands by to receive Maggie's call. Charley switches his portable radio to scan all channels and resumes his side-to-side search sweeps. Maggie calls the coast guard and fills them in on everything she knows about Josh's plans. They want to verify he actually left when she says he did. She is insistent on his leaving time from Friday Harbor since Sammie had told her he also texted her when he left.

The coast guard routinely contacts the deputy sheriff to find out if their department may be holding the missing person. Surprisingly, a not so rare occurrence. Checking the call log brings up Josh's name from the museum incident earlier. Deputy Danny is still on duty and receives a call from the coast guard duty officer, but he is unable to verify Josh's departure. Danny immediately calls Maggie and fills her in on everything he knows. He mentions the altercation but leaves out the details about Josh getting the best of a local bully only thirty minutes before he texted her that he was on his way. After hanging up with Maggie, officer Danny cruises the turn around and main street and spots Chet's van in the homeland security parking lot. Protesting has come to a quiet hush for the day, the hanger-ons sit on the lawn under the promenade lights discussing the day's events and what they will be doing in the morning. When Danny walks up no one seems to care that a uniformed policeman is approaching.

"What's up?" says Chet, Danny stops in front of him.

"Is Josh still around?"

"No, he left in his kayak hours ago. What's going on." In typical cop fashion, Danny answers Chet's question with another question.

"When did he leave, did you actually see him paddle away?" Chet replays the evenings events, starting when Brad drove off, explaining that they gave Carly a ride home. Chet tells Danny that he came to the marina with Josh and watched him paddle out right in front of the departing six o'clock ferry and he was booking fast like a pro-racer on a mission.

"He hasn't made it home to Orcas Island yet," says Danny, "the Coast
Guard is starting a search." Danny thanks Chet and asks him to let him know if he hears anything.

"Yeah sure," says Chet, stunned at the news. Deputy Danny pulls his patrol car out onto the cross-island road; he's going to pay a visit to Brad.

While on the phone with the coast guard, Maggie watches out her window. The dark night accentuates the vastness. The shoreline of their cove is lost in front of her; she can't make out her own dock. She glimpses the blinking red light Charley used as a turnaround point, and is grateful to see his light flashing her way and getting closer. Fifteen minutes later, he ties up.

"What did the coast guard say?" asks Charley when Maggie meets him at the top of the gangplank.

"Nothing—what can they say?" Maggie throws her arms around her husband. "They said they would contact the sheriff on San Juan, and then Danny called, but he didn't know anything either."

Deputy Sheriff Danny pulls into Brad's driveway, he leaves the motor running and turns on his perimeter lights. It's the same junky yard the neighbors have been enduring for thirty years, but some of their yards aren't any better, and some are decidedly worse. Brads lives with his mom and dad, two brothers, and a sister. All of them are hard working and hard drinking. Brad is the youngest and has suffered under ruthless beatings they call discipline. Perhaps that's his lame excuse for being so heavy handed with Carly. He spent the fifteen minutes it took driving home thinking of ways to get even with Josh. If he can get the jump on him, he was sure he could beat him into the ground, after all he was bigger and stronger. What he didn't understand was how Josh so easily dodged him and caused him to motion and the superhero moves so fast he is invisible. And Carly, she was his girl, and she needed to be taught a lesson in respect. Brad is still nursing his ego when Danny drives up.

"What business you got out here," says Brad, as he walks out on the porch. "I left town just like you said." Brads hand goes to his face in an effort to hide the swelling ear and scraped up face.

"You're my business Brad, I have a responsibility to every citizen, every kid in this county to make sure they are safe and not in harm's way. Like this afternoon, I couldn't let that kid hurt you, and I couldn't let you hurt Carly."

"I don't need no protection, and that little punk is gonna get what's comin, you'll see."

"Well I'm sorry to hear you threaten him like you just did, because if anything does come his way, the police will be coming for you." Danny walks around to the front of Brad's car while making small talk. "Did you come straight home Brad, stop anywhere? Maybe swing by Carlys?" The hood is cold, the engine has cooled, there's no telltale creaking noises.

"I might have driven by Carly's, but I never stopped."

"Goodnight Brad."

"Hey, why'd you come out here?" says Brad suspiciously.

"I told you, you're my responsibility. But since you brought it up, where's your old man and big brother."

"Out catching crabs."

Danny shuts off the cruisers search lights and heads back to town.

"What did he want," says Brads dad from the porch window.

"I don't know, maybe he was checking to see if I was home."

"This has something to do with your face being banged up, don't it," says his dad. "You done something today and you're lying about it." That's why that cop was here, you better not be getting in trouble. We can't afford anyone snooping around here, especially now when the salmon are running.

Chapter 33 - *Black Widow*

The Coast Guard incident command captain has called a team together. They know when Josh left and are able to exactly calculate the currents at the time. The big question is which way around Shaw Island did he choose to paddle. The decision where to search comes quick and easy. If Josh went to the west and got in trouble, he may be swept into Haro Strait. If he paddled east around Shaw and experienced trouble, he would be less vulnerable.

They deploy six four man rigid inflatable vessels and a helo from the cutter Tomahawk on duty in Georgia Strait. The high speed craft are on station in thirty minutes. Two of them attempt to recreate Josh's route, east and west around Shaw Island, they run very close to shore, just like a kayaker seeking refuge from waves would run. Using powerful searchlights, they examine the shoreline and off shore rocks. They explore anything that has potential to harbor an injured kayaker.

The helo and other boats converge on Haro Strait where they search areas the incident captain has determined the current and rip tides would carry a disabled boat or wreckage. Deputy Sheriff Danny calls the incident command captain, and verifies that Josh was witnessed paddling out of the marina as the six oclock ferry left. The captain thanks the sheriff and calls his support officer saying to get hold of wsdot to verify the ferry's departure time.

Danny parks on the promenade in the same place he left an hour earlier. He climbs the outdoor flight of stairs next to customs and immigration and walks out onto the spacious viewing deck.

"Hello Sheriff," says marina security guard Jorge Santos, "What brings you to the night shift at sleepy Friday Harbor, back door to the United States of America, you here to chase away those obnoxious whale protestors down below?"

"Not this time, Jorge, "Just be thankful they're not up here, you know this deck is part of the promenade and is a public space as well, we will have a hard time explaining why tourists are welcome and they are not."

"Everyone is welcome as long as they take pictures, or until the beams break, then we have issues, I know you're not here to pass the time Danny, what's going on."

"We've got a missing kayaker, in fact he's the one that got the whale watchers going this time."

"You mean the high school kid that handcuffed Rich Rogers man in his own car." Laughs Jorge.

"One and the same."

"Oh that's funny, not that he's missing, but Rogers was fit to be tied. He's been acting like he was personally taken down, not some green agent. Have you asked him what he knows?" says Jorge jokingly.

"Not yet, have you seen anything unusual out there. He left for Pearson Cove on the west side of Orcas at six o'clock. He's in a kayak, his family reported him overdue an hour ago."

"Well he's got good weather and decent seas, the tides coming in now, is the Coast Guard in on it?"

"Yeah, they began searching immediately."

"Well that's good, I haven't seen anything except the normal cruisers, fishing boats, and day boaters. Earlier a Cigarette Boat was tearing up the straits, I'm sure glad we aren't in the Caribbean where those boats are all over the place running drugs and guns."

"We've got our share of go-fast boats," says Danny, "but for the most part they just make a lot of noise and burn barrels of high octane."

Danny slowly walks down the wide steps to the promenade; he pauses looking out over the busy marina. Hundreds walk the docks, some are heading up to a bar or restaurant, some are coming back to their boat for the night. Many people are simply tourists wandering the city. Danny spots another marina security guard, and finishes the steps rapidly. He heads down the gangway intent on heading off the guard. When he catches up to him he asks him about Cigarette Boats and where any are berthed. All of them are on the same fairway.

The first slip holds a fire engine red boat, but you wouldn't know it's color from dark green due to all the algae, spider webs and seaweed growing on the unused boat. He moves on without stopping, the next boat is named Diablo, it's polished and detailed, even in the dark it glistens. Danny walks down one side. He reaches down to feel the engine cover, there's no indication when it last was taken out. He moves on to a boat named White-Lightnin.

"Good evening," says Danny, "have you folks been out tonight?" The four people onboard are lounging and drinking, a chip tray sits on the console. The front seats are swiveled facing the rear. The driver is about twenty years old and slides his open beer under the seat edge.

"Sure," says the driver, "is this about us going too fast? I never speed around other boats, too unpredictable. I stay at least a mile offshore, ask anyone."

"Ok, I will." Danny turns to a teenage girl in the back, "Were you kids out running around in this boat earlier today?"

She stammers, "I guess so."

"What time and where did you go?" asks Danny, still looking at the girl.

"I don't know, everywhere."

"Anyone care to be more specific," he looks at the driver.

"Haro Strait, San Juan Channel, Victoria, we went all over." Says the driver.

"Where were you at 6 p.m.?"

"That's easy, we were right over there," pointing towards the main dock. "We took on 300 gallons of fuel and then followed the 6 o'clock ferry out of the harbor. Did that ferry captain complain that I sprayed water on him?"

"Then where did you go?"

"We ran around Shaw several times timing how fast we could do it." Danny pulls out his flashlight, and lights up the hull, he closely examines every inch of the thirty-six feet looking for marks, scratched paint. He pays careful attention to the bow at the waterline, it's flawless.

"Then where did you go?"

"Victoria."

"When did you get back, did you go through customs?"

"We were back here in the slip around dark, customs isn't required, we never got off the boat or even stopped. What's going on," says the driver. "What's with all the questions?"

"A kayaker is missing," answers Danny, "Let me see your boater's education card." After noting the drivers information and boat numbers in his notebook he bids them good evening, and walks down the dock.

"What an ass," says the driver, "he could have at least told us what it was about first."

"Yeah, but then he'd have to kill us." The other guy jokes. "Still an ass."

Danny walks to the end where he finds *Black Widow,* her docks lines are loose and poorly cleated, he can feel the heat from her engine and hear the creaking metal as it cools. Fuel vapors hang in the air. While standing on the narrow finger float he scans more of the marina. Turning around and walking back he goes by the same empty slips but no more Cigarette or Stiletto go-fast Boats are to be seen.

"Sorry to bother you folks again," says Danny, back at the cigarette boat, "do you know of any other boats like yours moored around here?"

"Just *Black Widow,*" says the boat driver, "down where you were in that last slip, she had her out earlier before we went out."

"She?"

"Some chick 30 - 55, skinny, good looking, hangs out with an older guy sometimes, but she's the owner."

"How do you know this?"

"What do you mean—I got eyes. She does the driving in and out of the slip, just like me, that means she doesn't trust anyone with her baby, it's named *Black Widow,* come on man, you're the cop?"

"Yours is named *White Light'nin,* are you running moonshine?" After a short pause with no answer, Danny says, "thanks, you've been helpful," he jots a note, and moves on.

ORCA BOY

Chapter 34 - Rescue

Sadie's barking has been getting worse by the minute. She suddenly stands up and barks at the front window, and then runs to the door and back. Her whining and barking have become non-stop, she whines and feverishly scratches the door.

Sandy has had enough, she gets up from the keyboard and monitor where she is editing her *Islander Grand Resort* website and tracks down the commotion that has moved to the kitchen door.

"Sadie stop it," yells Sandy, "you're ruining the door, what is wrong with you?" Sandy flicks on the outside light and while holding Sadie's collar opens the door just six inches, but that is all Sadie needs. She yelps and barks in a fervor, pulling against Sandy holding her back. Her pulling and squirming overpowers Sandy until she wedges her head out the door forcing it open. Sadie bolts out of Sandy's hands and covers the one hundred feet to the forest trail at a dead run.

Sammie, runs downstairs from her room. "What's going on, I heard all sorts of barking down here, where's Sadie?"

"I don't know, suddenly she wanted outside, she was destroying the door, I couldn't hold her. She ran into the woods headed for Pearson's."

"Maybe that means Josh is back, I'll text Maggie, no, I'm going over there."

"Put some clothes on, you can't run around the neighbors in your robe." Sammie heads up the stairs to change taking two steps at a time.

Except for a few minutes, Maggie hasn't left her post at the picture window since before sunset. She hopes her vigilance will somehow help Josh.

"Charley, I hear barking." Says Maggie. "I can't see a thing down there; you don't think the Coast Guard would have a dog in the dark do you.

"No I don't, I hear it too, it sounds really frantic, something's not right. Give me a sec. to get my shoes on and I'll go check it out."

"I'm going with you."

Charley and Maggie take flashlights and go out the same kitchen door Josh had used two days earlier when he escaped from

Game Warden Rogers. The barking is nonstop, frantic does not fully describe the intensity of panic and urgency down on the dock . They see a flickering flashlight on the trail, and figure it must be Sammie so they wait for her where the trail forks to the dock.

"Sammie, is that you, is that Sadie barking, what's wrong with her?" says Charley.

"I don't know, she suddenly went ballistic in the house, and then broke away from Sandy and ran over here, I hope it's Josh." Sadie sees them or hears them coming down the rickety old planks, and runs toward them, but then she turns tail and runs back to the slip with the boat hoist. She repeats the maneuver, dashing back and forth yelping all the time. As they get closer, they see light flashes, and a greenish glowing cloud floating in the water. The eerie luminescence is light emitting plankton that glows when disturbed, and Pepper is doing plenty of agitating.

Her bright white markings flash as she rips back and forth outside the slip. Each time she turns she exposes her white underbelly and her flippers cause more plankton to light up. As they get close, Charley sweeps the dock with his flashlight. High hopes turn to dismay; the flat planks are empty as far as the light penetrates. Sadie has not let up, she jumps down onto the partially submerged boat hoist, and Charley follows her with his flashlight beam. The debris in the water is ninety percent submerged and looks much like any flotsam. Walking on submerged planks, Sadie wades to the end of the boat hoist. She bites down on what looks like backpack webbing and pulls hard in reverse, her body jerking with each super effort. She drags Josh's mangled body partly onto the hoist cradle.

"Oh my god its Josh" screams Sammie and Maggie simultaneously. Charley is already in motion. He runs the rest of the way down the dock and leaps to the sloping lift. Wading into the water he crowds Sadie to one side and takes over, but he is unable to pull him onto the lift. Shining his light into the water he sees that Josh is entangled in the broken kayak. His backpack straps and life vest straps are hopelessly wrapped up with the broken kayak and seat frame.

"I need a knife to cut him free, I can't let go of him, one of you needs to run to the house." Charley is aware that Josh has not moved and doesn't appear to be breathing. Pepper has moved in close, she is only five feet from her friend, she chirps loudly as if to say—*do something.* Or maybe she is saying—*please wake up.* Charley turns his head and meets her watery eye, he wonders if orcas cry, he senses and feels Peppers concern, the same as his. He breaks eye contact with Pepper and makes another attempt at getting Josh up the ramp, but the broken kayak is hung up.

"Check his pockets," says Sammie, "he always has his knife." Charlie sets his light on the dock and reaches into the water searching Josh's pockets, he comes up with his Leatherman, saying I got it. The knife is razor sharp and easily cuts the heavy webbing. Maggie and Sammie hold the lights, Charley drags him up the ramp clear of the water. No one has asked if Josh is alive but they are all thinking it. Sadie is pacing back and forth, her barking turned to whimpering. Pepper is watching motionless, the bioluminescence has faded.

Chapter 35 - Coast Guard Helo

The Coast Guard Helo hovers over Pearson Cove, its searchlights light up a big circle. All of the dock and much of the cove is bathed in bright light that penetrates deep into the shallows. Its rotor washes the surface creating a stream of outward moving concentric circles. *Look there,* points the pilot, *there's an orca , it must be trapped in this cove. Why doesn't it* swim away?

The Helo slowly descends toward the floating dock, the light circle shrinks while wind rippled waves blow out in all directions. At fifty feet, the Helo scares Pepper and she escapes through the coves narrow entrance for the safety of deep water. She surfaces to breathe a quarter mile away where she watches. At twenty feet the rescue crewmen on the dock nod to each other signaling they are ready and then kneel next to the basket. Next the pilot sets one landing skid on the dock just five feet from the basket and holds the craft steady. The co-pilot watches the water for any rogue waves that may enter the bay and cause the dock to suddenly rise endangering the operation.

Loading the basket takes ten seconds, the crew ten more, and then the pilot gets the signal to lift off. For the second time they fly over Pepper causing her to dive once more.

"There it is again says the co-pilot, *there's that same orca."* They set course for Emergency at the Friday Harbor Hospital, ETA, less than ten minutes.

ORCA BOY

The Coast Guardsman in charge at Pearson Cove along with another crewman inspect what's left of Sammies broken kayak.

"It was run over he says flatly, look here, prop marks, the victim and his pants were sliced up too. Here's green paint from one side to the other on the front deck, probably antifouling bottom paint. So was it an accident, or is someone out there trying to kill this guy?"

"You mean attempted murder or murder if he doesn't make it," says the one in charge.

"All of this is crime evidence; do you want me to tell the people up in the house not to mess with anything?"

"No, I'll talk to them myself, I need you to tape off the slip and kayak debris."

"Mrs Pearson, my name is Jason Jones, I'm sorry to bother you at a time like this, but can we talk right now."

"Sure sure, come in, have you heard anything about Josh?"

"No I have not, once the Helo takes off, he's in the ER. and leaves our jurisdiction. Your best bet is to talk to the Hospital directly. I wish I could tell you something."

"I called them," says Maggie, "he's unconscious, they said the cold water made him hypothermic, but may have held down brain swelling. I guess that's a good thing."

"Like I said, I'm sorry to trouble you at a time like this, but we have to investigate what happened; and someone will be coming by to look at the destroyed kayak, so if you could just leave it be out on the dock, ah that would be great. Someone will be contacting you."

Chapter 36 - Asleep

Sammie, Maggie and Charley take the first ferry in the morning over to Friday Harbor. To save time and hassle they arrive as foot passengers, leaving the car back at Orcas Landing. The island transit bus drops them at the emergency room door, just as Deputy Danny is parking his patrol car.

"Hey Danny," says Charley, "It's a little early for someone that was working late last night."

"How're you folks holding up?" says Danny.

"What can you do when something like this happens, there's no way to be prepared."

The four of them walk in together; Danny takes the lead and approaches the admissions desk.

"This is Joshua Pearson's Family, where should they wait?" Says Danny.

The day shift has come on, and they are expecting police and family. In the short time, Josh has been in the San Juan's he has become a local hero and news, even bad news travels fast.

"You must be Maggie and Charley Pearson," says the nurse, and then she looks at Sammie with a raised eyebrow.

"I'm Sammie, I live next door." The nurse nods her satisfaction.

"Follow me, we have a room set up right down here." The four file into a waiting lounge, Carly is sitting in a chair, her hands resting in her lap. Danny sits near Carly, nodding good morning.

"The doctor is with Josh," says the nurse, "she'll be right in." Maggie and Charley sit across the room with Sammie. Carly and Sammie make eye contact; each wonders whom the other is. Danny whispers questions to Carly, he wants to know if she had any more encounters with Brad last night. Sammie eavesdrops and her radar goes off when Carly answers that Josh gave her a ride home last night.

"Good morning, I'm Doctor Wendy Williams, Josh is across the hall, I just left him. He is unconscious, but his vital signs are what we would expect. When he arrived, he was extremely hypothermic and unresponsive but alive with good signs. He has multiple lacerations, bruising and swelling, his brain has received a traumatic concussive injury rendering him unconscious. You can go in and see him, but please don't make any loud noises, or touch him, his face is swollen and may shock you. You may go in now, any questions?"

"Is being unconscious normal, if he has good signs."

"Yes."

"When will he wake up," asks Maggie.

"I don't know, all signs are that he should be awake. Think of him as being asleep and getting rested, he'll wake up when he is ready."

"What if he doesn't," says Charley, asking the question everyone is thinking.

"I think he will, he's young and strong."

"Will he be ok," ask Sammie, "will he be back to normal once he wakes up."

"That's a good question, many times people with severe head injuries will have memory loss, especially of the accident, he may not remember yesterday or even the last week. Memory normally returns quickly, I wouldn't worry, I think he will be fine." Dr Williams opens the door, motioning across the hall to the open curtain. Everyone files out and circles the bed where Josh is lying.

"Dr—can I have a word with you in just a minute?" asks Danny. He quickly surveys Josh in the sterile white alcove, crammed with instruments, gauges and hoses. Mostly he wants to verify it is really Josh. He has seen accident victims before and is prepared for what he sees, the others are shocked. Tears well up in all their eyes. No one says anything. Sammie's lower lip quivers, tears flow down her cheeks, she catches breaths in gulps. She remembers their meeting on the ferry. She wonders if he will remember his awkward first attempts at conversation with her, or their first -almost kiss- at Proposal Rock. She is standing next to the hospital bed her hands only inches from his, she reaches out and gently cups his hand the way they learned to share tic-tacs. Do you want a tic-tac she whispers. Sammie closes her eyes trying to hold in the tears and block out her thoughts.

"What is it Deputy," says Dr Williams, when they are alone back in the waiting room.

"Thanks Doc, I'm investigating what happened, I'm not making assumptions but looking into possibilities."

"Go on, I'm listening."

"This may not be an accident, can you determine when it happened, and is there anything about his wounds or markings that may tell us anything. Any paint residue?"

"Blue paint, the attending ER Doctor said he cleaned blue paint off his face. The leg lacerations were done with a very sharp object, knife sharp. He was in the water 2-4 hrs, I would guess 2 ½ hrs, any longer he would be dead from hypothermia, any less and the swelling and bruising would not be fully developed. I think the cold water probably saved his life by slowing down and even stopping some damage from ever occurring. He's a lucky boy, he could have died on impact, drowned, bled out. I'm betting he's going to walk out of here with nothing but a few scars."

"Let's hope so, one last thing, if I showed you a picture of a boat propeller could you determine if it made the cuts on his legs?"

"Probably not, but I may be able to rule out the possibility, dull knives don't make clean cuts. If that's all, I need to go." Danny jots down Dr. Wendy Williams on his pad next to prop id and 2 ½ hrs. in water.

Danny slips back to Josh's bedside. After a few moments, he announces he is heading for town and will give a lift to anyone that needs one.

"I'll go," says Carly.

"Me too," adds Sammie surprising herself.

"Charley, Maggie," says Danny, "will you let me know if you think of anything—anything at all might be useful. I expect we'll be talking soon, and with good news."

The three of them walk out to the patrol car in silence. It's a five minute ride to the Whale Museum where both Sammie and Carly get out thanking him for the lift. While in the car Danny asks them if they have any ideas why someone would want to hurt Josh. Sammie reminds Danny that Josh had tied up a fish and game agent and accused the local director of stealing orcas. "Maybe," says Danny, "but that's not really enough to justify murder he answers, but then Carly adds, what if it's true, what if he is a poacher, he'll go to jail, that's a motive. Then she says, Josh spent all day yesterday online in the museum computer room, what if he really is on to somebody. The day before, he spent all day searching records too, adds Sammie, and there were two WU researchers camped out in Pearson Cove in an old Cruiser that followed him, they said they were worried about orcas missing from the pods. Danny asks Sammie if she got their names, and she remembers they were Dave Johnson and Kirsten Jacobs. Danny fills a page in his notebook with new information.

"You two have been a big help, thanks, I'll wait until you get inside," says Danny as they get out at the museum. Carly and Sammie stand in front of the museum door while Danny waits at the curb. Then Carly waves him off and the two girls go inside.

"Why did he wait," says Sammie.

"You don't know?"

"No"

"Last night my old boyfriend tried to beat me up, he dragged me into the museum. Josh and Chester had just left and when they heard me screaming they came running back. Brad locked us inside, but I got the door unlocked and ran out. Brad kept going after Josh, but he would duck and push him away, he didn't want to fight him. Brads a lot bigger, but Josh wasn't intimidated at all. He's really quick, Brad didn't have a chance, he flipped him to the ground right over there and hurt his face on the concrete. Then that policeman showed up and stopped it, he made Brad go home and told him to leave me alone. Josh and Chet gave me a ride home."

"Wow, what a night, are you ok now, what about Brad, is he going to leave you alone, do you think he could have done that to Josh?"

"I don't know, I'm afraid of him."

"This is unreal, Josh didn't say he was coming over here, he left Orcas before sunup yesterday, the first I knew was when he texted me last night that he was heading back."

"Is he your boyfriend?" asks Carly.

"Yes." says Sammie remembering their kisses and sharing tic-tacs, "Yes he is." *And you can forget all about him.* Sammie is more proud then jealous; the hours he stayed with Pepper after freeing her were hours of unselfish caring and concern for an animal's well being. Pepper had been there for him and brought him back to the cove. She saved his life, what more could she do. Suddenly she wants to get back to his side, to be there for him.

"You're really lucky." Says Carly, "He's nice."

"Yeah, I guess I am."

The museum door opens and in comes Chet and sister Christy.

"Hi Carly," says Christy, "Chester told me what happened last night, Brad is such a loser, you should have pressed charges." Chet has his eyes on Sammie. She's someone he doesn't know but would like to.

"Did you hear, they were looking for Josh last night," asks Chet to Carly.

"You haven't heard,"

"No—what."

"He was run down in his kayak, he's in a coma at the hospital."

"No way."

"Its true," says Sammie, "the Coast Guard helicopter brought him in at midnight."

"Is he going to be alright," asks Chet.

"We just left the hospital," says Sammie, "he was still unconscious, but the doctor said he would wake and probably be ok, I'm Sammie by the way."

"Oh I know you," says Chet, "you're the kayak chick."

"Is that what he calls me?" For a just second Sammie is heartbroken that Josh may not return her feelings, and to think she had just claimed she was his girlfriend.

"No no, that's me, he calls you Sammie, he thinks you're the best, and a super kayaker too. He told me all about you." Sammie is outwardly calm, but inside she is beaming.

"He told me about you too, he calls you the—*go to man*."

"Do the cops know who did it, I talked to Deputy Danny late last night, but he never said anything, just that Josh was late."

"No, they are asking everyone questions." Says Carly.

"I'm going to the hospital," says Chet. "The whale vans leaving right now if anyone is going," and he walks toward the door. Christy stays at the museum; Sammie follows Chet out the door.

The drive from the Whale Museum to the hospital takes ten minutes, the entire time Chet talks about how Josh took down Brad, humiliating him in front of Carly.

When they arrive at Josh's bedside, the hospital room is cool and the lights are turned down. Maggie and Charley are sitting quietly. Charley nods to Chet. Chet is still wearing his favorite *save the whales* shirt from when they met two days earlier. Sammie goes to Josh's side, Chet stands next to her. She gently cups his closed hand with both of hers. His warm hand is reassuring, the tic-tac container she slipped him earlier is still there. She gently giggles his hand rattling the contents.

"Chet's here Josh."

When Chet looks at Josh, he loses his normal rosy complexion, his face drains to pale white. His eyes widen in shock at seeing Josh's swollen face and bandaged body lying unmoving. He isn't prepared to see his friend who just hours earlier had run up four flights of stairs and taken down a bully. The sight takes his breath away. "Oh wow," he says, "I'm ok dude, you rest." Chet just stares, he clenches his teeth to keep his jaw from shaking, his lips pinched tight to stop trembling. He mentally runs down possible perpetrators. The color leaves his face as his emotions swirl from shock, to retribution, to fear. The person responsible is still at large.

"Pepper brought you in Josh," Sammie volunteers, rescuing Chet, "We found you in the boat hoist; you were all tangled up in straps and shredded Kevlar, she must have pushed you and the smashed kayak out of the channel and into the cove. She called Sadie to bring us down to the dock, you trained her well, she saved your life." Charley sets a chair for Sammie next to Josh, and then goes back to his seat beside Maggie. Five minutes later Chet leaves. Sammie holds Josh's hand and quietly talks to him, much the way he had spoken to Pepper, calming her while he cut away the deadly netting.

"It's okay Josh, you can sleep as long as you need, I'm staying right here. Do you remember when we paddled to Rock Island and you fell over in two inches of water.

Chet left, he said see ya later. Maggie and Charley are right over there." Sammie stands to stroke his face but swelling and bruising force her to draw her fingers along his neck behind his ear.

"You're going to have a big headache when you wake up. Please wake up Josh, please."

Sammie sits down and buries her face on his balled up fist.

ORCA BOY

Chapter 37 - Homeland Security

The Coast Guard has continued searching for wreckage after Josh's rescue. They recovered his scratched but still usable paddle and most of the kayaks shredded front half far out in Haro Strait. Using current and weather records the investigation team estimated where Josh was paddling when the incident occurred. They determine he ended up over two miles from where he should have been. When the coast guard spokesman is pressed by a reporter to explain the discrepancy and asked if the juvenile killer whale reported in the cove during the helicopter rescue may have been responsible for saving Josh he simply says,

"Orcas are highly intelligent animals, but they don't talk to us. We have no way of knowing how the victim ended up where he did with an orca next to him, draw your own conclusion."

Deputy Danny has learned that the propeller marks on the kayak were from a left hand pitched propeller. Most single engine boats use right hand propellers, but twin engine boats use both. He's looking for a twin engine boat.

"Hello Deputy," says the Marina Harbor Master, "what can I do for you."

"I'm investigating last night's kayak accident, I have a few questions you may be able to help me with."

"Yeah sure, I heard about that as soon as I came in, any good news on that boy?"

"I checked on him an hour ago, he's still out cold."

"Oh boy, that doesn't sound good, what do you need?"

"Out there on C row is an empty slip. I was told it usually holds a speedboat named *Black Widow*, can you tell me who owns it and where it is right now."

"That's easy—Victoria Masters, her husband died ten years ago, I guess that's why the boat name. She lives up on the hill. If the boat is not in its slip, she has probably gone to Seattle. She's a WU professor and commutes between orca watch outstations. We like her; she buys a lot of fuel for that monster."

"Would you happen to know if it's a twin engine or single?"

"Heck, it could have three or four, I don't know, sorry."

To the right, it's a short walk down the shore side promenade from the marina office to the ferry terminal. To the left, it's an equally short walk to the Customs, Homeland Security, and Fish and Game building. Directly in front of him is the Friday Harbor Marina, a sprawling morass of floating ramps, walkways, docks, and all matter of watercraft. There are six gangplanks, each leading to different parts of the marina. Danny turns to the left and takes the gangplank directly in front of the Fish and Game building. The first float at the bottom of the ramp is for dinghies and kayaks. Josh probably came ashore right here he muses as he pauses next to a dozen kayaks and looks up at the imposing building.

Further up the hillside he sees the Whale Museum and the long stairway leading to 2nd street. Anyone and everyone watching could have seen Josh kayak in and out yesterday. Anyone on the promenade or in the marina office, ditto. Then he notices the cameras mounted on light posts, he scans over to the Fish and Game building and sees more cameras. Danny continues down the six foot wide floating concrete sidewalk, the water is shallow, he sees long eel grass growing on the bottom, but reaching for light at the surface Eelgrass indicates a healthy eco system he remembers from a display on the promenade.

The first boat slips are occupied with recreational fishing boats bristling with expensive gear. Farther from shore the water gets deeper and the boats bigger. He pauses again, this time beside two go-fast boats belonging to Homeland Security. He walks down the narrow finger float between the high performance boats so he can see the motors. Both have four 300 hp outboards tilted up. What could they possibly need 1200 hp for, he asks aloud but no one is there to answer. Two left handed and two right handed stainless steel propellers on each boat. *Ten thousand dollars in props, a hundred thousand in motors, and my patrol car needs tires, go figure.* Both boats have black bottom paint.

The next slips are for transient boaters visiting overnight, music drifts from an open hatch, he gets hellos from people he doesn't see at first. Next, he comes to eight slips marked *Fish and Game boats only,* some of the slips are empty, a double slip holds a floating pen with its own little dock. Four of the boats in slips are identical aluminum sleds. They are twenty five foot flat bottom work boats with drop down bows. Danny makes his way down the narrow finger floats between boats. All the motors are tilted up. Three have singles with right hand props, one is a twin engine with counter rotating propellers. The left hand prop has a broken off skeg. All the boats have blue bottom paint. He gets down on his knees and using his pocket knife scrapes a loose paint flake from the boat with the broken skeg.

"HEY—watcha doing down there?" Caught with his head down and on his knees, Danny looks for feet and legs in his limited field of view but doesn't see any, finally, he rises up and finds the voice coming from a uniformed young man standing in the next boat.

"You can get yourself shot scaring a cop that way." Says Danny, only half joking.

"Yeah I know, but I figured it was worth it, don't you feel energized now."

"No, not really, what's your name?"

"I'm John Marshall—Field Agent"

"I'm Danny O'Brien—Deputy Sheriff, you're new here, I haven't seen you around."

"I could say the same about you."

"Except you would be wrong and you know it."

"Touché, what's up Deputy?"

"Have any of these boats been used since 6PM last night."

"Hard to say Deputy, you could check in the office up there, and see who was working last night. We don't punch time clocks and these boats are pooled. We have our own projects and just grab what we need. Most of the agents just throw the keys into the cup holder, that is the ones that need keys."

"You mean, anyone could sashay right out of here with a boat."

"That's right, or off the breakwater, sometimes we leave em out there if there's no room in here, or if were going right back out."

"Do you ever share these boats or loan them out to say the Coast Guard or maybe whale researchers?"

"Not usually, the Coasties use ribs, but once in awhile WU researchers take em out. Does this have something to do with that kid, Orca Boy, getting run down?"

"It might, what do you know?"

"Nothing."

ORCA BOY

Danny continues out to the end of the dock, nothing else catches his eye. On the way back he pauses in front the Fish and Game sled with the broken skeg and studies the banged up aluminum bow. Some of the scratches look fresh. The other boats are banged up just as much. He makes an entry in his notebook. Next he walks to the far breakwater to check for any Fish and Game boats, he finds two. Both have twin engines, each with a left hand propeller and a right hand propeller. Both have keys in the cup holder. *Oh jeez, these guys ought be fired, it's against the law to leave keys in a car, it's just plain stupid to leave keys in a boat.*

There are too many docks to walk up and down without some idea what he's looking for, Danny makes his way back to the dock with the cigarette boats from last night. Diablo is there, *Black Widow* is still gone, The kids are gone, White Lightnin is empty except for beer cans . He works his way down the tippy finger float to the transom of White Lightnin. It's not an outboard, the single propeller is under water, where he can barely see it, but there is only one, and more than likely it's not left handed.

"You're back," says the Harbor Master, as Danny pops back into the marina office.

"Sorry to bother you again, Is there a camera that shows the breakwater entrance and the open water leading out to San Juan Channel?"

"That's the harbor camera; It's live on our web site 24/7."

"If you save a copy, I'd like to look at it from 6pm on last night."

"Sure, you can look at it on my computer in the office, come on back."

The camera images are still frames saved every five minutes. The departing ferry shows up in only one frame, He sees a kayak in two shots, most frames show boat movement but the next frame is empty. Danny scrolls two dozen images, the total saved from 6 to 8 PM, before turning away from the monitor shaking his head.

"Too much time between shots he announces to the Harbor Master, a boat can leave or arrive totally undetected in between frames. I need a continuous stream, any ideas?"

"Homeland Security, they probably have a satellite camera," jokes the Harbor Master.

Back on the promenade, Danny pauses next to one of the many benches lining the two block pedestrian walk. He rests a foot on a low rock wall and stares out over Friday Harbor. The bustling port is fully awake and in full swing.

"I'm sorry Deputy," says the Homeland Security receptionist, "no one is here that can answer your question or authorize a response."

"I'm investigating an attempted murder, and you won't tell me if you have a camera that may be pointed at the marina."

"I'm sorry Deputy, I will ask the director to contact you," and then she dismissively stares at him.

Danny leaves his Sheriffs department card on the counter and keeps his thoughts to himself about Homeland's apparently well-deserved reputation for being unfriendly.

Outside on the promenade he calls the Coast Guard captain in charge of Josh's case.

"This is Deputy Danny O'Brien, I have a quick question."

"Go ahead, I'm listening."

"If an outboard runs over a kayak or person, would the skeg leave a mark, or just the blades?"

"Good question Danny, many times whales will show skeg scars and propeller slashes, making lacerations that look like a zipper. Sometimes we can tell if the boat was inboard or outboard."

"Ok, what if an outboard motor has a broken skeg?"

"It depends on the skeg's broken stub and what it hits, it may leave no mark at all if it's really short, or a shallow scratch."

"Is there anything conclusive so far."

"We think it was a stainless steel prop, a sharp one, probably fairly new. The bottom paint is basic blue ablative, found on ninety percent of the boats. How's our boy doing?"

"He was still out a few hours ago, I'm heading that way, thanks."

Four sets of binoculars have been trained on Danny, following his movements up and down the docks and promenade. One person is behind dark shaded windows of the Fish and Game office. They watch as he goes from the fish and game slips, out to the boats at the breakwater. Another pair of binoculars in the same building betrays the receptionist lying when she said no one with authority was in. In the marina security office the day shift watches the marina from their perch high above the main marina gangplank. A fourth set of binoculars watches from the viewing stand near the main street turn around.

Chapter 38 - Money Trail

Five hundred feet away, at the top of the second street stairs, Chet is alone in the whale museum theater. His laptop battery is dead again, so he has logged onto his e-mail from the same terminal he and Josh used yesterday. All the names, financial records, everything Josh acquired; he dumped into a word doc. and sent to Chet's e-mail. Now he sits starring at it. *Josh is one smart dude, he said to keep looking for a connection or something out of place, something not normal were his words.* Chet starts with Rich Rogers, *my favorite animal cop—NOT.* He studies the list of banking deposits; he tries to imagine each one, in his head he visualizes the time of year. March -- spring vacation – travel, Sept. – back to school. Chet looks at Roger's payment history. He hesitates at first, but his anger solidifies thinking of Josh busted up in the hospital, and uses the password supplied by datamaster24. He digs into Visa credit card purchases. He envisions birthdays and vacations, Christmas gifts and a new car.

The more he looks, the more nervous he becomes, he wonders about the PC monitors built in camera, and if he should cover it with tape. Josh assured him he wasn't hacking, but what he is doing sure feels like unauthorized trespassing. He makes a note to get some hand sanitizer and wipe down the keyboard. Logging off Rich Rogers Visa credit card account resolves some of his anxiety, but not until he deletes the history and verifies no one is watching over his shoulder does he feel like he is home free.

Snooping in other records is equally nerve wracking, but he keeps at it. Chet learns family secrets and sordid details. Rogers made a $25,000 payment to his ex-wife, Dave Johnson supports a family in the Midwest. He learns that ten years earlier Kirstin Jacobs shared a checking account with Annabelle Smith and wrote checks to San Juan eldercare for $2,500 each month ending nine years ago. He figures her mother died, but not until exhausting her savings. Chet scrutinizes Nasel Peters personal information, but when he looks at Nasel's research department accounts at WU his brain goes numb.

The sheer number of transactions is impossible to track. He tries rapidly scrolling the screens of data looking for a pattern to jump out at him to no avail, but then he remembers Josh using the keyboard shortcut key ctrl f.   He tries it and gets numerous hits when he looks for *killer whale* even more hits when he types orca   into the search box.

His excitement builds when he discovers that WU has been doing business with an international exotic animal anti-suffering organization called WAR - *World Animal Rescue.* The nonprofit is headquartered in Sierra Leone. The excitement is short lived, when he looks at the transaction notes he realizes that Nasal Peters is making donations to WAR, not selling them stolen orcas.

Chet keeps at it, but his spirit is not in it, he keeps thinking about Josh lying in the hospital. *You better make it man so you can find who did that to you.* Unable to concentrate, he slams the keyboard tray shut. Two people watching the orca   movie turn and look at him, and then turn away.

"See ya Carly, I'm going to go check on Josh."

Chapter 39 - Wake Up

"He's still asleep," announces Dr Wendy Williams, after checking Josh. "Has he been working long hours lately or staying up all night."

"Really long," Sammie lights up, "he paddled from Orcas and back, he's been going 24/7 for days."

"If he was exhausted when he started out, the physical trauma and hypothermia may have overwhelmed his body to the point where it went into deep sleep." Maggie and Charley have moved to Josh's bedside. Hearing good news brings new tears to Maggie.

"It's been over twelve hours since he went into the water," says Charley, "does that mean he's had twelve hours catching up on his sleep."

"No, not at all, REM sleep, that's when our body's get rested, may not have begun yet. He may wake up, and be terribly tired, and go back to sleep for twelve more hours."

"So this is good news then, he's not in a coma?" asks Maggie.

"I think so—yes, he was never comatose."

"Should we try to wake him?" asks Sammie.

"He will probably wake on his own, but If he doesn't wake by tonight we will attempt to stimulate him. Right now, the anti-swelling medications are keeping him out. Just treat him like someone taking a nap, talk quietly. He will have a bad headache and hurt all over when wakes up."

"Like a hangover?" suggests Charley.

"No—more like he was run-over, sliced up by a propeller, hit in the head and then damn near froze to death."

"Oh—that kind of ache."

Sammie continues her vigil with renewed hope. The doctor brought in fresh energy and raised hopes for everyone.

"Did you hear that Josh?" says Sammie, after the doctor leaves. "You're just asleep, that's great news." She squeezes his hand around the tic-tac box. He bends his wrist in response.

"He moved," gasps Sammie, "I felt his hand move." Sammie puts both hands around Josh's hand and gently squeezes, comforting him. Josh's eyelids flutter, he turns his head and squints trying to block out the light.

"Josh, Its Sammie, wake up." Maggie and Charley are at the bedside. Maggie has a fresh load of tears, Charley is tearing up. Sammie cradles his hand, rubbing it rapidly, she is trying so hard to stay composed that her breath comes in gulps and she is making the back of his hand turn red.

"Josh, wake up." His head moves ever so slightly side to side.

"Josh, wake up." She whispers again, and again his head moves ever so slightly.

"Josh are you awake?" She whispers.

Mom, mom, don't go, I've missed you. —You must wake up Josh, you have more to do—

"Josh wake up."

I have to go now mom, I will make you proud of me.

"Josh wake up." She squeezes his hand a little more. His eyelids flutter and open, and then he squints turning away from the light. "Turn off the lights please Charlie," says Sammie.

"Is that better?"

"No——my head hurts."

"Lay still," says Sammie, "you were in an accident, you're in the hospital." No one says anything, they watch Josh slowly come back to life; they see his eyes open and close as he becomes accustomed to seeing. He rolls his head on the small low pillow, and winces closing his eyes again.

"The doctor says you will have a bad headache, plus you got hit in the head and face so you're hurting a lot. Your mouth must be dry; I'm giving you an ice chip on your lips." From the paper cup the nurse left, Sammie picks a sliver of ice barely big enough to grip between two fingers. It melts as she places her fingers against his lips. She drags her wet fingers slowly across his lips like when she fed him tic-tacs, bringing a smile of recognition along with less enjoyable twinges of pain.

"More please." She delivers the next ice slivers with a spoon, laying a small pile on his closed lips. They quickly melt, disappear into his mouth and drip onto the pillow, he crunches the rest.

"More please." She repeats with a spoonful, and like feeding a baby, most end up sliding down his cheek.

Josh rattles the container in his hand getting Sammies attention.

"You want one?"

"Yes."

Sammie takes the container and pops the lid with her thumb and shakes out a single tic-tac into her other palm. She places the container back into his hand, and then with the white candy between her thumb and forefinger lays it on his closed lips. Then with her finger she gently pushes the tic-tac between his lips, pausing with her finger on his lower lip for a short moment, before going back to holding his hand she leans forward and kisses him.

"Whew says Charley, I don't know what I just watched, but it looked like good medicine."

"It's very good medicine," says Dr Williams, who has been standing by the curtain watching. "Perhaps the best." Dr Wendy moves next to the bed, everyone shifts to make room.

"Hello Josh my name is Dr Wendy Williams, you are in the Friday Harbor Hospital. You were in a boating accident yesterday. You banged your head and got some cuts on both legs, but don't worry, you are going to be just fine, albeit a little sore for awhile. I need to take a look at your eyes, is that ok with you.?"

Wendy has been leaning over him while talking, watching his eyes track. Josh shakes his head up and down and immediately regrets making the subtle headache inducing movement.

"It's ok to talk; you don't have to shake your head, says Wendy as she brings her pencil flashlight out. "I'm going to shine a light in your eyes now, do you remember what happened yesterday, I mean the accident?" She trains the light on one pupil and then the other, well, do you remember the accident?" After ten seconds of silence, Wendy says to Josh that it's not uncommon for a person with a head injury to not remember the incident or the events leading up to it. She says it is shocking to suddenly realize you have a void in your life that you can't fill in, and that it is perfectly normal to struggle with the reality. The good news, she says, is that for most people, it is temporary.

"What is the last thing you remember Josh," asks Dr Wendy.

"I was paddling Sammie's kayak toward Turtleback Mountain."

"That's good isn't it Doctor," says Charlie, "he remembers right up to when he got run down."

"I was run down in the kayak?" asks Josh.

"That's right," answers deputy Danny, the evidence points to someone driving a boat right over the top of you about two miles from home."

"On purpose, who did it, do you know?" Danny steps completely into the room and stands around the bed with the others.

"Were working on it, right now I'm fitting the pieces together. Doc is it ok if I ask Josh a few questions?"

"That's fine, do you want us to clear the room?

"No, in fact my questions are for everyone. First, does anyone know who did this to Josh?" Everyone looks back and forth at each other. Chet had arrived and stood beside Danny while Wendy was examining Josh. Now he too is around the bed. "Does anyone have any suspicions?"

"Fish and Game," says Charley, "Josh made them look pretty silly."

"You made them look stupid dude," says Chet, giving Josh half a high five in the air. "What about Brad, or WU."

"Why WU," asks Danny.

"Josh figures they are involved in orca trafficking, if he is correct, then maybe someone is worried enough to do this."

"Two of them followed us to Rock Island," adds Sammie

"Do you know who they were," asks Danny. Sammie raises her eyebrows looking puzzled at Josh, she only remembers the girls name was Kirstin.

"Kirstin something." Danny writes in his notebook. Chet knows their names but looks at Josh for an indication.

"Kirstin Jacobs and David Johnson," says Josh softly. He is secretly relieved that he passed a memory test. Danny makes another note.

"Pretty much everyone in the salmon fishing industry hates orcas and by default anyone standing up for them," says Charley

"Josh, you got any ideas?" asks Danny.

"You don't have to talk if it hurts," says Dr Wendy.

"I can talk," says Josh, "I don't remember anything except paddling."

"I know something," says Maggie, "There was a speedboat shooting a big rooster tail out in the channel, it went back and forth several times, and going very fast, too fast if you ask me.

"All right thanks everyone," he makes another note. "Dr may I speak with you out in the hall," as he motions for Wendy to follow him.

"Thanks Doc," continues Danny, "the Coast Guard investigator told me of something they call a zippered laceration, are you familiar with the term."

"No, not really, I can imagine what it would look like, but how is it made?"

"They see it on Whales that have been in accidents with boats, what happens is the propeller makes short parallel curved cuts, and some boats have a skeg that makes a long cut perpendicular to the propeller cuts."

"Got it, and you want to know if Josh has any telltale zipper marks, the answer is no."

"Ok, thanks. Anything that you care to share about Josh." Says Danny while they walk down the hall.

"He's going to be fine. He's had quite a trauma and will be extra tired while recuperating. His family and girlfriend are supportive, he will do just fine."

"That's a relief, he's a good kid."

Dr Wendy Williams and Danny enter the main waiting area to a throng of reporters and crew with video gear. The pretty lady reporter that shared the water taxi ride with Charley is among them, she catches Danny's name tag, but Danny doesn't make eye contact with anyone and ignores shouted questions. Four long strides and he is out the door. Dr Williams takes questions and updates the reporters.

"Officer O'Brien." Says the lady following him outside, hardly raising her voice. Danny stops in his tracks. He won't ignore a polite question, especially from an attractive lady.

"Yes mamm, what can I do for you?"

"My name is Roberta Wilson, I'm a travel writer. Pete's my photographer, companion, bag carrier, and older brother. Pete just nods and places a finger on the bill of his baseball cap. We came to the San Juans to see firsthand some of your tourist attractions and stumbled into this exploding orca controversy."

"Well then let me apologize to both of you, we normally are a laid back sleepy corner of Washington, not at all the center of demonstrations and drama. What's on your mind? Roberta?"

"I would like to interview you, not now, sometime when it works into your schedule." She extends her hand with a business card. Danny does the same. "One of us will have to make a call to the other." She holds Danny's gaze, her dark eyes don't tell him anything except, she's intelligent, friendly and very pretty.

"Ok." says Danny, "One of us will have to make the call."

Danny sits in his patrol car with the engine idling, visions of Roberta Wilson, silent Pete, and the interview request on his mind. He shakes his head forcing himself to focus, and then writes her number in his notebook, then he flips through it one page at a time. He stops on the page with notes about the Homeland Security camera. After a few minutes, he closes it and pulls the shifter down into drive.

ORCA BOY

Chapter 40 - Kayaks

"I'm hungry," announces Josh to his room full of nurses and friends. The closest nurse offers Josh jello and vegetable medley with crackers. "Is my pack here somewhere?"

"I brought it, it's a little damp still," says Sammie, "I figured you would want your tablet. Everything in dry bags is fine. Maggie is drying the stuff that got wet. Do you want me to get something for you?"

"Yeah, my wallet, I am buying lunch. Chet is the Orca Van here, how about if you run down to the Burrito Bandit and get a couple of Peppers Revenge's for us. "

"Excellent choice my man," says Chet. "I'll be back in twenty."

"I don't believe this, you are incredible," says Sammie, grinning and cradling his hand with both of hers. You were in Friday Harbor one day and you got a burrito named after Pepper.

"And," adds Josh, raising a finger on his free hand, "a plan for an orca mural on the side of the whale museum. It will be a ongoing fund raiser, you see Chet's group needs money to do things, and I thought they could have an annual contest to choose a local artist to paint a mural. Patrons will buy raffle tickets to have their names listed and a chance at a small prize. The winning artist will get a paid job and exposure. The museum gets a mural and extra donations. It's a win for everyone."

"Does Chet know about this plan."

"Sure, we talked about it while we were waiting for Dave Johnson. I'll have to fill in some details for him, explain how they will make money, but he gets it, pretty much, I think."

"What else have you done recently?"

"Not much, it's been a slow morning, oh, oh, that reminds me, would you plug in my tablet."

"Do you remember borrowing anything?" She hints, and then Josh suddenly loses his glibness.

"Oh gosh Sammie, I'll get you a new one, in fact well get two. I want my own, and I want yours to be a little lighter and faster, you know, just to be fair, but you decide, you're my expert."

"Oh, your expert am I, how condescending you arrogant bruised runner up." She reaches through the bed sheet into his side and pinches him.

"Ouch, why'd you do that. I just want you to win."

"Ouch, stop it, you win."

"Now you're getting it." She cradles his hand again and then shakes it rattling the tic-tacs.

Chapter 41 - cameras

Deputy Sheriff Danny O'Brien to see agent Rogers is all Danny says when he enters the second floor office above Customs. The receptionist jots a note and takes it down the hall where she disappears into a closed office. When she comes back a minute later, she says that agent Rogers will be with him in a minute. Danny looks out over the marina, the view is commanding, he figures there must be a camera on the roof, it's a no-brainer.

"Hello Danny," Rogers comes out and faces Danny, neither offers to shake hands. "Is this about that Pearson boy getting himself run down?"

"I'm afraid so Rich," both hands are on his hips, he squares up, "I have to ask around, see what I can. We don't know what happened, except a boat ran over him. I'll tell you what I think though."

"Go ahead, I'm listening."

"I think that whoever ran over him, most likely came outa this harbor right behind me." Pointing over his shoulder with his thumb. "If it was an accident, they could have come out any time, even yesterday, or never even been here. But, if it was on purpose, I figure they knew he was out there and they went looking for him. And if they went looking for him, they wouldn't look until he left which was 6 oclock last night. I also think there is a good chance that after hitting him they came right back here."

"Ok, but what's that got to do with me or the department of Fish and Game?"

"Nothing," pointing up to the ceiling Danny says, "Have you got a camera up there."

"We have two, one looking out on the breakwater, the other on our slips below us."

"Are the images of the last twenty four hours saved?"

"Yes, about two weeks worth. If you want I'll have them copied to a thumb drive, what time frame did you have in mind?"

"That's great Rich, sometime before the 6 o'clock ferry last night until midnight, just a six hour window, and both cameras."

"I'll have someone call you when its ready, hey Danny, how's that kid, is he going to make it. You know, I don't like him interfering with our work and all, but I hate to see him end up dead, you know what I mean. He's just a kid."

"I don't know, the last I heard, he was unconscious, he may never wake up."

"Really—well that's too bad." Rogers bites his lip as if contemplating saying something profound, but simply repeats himself instead, *well that's too bad.*

"Tell me about your work with orcas."

"What's to tell, we monitor the population, keep people like Pearson from giving them too much love, enforce boating rules for their safety."

"Why does Fish and Game capture them."

"We only capture orphans and injured that WU identifies."."

"And then what happens to them?"

"It's up to them—WU, some get rehabilitated, and some get shipped to other research institutions. It's not our problem. They have some sort of decades old congressional mandate to manage the population here in the islands. We just enforce and follow orders, most of our work is chasing salmon and crab poachers, not looking after funny looking black and white dolphins."

"Who decides what orcas to capture?"

"WU."

"No, I mean what person."

"Well I guess it's Nasel Peters now, he's the department head, but we never hear from him. It's always some associate researcher, you know PhD's, doctors. For a long time his office manager was Eloise Jacobs, then Kirstin Jacobs took over, I figured she retired and her daughter took over. Like I said, we don't have much say so, our higher ups say work with them on the orcas, and so we do."

"Do you know a Dave Johnson?"

"Sounds familiar, but I can't place him off hand. Who is he?"

He's WU researcher person. How come you keep the keys for your boats down on the boats, what if a boat gets stolen?"

"So we don't lose them, agents used to forget and take keys home or mix em up, it was a big headache, besides, walking up to this penthouse is a lot of work, we should really have our office down on the dock where we do our work. Who in their right mind steals a Fish and Game boat, they all look alike, smell bad and exude fed cop all over them."

"Makes sense, anyway thanks, and put a rush on that video if you can." Danny steps out onto the observation deck and jots notes.

Chapter 42 - Warning

The return address is a PO#, it's a WU #10 business envelope. The type the school prints by the thousands.

It's addressed to—*FH Hospital, the jerke that got run over in his kayak.* It was placed without a stamp in the incoming mailbox.

Josh is sharing the *Peppers Revenge* and hands it back to Sammie when the nurse brings him the envelope. He removes the folded single sheet while everyone watches. The pale white paper is stiff, like parchment, the type that gives a nasty paper cut. He glances at it and then lays his head back on the pillow exhaling the word *crap.* Sammie takes the paper from his hand, its written with red crayon— *you better stop what your doing or you wont be lucky next time.* She lays it on his bed.

"What's it say?" asks Charley, getting up from his chair. Josh uses his fingertips and retrieves the paper.

"It's a warning that may be legitimate, or some ass activist taking advantage of my situation, in any case, Deputy Danny wont want extra fingerprints on the paper." Josh holds the paper open so everyone may read it.

"Oh Josh," says Maggie, "this is serious, you have to stop, I wish your mother was here, she could talk sense into you."

"Your right about that Aunt Maggie, I wish she were here too, and this is very serious, but mom would have said, *do what you know is right, even if it hurts.*"

No one except hospital staff and friends know that Josh is awake and alert. Danny reads the letter and then, using white latex gloves, he tucks it away in an evidence pouch. It's been less than two hours ago that Dr Williams talked with reporters, and even less time since TV reporters went on the air. Danny remembers the large crowd he waded through when leaving the hospital. One of them in that crowd, perhaps. Maybe someone is just fanning the flames, making more news, but why? Maybe it's a hospital employee. The threat can't be ignored, he alerts hospital security and the nursing station, restricting access to Josh's room to known friends and family. Danny pulls onto the Cross Island Highway; his destination is the WU Haro Strait Outstation on the west coast.

"He's asleep," says Sammie, "I guess the Doctor was right about him being tired, he only had a little of the burrito." I'm going to stay here, I don't' want him to be alone when he wakes up, that's what he did for Pepper, and she can't be here for him, but I can. I'm going to go get something to read. I'll be right back." she whispers while carefully wrapping up the unfinished Peppers Revenge and setting it on the stand.

"We'll wait until you return, and then Maggie and I will head back to Orcas."

"Uh, Sammie," says Chet, "things are a little tight for me, Is there any chance Josh got $15 out of his wallet while I was getting burritos?"

"I got it Chet, here's twenty bucks, keep it for gas. Josh can catch me later." Charley hands a relieved Chet a twenty.

Chapter 43 - Norma

Sammie has been reading for twenty minutes, everyone has left. She has pulled her chair tight to the bed and turned it so she is facing Josh, their arms entwined her hand is on his forearm. She is comforted listening to his deep even breaths, when his breathing rhythm changes, she raises her eyes. He's awake, he's been watching her read. Their eyes connect, and she smiles. Josh returns the smile, no words are spoken, none are needed, she finishes the page and looks up again. His eyes droop and close, the rhythm returns. When she turns the page his hand caresses her arm, but his eyes stay shut.

"Wake me in an hour, we've got work to do."

"And if I don't," —the rhythm continues.

The parking lot if half full when Danny arrives, tourists crisscross connecting trails in the windblown scrub pine looking for the perfect cliff side orca sighting viewpoint. Haro Strait is nine miles wide here and Canada's Vancouver Island is but a distant hazy mirage as the low lying fog forms for the evening. The flat water is perfect for spotting telltale spouts or four foot dorsal fins. Scattered offshore are four or five excursion boats, some from Canada, some from Friday Harbor. From shore they all look alike, each promising their passengers an orca sighting of a lifetime, but guaranteeing nothing except maybe seasickness and a three-hour tour.

Danny noses the cruiser into a tire shredding rocky spot beside the main building. He slips in an unmarked side door and pauses while his eyes adjust to the dim light inside.

"Hi Danny," says Norma, his old school friend and the long time bubbly staff person. "Did you bring some orcas, it's been slow today."

Laughing, "Hi Norma, I wish I could, we could charge a fee and get rich."

"I heard about Josh Pearson, he's quite a hero, is it true he's ok?"

"I just left him, the doc says he'll be fine, but how did you know."

"A tourist that came from the Whale Museum told me. That's wonderful news, his family must be relieved. What about him being saved by that same juvenile orca he helped, the news is full of stories, is it true? Everyone that comes in here has another version to tell."

"Well, no witnesses have come forward, but Pepper, that's what Josh calls her, was swimming next to him when he was found unconscious on the boat hoist at the Pearson Cove Marina. Sadie, that's the neighbors dog that is all over utube playing fetch with her, sounded the alarm.

"What do you think then, is it true, is it possible?"

"I don't think there is any question that the orca rescued him, she probably pushed or towed him somehow for a couple miles, and then shoved him up onto the hoist. She's probably an eye witness to what happened."

"That's funny, an orca as a witness, are you going to interview her?"

Danny flips open his notebook and jots, *check slip/hoist again* and then says.

"Maybe, but right now take a look at this envelope." He pulls out the bagged envelope and sheet of paper with the red crayon warning threat. Danny holds it up, slowly rotating the bag for Norma, he keeps the threat letter folded, there is no need for anyone to know the contents. He opens the zip lock an inch and sniffs, and then holds it up for her to do the same.

"Ok, so you have a musty old university envelope with a hint of annoying perfume."

"How do you know it's old."

Norma opens the top drawer of her desk and pulls out an envelope and hands it to Danny.

"Here's a new university envelope, see the difference?"

"Yeah, I do, no address, just a PO Box, and the picture is different. When did they switch over?"

"About ten years ago, but they pass out printed envelopes by the ream, we may still have some old ones around here if I dug around in my file cabinets, do you want me to look?"

"No, what about letterhead, do they supply it also."

"Yes but, its just 20 lb copy paper, why? what's the significance?"

"Probably nothing, but I need to follow up everything. Do you know Dave Johnson or Kirstin Jacobs."

"Sure, I've known Kirstin since she was little, her mother, Eloise used to work in the research lab before Peters was there. Eloise and Victoria, what a pair, best friends and inseparable, Kirstin sort of took over the job when her mother got sick."

"What kind of sick and who is Victoria?" says Danny.

"Oh, she's one of the old guard, Victoria was in charge before Peters came on board, they used to call her the *Black Widow Professor,* I don't think she teaches much anymore, just hangs out and attends functions. Eloise has dementia or nowadays they just say Alzheimer's, Everyone ignored her condition and worked around it but eventually Kirsten moved her into a facility. "

"What about Johnson?"

"I know of him but, working in a whale watching gift shop doesn't really give me mingling status. I think he teaches and takes students on field trips."

Norma is a treasure trove; Danny forces himself to jot notes while listening. He hates to leave, but after getting his questions answered, the conversation strays into old times and storytelling. He thanks Norma and exits the way he came in. Danny heads south along the coast, but on San Juan Island all roads lead back to Friday Harbor. He drives by the hospital and four blocks later turns onto Sixth Street. The street is lined with older turn of the century houses from when Friday Harbor was a bustling fishing and logging hub. It is easy to imagine a tree lined cobbled street with freshly painted new homes, and young hardworking families staking their claim in new subdivisions touted by developers as the newest in modern living. Today the recent rich have abandoned much of downtown and live on five acre mini ranches where they raise Kobi beef and Alpacas while commuting to six figure jobs. The cobble stone street has been replaced with blacktop paving, the cobbles tossed in the harbor to shore up eroding banks. Trees that grew majestic, became hopelessly overgrown and disfigured years ago heaving the sidewalks. Some once proud bungalows have been reroofed, and resided, but a century of good times and bad times, peeling paint, fishing skiffs, and abandoned cars as yard decoration has blighted Sixth Street, marking it the poor part of town.

ORCA BOY

Chapter 44 - Datamaster24

Fortunately, the nurses have left them alone in the darkened room, an hour passes easily for Josh, and Sammie. She falls asleep while reading and slouches in the chair, with her head lying on the hospital bed.

"What?" Sammie half lifts one droopy eye lid, "Huh." He tries not to disturb her as he eases his arm out from under her hand and head.

"Nothing, go to sleep." he logs on to his browser and goes to savingpepper911@hotmail.

Datamaster 24 has a response to his last query, the e-mail is just like before. He will have twenty four seconds to copy the info and then it will be lost forever in the datamaster cover your butt system of leaving no trail. He copies the code, opens a blank word doc. and reads the saved info.

"I'm sorry I didn't wake you, I fell asleep."

"That's ok, I enjoy holding your hand and being close to you, while you slept I was thinking of Rock Island. We should go back as soon as we can." Sammie gets to her feet and kisses him.

"Your sweet, what's that on your tablet?" Josh cautiously shows Sammie a screen of pilfered financial information he and Chet have been scrutinizing. When she doesn't appear too shocked, he scrolls and shows her more.

"My gosh Josh, is this legal," she whispers. This is private bank stuff, how'd you get this." He explains the Datamaster 24 system, and shows her the response yet to be retrieved.

"This is cool, move your chair around so you can watch this destruction." Josh gives the blank word doc a title and then enters the code.

"What's that mean, warning you have 24 seconds, what happens?"

"Just watch, you'll see." He clicks on the retrieve button and instantly the datamaster 24 site brings up the last query response, he notes that it's the same associate, and he is dinging him 750 points. He gets a kick out of thinking that everyone on the system will work for no points, it's the challenge that pumps them up. They Know they are an elite group of users in a secret and hopefully untouchable network, the thrill of breaking rules adds excitement, the point system is really a way of assigning a level of danger to each hack job. He touches ctrl a, ctrl c, and pastes the info into his open word doc. The little countdown clock is only down to 17 seconds. Sammie watches the screens change as he copies and pastes. When he's done he leaves the countdown clock ominously covering the entire tablet.

"What was that stuff, I just saw it for an instant, what happens when that clock runs out?" Sammie's eyes are wide on the screen, she is leaning over Josh half blocking him.

"Keep watching, when the clock hits zero, all the data blows. Ok here goes, watch."

"Wow, I mean gross, look at that—ugh, that is creepy scary, I've never seen a Bizzarro Pac-man, let alone seen two go berserk."

"What!—oh crap, they changed the sign off, it used to explode, but this was way cool too."

The next active screen replaces Datamaster 24 when the cannibalism is complete; it's an enlarged image of a high performance kayak. Josh has been busy researching the surprise while Sammie slept.

"They have it in stock at *Island Kayak* right here in town. It's the new carbon fiber model of your old one, only twenty seven pounds and two cargo hatches."

"I love it, can we test paddle it." She slides her arm around Josh's neck and hugs him prompting an ow to which she says, sorrrry.

"Yes, you can test it all you want, in fact I will personally guarantee your satisfaction or double your hugs back."

"Promise."

"I Promise," says Josh. This time her hug is tender and finishes with a warm lengthy kiss followed by staring into his eyes until when she is about to kiss him again with real passion, Josh freaks. He breaks away, looking anywhere but at her. The pain in his cut legs and battered head is understandable, but suddenly he is in a cold sweat, his chest shakes with each short breath as if he's on his tenth double espresso. With a simple kiss and a probing look she has turned him into a shaking puppy unable to look at her and afraid to say anything for fear of it sounding stupid. *I can't believe it, she twists me tighter than a championship fight.* He faces his fear, he faces her, and takes a deep breath, he mouths quiet aum's, omm—omm—omm, and then takes another breath and a long exhale.

"What are you doing, are you ok?" says Sammie with a

bewildered semi-coy smile.

"Focusing—let's get to work." Josh is eager to make Sammie happy, but he is just as excited about nailing orca poachers. He brings the word doc. screen back, Sammie reads over his shoulder, but he clicks through the first pages so fast she only registers headings. Nasel Peters has no smoking guns or unknown children, so no financial data. Johnson is childless, Jacobs unknown. A statement from the *data gatherer*, as they sometimes jokingly call themselves, stands out, it says—*it appears you are looking for a money trail so I took the liberty to look for siblings, the results are included.* "These guys do great work," says Josh, "but it is time consuming using secret web sites and posting on forums to pass data."

"I thought you were using e-mail."

"No—E-mail leaves an electronic trail, we use it just for making connections, it's kinda like a pager or doorbell calling your attention." Says Josh.

"I don't get it, why can't you just text or talk."

"Well first of all it takes some time to uncover stuff, and some of the Datamaster members desire to be anonymous because that gives them the freedom to play a little loose with rules."

"You mean hacking right?" Says Sammie, confident that she has recognized what the other members are really up to.

"I'm not hacking, hacking is illegal."

"But your friends are hackers."

"They're not friends, I don't know them, I just post queries and read responses. No one knows anyone."

"Aren't you worried that the Datamaster administrators will get busted and implicate you?" Says Sammie.

"No, I use disposable e-mails and they burn their hard drives randomly or when protocol is broken triggering a doomsday self destruct. There is no electronic trail beyond an empty URL address. After a self destruct they get new hard drives, load a common open source forum, tweak the program and add a doomsday self destruct device, and start fresh with no history."

"What about the ip address?"

"I'm impressed," says Josh, "proxy, proxy, proxy, and it all leads back to an entity that doesn't exist in the real world."

"Ok then, what about your tablet?" Sammie whispers, "haven't you saved a bunch of confidential information like ss numbers and passwords that you don't have permission to have? How can you explain having that info, that's the same as stealing isn't it."

"Shhh, if things go bad, it will have to be destroyed, there is no way to delete files for sure, burning is the only positive way." Josh turns to the monitor and rapidly reads the new information. The Datamaster member has supplied; Kristin Jacobs, son Ryan Jacobs, and mother Eloise Thompson, all living on San Juan Island. Dave Johnson has a brother living in Florida. Lastly is Victoria Masters a onetime sister relationship to Eloise Thompson. As of research time, all financial data and last known address is current.

"Lets go back over the data I got yesterday. Sometimes a second or third pair of eyes spot things others miss."

"Hey guys," says Chet walking in, "I couldn't stay away. I met a reporter out in the lobby. Well I don't know what she is, but she said she is a writer, but I think that's just a line. She calls herself a writer but and she has some camera dude with her. Anyway how you feeling, you look great, I mean except where you don't look so good."

"Hey dude," says Josh, "slow down, is your laptop charged, I'll e-mail you some more files to study. What does that reporter lady want?"

"Well she wants to talk to you but I answered a lot of their questions."

"What do you mean their questions, are there more out there?"

"I don't know, I guess, there's a bunch of them just hanging, I just talked to a couple."

"Dude, you just did an interview, were there cameras."

"Yeah, I guess, I wasn't looking at anyone but her, she's really pretty. I mean really, really pretty.

"We get it, you're in love, watch the news if you want to see what you look like drooling and helpless, by the way, TV cameras can spot a zit from a mile away." Sammie nudges Josh, and whispers *you're hopeless.* He whispers back, it's different when a pretty girl kisses you.

"You think I'm pretty?"

"Yes."

"Just a sec," she touches his lip with her finger, "well come back to this. On that first day when Rogers arrested you, a writer lady stayed at the resort, she was pretty and had a camera guy, her brother with her. Chester what was your pretty lady's name?"

"Roberta something, Wilson."

"That's her, that's the writer, she's really cool and pretty like Chet says."

"Well, she's out front with the rest of them."

Chapter 45 - Animals

Rich Rogers sends the flash drive loaded with camera footage to the sheriff's office. Make sure it is delivered to Deputy O'Brien are his instructions. Next he walks down the stairs himself, in his hands, he carries a long bicycle cable and padlock. At the promenade, he pauses and exhales showing sadness and resolve. Emotions weigh on him but he knows what he must do. He heads down the gangplank and turns toward the outer breakwater. Five minutes later, he is standing by the twin-engine fish and game boat with the broken skeg. Honda 175's power the big aluminum work boat, a single outboard with half the horsepower would suffice, but the endless pot of money the state uses to buy the department first rate equipment just keeps on giving. Whatever they ask for, they get. There is no question the stout aluminum boats are required, anything less would not survive the abuse his agents heap on them. *Bumper cars,* he says under his breath, then he slips the cable through a cleat and padlocks the boat to the dock. Using a heavy cable tie he attaches a clear plastic sheath with a note inside, it reads DO NOT BOARD!—Rich Rogers dept. of Fish and Game. He walks further down the dock checking out the rest of his boats; he takes note of broken, bent, and missing parts. Some of the boats have lunch sacks and clothing lying about. *Pig sty's—bunch of animals!*

Chapter 46 - Video

The address for Kirsten Jacobs house is in the middle of the block, a five minute walk to the hospital, and ten minutes to the marina. The faded mailbox says Eloise Thompson. Danny parks and steps out. He scans the dozen or so houses that face this section of street, he sees the tell tale curtain flutters, and fleeting faces. He's used to it, people snoop, and cops draw attention. Across the street, he waves to a face that does not turn away. He walks by an old bicycle, rusty but with air in the tires, the Friday Harbor teen-age equivalent of a daily driver. A wisp of black smoke comes out of the single brick chimney; the oil furnace is turned on. He knocks, and listens, and then knocks again. He finishes knocking by resting his knuckles on the door, no sound, no vibration, he shoves, its latched, he doesn't try the knob.

Danny dismounts the three steps and walks alongside the house. There is no side fence the back yard is open, there are no land mines, *apparently they don't have a dog.* The back door is in a little porch at the top of three steps. Half the paint is missing, the other half is peeling like the outer skin on an onion. The door has a window with a dirty white cloth on the inside. A plastic trash bag sits outside the door, *apparently the neighbors don't have a dog either.* Danny walks back to his car and pulls out his notebook, using the cars roof he starts to write but he is stalling and watching the Jacob's house. After a minute or two he looks across the street, the face is still there. He nods and walks toward it.

"Hello, I'm Deputy Danny O'Brien, have you got a minute."

"Of course I do, I have nothing but minutes, minutes to watch, minutes to wait for my coffee, minutes to live."

"That's funny," cutting her off, "What I meant was, will you talk to me for a little bit."

"Ok, but just for a minute, I don't have all day." The gleam in her eye is wicked.

"You're wonderful, and this may take all day. I'm guessing that you know Kirsten and Ryan."

"Of course, and Eloise too,"

"Have you seen them around lately."

"I see them every day."

"What about last night."

"Yes, I saw them last night."

"Do you know about when they came home?

"I think they are home right now."

"Do you know when they came home last night?"

"Yes they were home last night."

"Did you see them leave yesterday."

"No, I'm sorry, I don't think they were home yesterday."

Before Danny can ask any more pointless questions, a car pulls into the driveway across the street giving Danny a reason to thank the neighbor and excuse himself.

"What's going on," says Kirsten outside her car, "I don't normally have a police car in front of my house when I come home."

"Hi, I'm Danny O'Brien, are you Ms Jacobs, I'm following up on a boating accident yesterday, did you by any chance hear about it."

"Yeah that's me, do you mean the one on the news with the kayak, what's that got to do with me?"

"Precisely, that's the one, I understand you and Dave Johnson met with him over on Rock Island a few days back."

"Yeah," she says hesitantly, "You don't think Dave did it do you?"

"I'm just gathering information; I'm talking to everyone that has been in contact with him. Would you happen to know where Dave Johnson was last night between six and nine, and if you don't mind, where were you."

"Oh my god, I was right here.

"Would you give me his number, and one more thing, are you familiar with a cigarette boat named *Black Widow?*"

Before she can answer the house door opens and Ryan Jacobs comes out. He's slender and tall like Kirsten, his hair is in a pony tail. Danny glances at the rusty bicycle, they're a good fit he decides.

"What's going on. I was just playing a game when I saw the car out here."

"This is my son Ryan." Danny extends his hand and they shake, its cold and wet.

"Sorry, I just washed up."

"I knocked earlier, why didn't you answer?"

"Like I said I was playing a game."

"He wears headphones." Says Kirsten, Danny just nods like he understands.

"What about the boat, *Black Widow*." Ryan looks at Kirsten then away.

"*Black Widow* is Victoria's boat."

"Any idea why she would have it out last night."

"No."

"She's your old boss right, do you know if anyone else uses the boat."

"No, she was my mother's boss, and I suppose anyone she gives the keys to."

"Some people hide their keys onboard, does she."

"Yes."

"Do you use it, were you out last night?"

"Sure, she lets me use it, but I told you, I was at home all night."

"What about you Ryan, do you drive *Black Widow* sometimes?"

"No," says Kirsten, Victoria says it's a woman's boat."

"An ocean racing cigarette boat is not normally a woman's boat?"

"And what is a woman's boat deputy?" He ignores her question.

"Do you know where it is now?"

"If it's not in its slip, then Victoria probably has gone to Seattle with it, her late husband set it up for high speed commuting."

"When you met Josh Pearson on Rock Island you had a different boat, why?"

"At the time, you police were looking for him, Dave and I didn't see any reason to help you capture a kid that is standing up for our orcas. and *Black Widow* draws attention."

"For the record, that was the feds." Kirsten's icy stare says it all.

Looking at Ryan, Danny says, "Where were you last night?"

"Just hanging," he mumbles, "there was a group playing drums on the promenade." Danny holds his gaze intentionally, and then extends his hand and says thanks. Before shaking hands, Ryan wipes his hands on his pants, but still leaves clamminess for Danny to wipe on his own pants before finger tipping Kirsten's warm inviting hand. Her iciness has evaporated as fast as it appeared.

Danny's office text's him; *FYI, You have a package from Fish and Game marked video.* He texts back; *Be there in ten.*

ORCA BOY

Before looking at it, he saves the entire drive to disk, placing it in a folder titled Joshua Pearson. He opens the footage in windows media player and stretches out in his darkened office, one hand on the keyboard, his fingers playing the arrow keys. He runs fast forward until the ferry disappears from its berth, racing around the corner like a fat slot car on speed. And then he stops and backs the ferry all the way back to the terminal. Danny pauses the file and leans forward studying the docks and the boats in the fairways. The focus and resolution is excellent, not at all like the convenience store and bank surveillance films on the news.

He zooms in and pans to the wharf with the go-fast boats. Next he pans to the top of the screen and studies the outer breakwater float where Fish and Game ties up its overflow boats. In the middle of the screen are the Fish and Game slips in front of their office. The dinghy and kayak docks are almost directly under the camera and out of view. *Damn says Danny to no one, can't see the promenade or kayak floats.* He studies the many fairways on the screen. For a kayak to get through the maze, a paddler has to paddle left around the marina, or to the right and go under four gangplanks eventually coming out by the fuel dock next to the ferry.

He scrutinizes every inch, all the way to open water beyond the breakwater and red painted customs dock. Danny taps the forward key and the screen comes to life. He see's people moving about, after a minute of familiarizing, he taps the key and the people comically speed up in jerky spasms. Boats move in and out of the fairways, turning into slips and narrowly escaping the watery equivalent of fender benders. Two kayaks appear and then jerk to the outside and move beyond the cameras field of view. A seaplane lands and is quickly swallowed by the sea of yachts. Down on the docks a crowd of a dozen or so tourists walk and then stop in front of a large boat, and then move on to the next. Danny can see a tour guide in front, then in an eye blink they are all on board. Every fairway has at least one boat moving, most several.

He keys normal speed, a group of four is walking toward the cigarette boats. One person is dragging behind them a white cooler on wheels. It's the four he interviewed, they turn down the finger dock berthing *White-Lightnin.* Danny looks at the ferry, no movement so far. Five kayaks appear on the screen where the kayak docks should be. The last kayak quickly out paces the others and makes the first corner continuing to leave the others further behind. *That's my boy,* says Danny still talking to a dark room.

On the far right side he notices foot traffic and cars are no longer clambering onto the ferry. A worker pulls the chain across and seconds later, a gap appears between the ferry and the dock. White water churns out the back into the widening space. The lone kayak has cleared the breakwater and shares the expanse with the ferry and other small boats. All boats, including the ferry line up in orderly rows moving in or out of the quarter mile wide entrance, no one is foolish in attempting to cut across in front of the ferry. The kayaker keeps well off to the side and moves out into San Juan Channel, The ferry quickly makes the turn to the east and is lost from view. Danny keeps watching the kayaker even though it has become an almost impossible dot to follow, he sees the current drag the paddler seaward to the west. When the kayak is virtually invisible he zooms in, until the resolution is hopeless, but he can tell it went west around Shaw Island toward Shaw Rocks. Panning back and rewinding he picks up *White-Lightnin* leaving the fairway and then picking up speed slowly just like the driver said when he drove around other boats. Once out of the harbor and almost beyond the cameras field of view, the driver stands on it. The go-fast boat rockets ahead like a drag racer with all green on the tree. It's rooster tail shoots as high as the ferry's passenger deck when it roars by thrilling the tourists and surely irritating the skipper. Danny keeps watching the screen, occasionally fast forwarding and then backing up for a second look. Soon another ferry takes the empty terminal space and the procession of cars and foot passengers begins anew.

He studies the Fish and Game boats, but there is no activity. The video time stamp reads after seven, everyone has quit for the day. While watching fast forward a sleek black boat appears jerkily heading out, Danny keys pause and then reverses and slowly backs *Black Widow* into her slip. He keeps in reverse and tracks the lone occupant back up the wharf and out of the cameras field of view. The time stamp says 7:10, the person is wearing a dark colored long fisherman's rain hat and oil skin type trench coat, he can't see the face, but any of hundreds of Friday Harbor waterfront deck hands have a similar outfit in their closet or pickup truck. Danny studies the persons walk and estimates their height. Frustrated he admits to himself, he doesn't know if it's man or woman. He repeatedly watches the figure swing onto *Black Widow*. He concludes the person is fairly nimble and doesn't move like a heavyset person.

He fingers the keys forwarding back to where he first saw *Black Widow* leaving the fairway, he notes the go-fast boat wandering, its bow yawing back and forth, while making its way past the breakwater. Perhaps inattention, perhaps driver inexperience, perhaps it is just hard to make hundred mile an hour boats go straight at low speeds.

Danny keys a faster speed keeping an eye on the harbor entrance. Another ferry arrives and berths in the double terminal, and evening shadows stretch across the busy marina marking the suns final descent over Vancouver Island to the west. Over an hour of footage passes in mere minutes, Danny stops often to zoom in or back up for a closer look. At 8:30 *Black Widow* returns to her slip. The same oil skinned figure hastily steps off and ties her up almost as an afterthought in their hurry to move down dock. Danny follows at normal speed, his face six inches from the monitor screen. He's looking for a reason to freeze and zoom in, but the person keeps their head down, arms in pockets as it hurries along.

At the head of the wharf is a main concourse with a restroom blocking Danny's view. The figure disappears under the overhanging roof, while he waits several people come and go, some using the bathroom and some just walking by, but they are all momentarily obscured from the camera's vantage.

Where's my guy, where did you go, he growls to no one. He hits pause and studies the people on the wharf, and then backs up the footage to where the oilskin person was last visible. He keys forward again keeping track of each person's arrival and departure from the bathrooms blank spot. *There you are you son of a gun, I got you now.* The person has changed hats and coats from a dark rain hat to a bright floppy sun hat and is carrying the oilskin draped over their shoulder. *Definitely the same person, definitely maybe,* Danny is still talking to himself.

Instead of leaving by walking up one of the gangplanks, the figure turns toward the Fish and Game float and makes his way down to the row of slips holding eight or so work boats. The person steps into the back of a twin engine skiff, and seconds later a puff of smoke identifies the port engine started, followed by the starboard engine. Danny looks over the area and sees no uniformed presence, no one to stop or identify the person, he remembers Rich Rogers words about keeping the keys on board to avoid losing them. *I got news for you Rogers I'm watching you lose an entire boat.*

The person shoves off and is halfway up the fairway just two minutes after brazenly stepping aboard. Danny watches the Fish and Game boat clear the breakwater and climb up on plane. On flat water the over powered twin engine sled can make seventy five miles an hour, easily fast enough to become airborne and ultimately crash in the wrong conditions. The boat leaves the cameras field of view and disappears around the corner to the right, the same direction *Black Widow* had come from less than fifteen minutes earlier. Danny checks the footage time clock and makes a note in his notebook next to other times he has been keeping track of.

He pauses the video and studies the waterways and docks, darkness is quickly falling, the entire marina is in shadow. The descending sun is racing the forming fog to see which will be the first to steal his view. *And to think, I was down there checking on that boat just an hour or so after it came in.* He keys play again and speeds it up, he sees *White-Lightnin* come back to her slip, and watches all of the kids speed walk to the bathroom and then speed walk back for more beer.

Thirty minutes later in almost total darkness, he sees red and green running lights come inside the breakwater, dockside floodlights illuminate the Fish and Game work boat nudging up to the end of the other Fish and Game boats. Its way to dark to see any detail, but Danny can see the figure is wearing the same floppy light colored hat. It takes just seconds to cleat off the dock lines and then the figure simply walks away, joining the stream of tourists making the trek to the end of the breakwater and back. Danny watches the screen intently, somewhere along the float the person changed back to the dark rain hat and donned the oilskins, he catches a few glimpses under floodlights until the person heads up the first gangplank and walks out of the cameras range of view.

Danny jots the final time in his notes, and leans back, tapping his pencil on the table while watching the screen. *I don't get it yet, but I will. First you go out in a go-fast boat, then you switch it for an almost as fast work sled that you bring back and park in a different place, all the while hiding your face. Did you run down Josh? Who are you?*

He keeps watching on fast forward until he sees himself talking to the kids on *White-Lightnin*.

ORCA BOY

Chapter 47 - Tears

"Josh, this is Roberta Wilson," says Sammie.

"Hi, excuse me for not getting up, I'm a little sore right now."

"That's understandable, has Sammie told you, I was staying at her resort?"

"Yes she did, they said your brother was with you."

"He is, he's outside."

"So—you can't miss Sadie," jokes Josh, "but did you get to meet Pepper."

"No, but I rode in the water taxi with Charley. Dave and I came here to research travel articles, not report on orca protests, but since we are here and met some of the key players, well, I'd like to hang around and see where all this is headed. Maybe we can be of some help to you, I know some editors and I write, we can..." *whispering, "he's asleep, normally I don't put people to sleep."*

Sammie and Roberta sit in the corner with chairs facing each other, their knees touching while they talk in whispers trying not to wake Josh. When Roberta stayed at the *Islander Resort,* she learned all about how Josh saved Pepper so they discuss more recent events around the islands. Sammie fills her in about the goings on at Rock Island when they met Kirsten and Dave, and how Josh had intimidated them, and then was so romantic with the tic-tacs.

"You like him a lot don't you," whispers Roberta.

"Does it show that much?" They both lean forward meeting in a conspiring huddle. "I don't have anyone to talk to. He says I scare him, and there's all these girls drooling over him, there was one here this morning before I got here, and his sister too," nodding at Chet, "I don't know what to do." Roberta grasps Sammies hands in hers. In spite of her smiling, tears flow down Sammies cheeks and her lower lip shakes. "I thought he was dead."

"Sammie," says Josh, he is sitting up with his arms towards her, "come over here." She runs to him and melts into his hug, burying her face in his arms and white bed sheets. He grimaces with pain, but wraps one arm around her head, the other around her shoulder, and just holds her tightly.

"I thought you were dead." She gulps deep breaths and with each exhale, cries some more. Josh lays his head, tight on hers and rocks her, comforting her. Very softly she hears ommmm... soon her gulping ends, and she relaxes in Josh's soothing embrace. Roberta's tears are of a different sort, but she manages to outline an article about loss and young love.

Chapter 48 - Crane Barge

Deputy O'Brien pounds up the steps one at a time.

"As far as I know, she hasn't been moved or boarded since last night." Says Rogers when Danny gets to the top and the two of them are looking out over the marina.

"You looked at the footage?" says Danny.

"Yeah—what do you make of it? First he takes out a Ferrari and then steals and joy rides a parks boat. I padlocked it by the way, the code is 505."

"I don't know yet, but I will. I need to take it for safe keeping, have forensics go over it."

"That's fine, I got more, You need me just holler."

Danny's been up there barely long enough to get his wind back and enjoy the view, *I should have just called,* when he heads back down the flights of stairs. *He stops by his cruiser for a bag with his notebook a roll of yellow police tape, chain, and padlock, and his camera.* Next he heads for *Black Widow.* The go-fast boat floats easy and guiltless in her slip. *What part did you play.* He stretches a single plastic strip from floating finger dock to floating finger dock sealing her in the slip, across *Black Widows* wave piercing bow he stretches another strip. When he snaps the chain empowered padlock on to her stainless steel bow eye, he takes a hard look at her bottom paint. *It's black paint pretty lady,* he says, *not blue, you're probably going to see more hundred mph plus runs, but not today.* Danny takes lots of pictures but doesn't go onboard or touch anything. He adjusts his resolution to maximum and discreetly snaps images of each of the gangplanks and the promenade. Later with his computer he will zoom in and see who is watching him.

The walk to the outer breakwater takes him past the bathroom that blocked the video camera. Knowing he must be thorough, and it will bug him later if he doesn't look, he pokes around in the garbage barrel under the roof overhang, and then does the same inside each bathroom. As expected, he comes up with nothing.

While walking, he tries scenarios for using two boats. *The perp needed gas... pretty simple, he stole a boat with an empty tank, and then stole another. Check fuel levels... check. The go-fast boat was too loud and identifiable... he had a disguise, and over water distances are way too far to id. The perp searched for Josh first and the faster boat makes sense. One boat is a v-hull, the other a sled... so what. Black Widow is flashy and attention getting , but not a parks boat... maybe he or she realized it was a bad choice! He wants to shift blame to Fish and Game... maybe! Maybe someone saw him, blowing his cover... maybe! One thing is for sure... he saw the same person take out both boats, what's the connection?*

Finally, the long walk out to the breakwater is over, it's hard to miss the boat in question, Rogers has it secured with a logging chain and a case hardened industrial lock that would stymie the largest of bolt cutters. It looks like it will take a determined thief all day with ten hacksaws to cut it off, except Danny knows a bad guy with a battery operated angle grinder could slice through a chain link like a hot knife goes through butter, and with relatively little noise. Like at *Black Widow,* Danny stays on the dock, he looks her over. The twenty five foot aluminum sled has a small cabin making it hard to see the driver. Telltale prints could be anywhere; there are polished grab handles throughout the vessel. Steering wheel, twin shifters, throttles, all likely places to lift evidence, unless the person wore gloves. He kneels on the dock by the boats bow—blue bottom paint. *Strike one.*

Danny brings up *Billy's Island Salvage* service on his phone. "This is Deputy O'Brien, how you doing Billy? — Can your barge crane lift a twenty five foot aluminum parks boat out of the water?"

"Sure Danny, no problem."

"Can you do it without slings, I don't want to disturb the bottom."

"I don't see why not, all those boats have factory installed lifting hooks, and if it doesn't, we can hang it by its cleats. What's going on?"

"I need you to bring your crane over to the breakwater and hoist a possible hit and run boat. I'll have a forensic investigator there in about an hour, you come by in say two hours, if that will work?"

"This is Danny, I got *Island Salvage* on their way to the breakwater in about two hours, I think you should go there first, before you do *Black Widow,* you know, in case you get hung up lifting prints.... Yeah, that's right.... Ok, ok, the boats chained up, you can't miss it, oh and the padlock combination is 505.... Yeah, I'll see you there." With his camera still on high resolution, he snaps images of the Fish and Game boat making sure he gets zoomed in background shots of the far off promenade and the surrounding waterfront.

"Deputy... what have I done to deserve this honor?"

"Well thank you—If you are, Victoria Masters and own *Black Widow,* that's enough.

"Oh boy this sounds ominous, right on both counts, come on inside, take a load off."

Victoria graciously ushers Danny into her study saying, *Robert says this is where all the important talk takes place.* After a puzzled look from Danny she explains Robert was her late husband, it was his study and favorite place to talk. The walls and shelves are lined with boat pictures and models of sailing yachts. There is a computer desk and printer, but the main focus of the room is comfortable leather armchairs. Danny stands taking in the pictures, Victoria has watched men before as their eyes go from boat to boat, she keeps quiet while he takes it in.

"*Black Widow,* was Roberts boat?" he questions, trying to understand why an older lady would own a go-fast boat."

"In a way, *Black Beauty* was Roberts boat that he bought for us to commute to Seattle, but he really bought her for me, he was a sailor, power boats to him were simply a way to get somewhere fast. Sailing was his passion."

"You said *Black Beauty.*"

"Oh, the name change was after he died, he wanted to name her *Widow-Maker,* so we compromised. After he passed I changed it to *Black Widow* to honor him.

"He died onboard her?"

"Heavens no, he died on his sailboat, this one here," pointing to a picture of a racy looking sloop. "This was his baby, *Island Time.*" Victoria reminisces for exactly two seconds and then says.

"Why are you here deputy?"

The simple to the point question snaps Danny from any lull or thought that he was interviewing a fragile old woman. Victoria is sharp, quick and probably hard as nails, just what you would expect of a female owner of a Cigarette racing boat. Danny explains the marina camera video of her boat coming and going. He describes the lone oilskin trench coat wearing figure. He explains there is no doubt it is *Black Widow* in the video and that witnesses on Orcas Island had seen a black boat shooting a rooster tail at the same time period. He asks her, straight out, who was driving her boat.

"Well deputy, you certainly have made a case for my boat being used yesterday, just exactly what are you accusing me of, should I retain counsel?"

"I'm sorry, that's not at all where I'm headed," looking at the petite woman, Danny dismissed any possibility that she was the driver last night. "Do you know who might have been out in your boat yesterday afternoon?"

"If it was stolen—anyone."

"Who besides you drives it."

"No one." Danny watches her quickly look away, any beginner investigator recognizes uncomfortable body language.

"Mrs. Masters, you are not required to talk to me, I am investigating an attempted homicide that your boat may be involved in. *Black Widow* has been quarantined and a forensics officer is on the way right now to process her in her slip. It is against the law to give false information; if you do, you become complicit and open to indictment. Let me ask you a different question. Is there anyone that drives your boat with or without your permission?"

After a moment Victoria says, "Just Kirsten."

"Kirsten Jacobs, from the whale research center, why her?"

"I've known Kirsten all her life, I'm her god mother, she is not your person officer."

"Why not.?"

"Her mother didn't raise her that way. Eloise is Roberts sister and my best friend, Kirsten is the daughter Robert and I never had. She would never deliberately try to hurt someone."

"What about Ryan."

"Her son is a just a kid Ryan's a handful like any kid.

"Does he drive the boat?"

"He has steered it when we are out together, but I've never let anyone but Eloise and

Kirstin take her out without me aboard."

"Where do you keep the keys?"

"In a zippered bag in the console." —*Sheesh, does anyone secure their boat.*

Billy's floating crane maneuvers alongside the breakwater, from the large hook three cables dangle above the Fish and Game boat. Danny and the forensic detective stand on the dock watching. Billy's single crewman snaps the smaller cable hooks onto the factory lifting eyes and then raises his thumb for Billy to take up slack. The twenty-five foot boat is dwarfed by the eighty-five foot crane barge. All eyes are on the dripping aluminum hull rising straight up out of the water. Danny and the detective watch intently in case something is missed or falls back in the water. Billy swings the load over the barge deck while his crewman secures a tag line to keep it from spinning.

"Hold it right there," yells the forensic guy. He and Danny jump in the waiting county police boat for the ten-second ride over to Billy's barge.

"Don't get under there, that's not safe," yells Billy from the cranes control cab.

"I have to, I need to do my job," he yells back.

"Hold on a sec then," yells Billy, "hey—get some barrels and beams under there, I don't want no squished cops on my barge."

Both policemen snap pictures, the tech's camera obviously more complicated than Danny's. The barge crane and police boat have caused a lot of commotion, so once again Danny points his camera towards the army of shore watchers gawking from every possible vantage point. This time he makes a point of capturing shots of people that are a little too curious, squeezing onto the nearby floats. Of course watching a police action doesn't make a person guilty, but he knows perps often hang around, even get involved in solving their own crimes.

The Fish and Game boats underwater condition is typical of a heavily used work boat, the bottom paint is warn away from encounters with floating flotsam, beach gravel and wayward logs. Several of the reinforced stringers have paint stripes from high speed strikes. The tech guy painstakingly photographs and takes samples, labeling and saving dozens of Ziploc bags.

"Look here." Danny and the tech stare at a loose fiber hanging from a rivet. "This may be what you're looking for," says the tech. "If this boat were planing at speed, this is where I would expect impact evidence, and there it is." He gets several pictures and then using tweezers plucks the shard. "I'll compare this to samples from the kayak, but if I were to guess, I'd say they're gonna match."

"Prints." Says Danny. "I need prints to put this creep away. As near as I can tell from the video footage, the boat has not been boarded since the incident, so our guys are on top."

"If they are there I'll get them, if he wore gloves, maybe not." The tech shrugs.

Chapter 49 - Victoria

Six am at the hospital finds Josh awake and studying yesterday's datamaster24 download. Something has been bothering him since the accident. Something Chet said about the money trails he followed. Roberta and Chet left in the late afternoon. Sammie caught the last ferry promising to be back in the morning when he is released. Josh had to beg Maggie to stay with Charlie on Orcas Island, he didn't need or want them to pick him up. Maggie finally gave in when he told her that he and Sammie had a day of shopping and hanging out planned.

Napping off and on during the day has messed up his schedule so at two am he was awake texting his dad. Fortunately the San Juan Islands are far enough off the beaten track that the news of his accident never reached his dad, so the first and only news was from Josh that he was ok. They texted back and forth, ending with him asking Josh to say hello to Danny O'Brien. The hospital wifi has been working reliably allowing him to work on a code-writing job for a past customer.

Web site work is quick easy money and buying new kayaks will seriously deplete his PayPal account. *That's it, that's where we need to look, fast easy money, and big purchases.*

"Knock knock, anyone home," Danny has already peaked to make sure Josh is awake.

"Hey Deputy O'Brien, I just texted my dad, he says say hello."

"I figured you might be awake early, I thought I would beat the rush."

"Well I'm glad you did."

"Your swelling has gone down some; you're starting to look like you may not have lost the fight after all."

"Oh, I lost alright; I've never felt this beat up after a match I won.

"It wasn't a match Josh. Someone tried to kill you"

"Do you know who it was?" Danny shakes his head and then tells Josh about finding the Fish and Game boat, and *Black Widow* on the video. He goes on explaining that the perp was in both boats, and asking him if he can remember the boats or if he has any ideas why or who is behind the attack.

"Well the why is easy," he says, "I've got myself in the middle of a poaching operation, and like dad says, some people or someone is getting worried. Do you think they will try it again?"

"I hope not, but I don't know Josh, Your dad and I both would like to see you keep a low profile, you know, at least until this thing is figured out."

"Gotcha. It has to be someone involved with orcas, and has to be someone already introduced in the cast of characters."

"Josh, this isn't a play."

"Figure of speech, bare with me. We got Rogers and his group of agents, and their families—top of my list for sure. Me and Sammie, Maggie are all vouched for. Dave Johnson, that Jacobs girl, Kirstin. Brad and his family, Chet and Carly—not. Who owns that Cigarette boat?"

"Josh, I can't give out names and certain info, even to you, the victim. She is the retired director of the whale research department, but I don't think she is involved. I interviewed her yesterday."

"What about family?"

"None, except she said she was Jacobs and her sons god mother and best friends of her mother, who's in a nursing home. Tell me, why do you dismiss Brad and his family."

"It's personal for Brad, he is disgraced and unfortunately, I expect he wants a rematch, to save face, not kill me. Chances are his family is ridiculing him for being a loser and he blames me. I just hope I get some healing before we meet again. What about that crayon letter, anything."

"We got prints and perfume and crayola to match, but he's not in the system, at least not yet. When we find someone, we can corroborate and tie them to the crime."

"Excuse me," says the day shift nurse, "would you like some breakfast?"

"Oh boy—yes, I've been smelling great things, bring it on, I'm starving."

"I'll be right back with a tray."

Danny wraps up his few questions for Josh, but mostly he wanted to make sure he had a ride when he is released. Josh's father and him had been good friends, and still were even though each had gone separate ways. It was natural to look after Ray's son, in a way, Josh was an extension of Danny's old friend.

Danny had said something that caught Josh's attention and now he was eager to check the financial records with Chet. It would be easier to share with Danny, but him being a Deputy Sheriff complicated things and frustrated Josh when he thought about it. He was laughing to himself when Danny had said he could not share confidential information, little did Danny know, but he was awash in confidential information. So much so that Danny would be obliged to arrest him if he was a stickler for rules. It would be a real test of Danny's integrity, but Josh was not about to force Danny to choose loyalty's.

Certain information will not be shared, and destroying his computer was a small price to pay if it should come to that. He already knew that once he figured out the money trail and could conclusively expose the top people, he was probably going to anonymously e-mail the pertinent information to several news stations using untraceable ten minute e-mail addresses. Once the money trail is known, others will pick up the ball and run with it, and he will stay invisible. At least that's his plan.

Alone with his breakfast tray, and his tablet, Josh is energized. First he opens files, and then he opens his mouth and shoves in mounds of scrambled eggs and toast, washing it down with orange juice he studies the records. *There it is like Chet said, the payments to the home quit. She died is what he said, an assumption is more like it, maybe even a smoking gun about to unravel—bingo, here it is.* He finds the monthly payments that suddenly end about eight years ago, and yet Danny just said Kirsten's mother is alive in a home. I wonder how she pays for it. Between bites and gulps, he google's - *Black Widow Friday Harbor* WU- and discovers a familiar name—Victoria Masters. *Thanks anyway Danny, but I got it.* He logs on with data master 24 for the fifth time in a week.

Chapter 50 - Test Ride

"I watched you devour your breakfast, so I brought you another, how you can type, eat, and recover in a hospital bed, all at the same time is beyond me." says the nurse.

"This is great, I'm starving, thank you." His latest request finished, he exits the hacker site feeling a little sneaky, even guilty that he is lying in a hospital bed with nurses waiting on him while he is secretly digging into one of their neighbors, even a friends perhaps, personal history.

"Dr. Williams will be in to check you out, and then you'll be able to leave. Do you have transportation to Orcas Island?"

"I'm not going back right away; first Sammie and I will take the bus into town to go to Island Kayak. I promised her a test paddle in her new boat, the one replacing the one I wrecked. Then I guess we will think about catching a ferry home."

"Ok—you're in charge, but you really have to take it easy, your lacerations are deep and might bleed a lot if you aren't careful and tear something."

His recovery is nothing short of remarkable, Josh has come back from near death after being left for dead floating in waters so cold that victims often die from hypothermia long before they are rescued. His legs are stitched up and super tender to touch where the propeller cut him, and he has some major bruises, but swelling is down, he feels strong and most importantly his head is clear. Dr Williams Ok's him to leave just as Sammie arrives and suggests exiting through a side door if they want to avoid reporters hanging around the main entrance. Sammie hands him a bag of clothes Maggie dug out of his room.

"Oh my gosh," she exclaims seeing his battered torso while he modestly gets dressed. "Have you seen yourself in a mirror?"

"No—do I look hot like you?" Sammie starts to punch him but stops short, there's nowhere to land a friendly punch.

They hold hands and walk painfully slow, unnoticed, around the building. They look like any of hundreds of kids with backpacks roaming the islands. Except, judging by the way they laugh and lean together, these two are more into each other, than actually into going anywhere. They follow the sidewalk and then cut across the parking lot just as the Island transit minibus pulls up beside them. A smiling lady driver opens the folding door.

"Want a ride to town," says the driver, "Dr Wendy said to come find you." The transit van bus van is empty as can be expected mid morning on a weekday. "Where to, I'll drop you off."

The two of them pile out at Island Kayak on Front Street, less than half a block from the marina. Sammie has been there before and the owner waves to her when they walk in the door, but Josh is the instant center of attention. I've been expecting you he says excitedly shaking hands, you look like you been in a scuffle, did you win I hope, are you ready to check out our newest boat. The scuffle reference surprises Sammie, she thought that Josh's celebrity attention was due to the recent news, but the shop owner was simply treating him like a customer about to drop a large wad of money on his counter, he has no idea who they are. Sammie listens to them talk, she is impressed with Joshes knowledge, not only does he speak fluent kayak speak, but he relates his questions to actual on the water experience as if he has spent years in kayaks, and not less than a week in only two boats.

"Well, what do you think," he says as they stand by a beautiful sky blue carbon fiber boat sitting on a cradle.

"It's too small." Says Sammie

"It's the same length as your other one is, err was."

"It was too small too." She is tilting her head and smiling at him, the same way she has done before.

"I'm not a mind reader, and that look scares me." Hearing Josh say *scared* snaps her back to earth as she remembers the advice Roberta shared with her about men.

"I thought it would be nice to do some camping and even bring Sadie along, what do you think of a couple of two person boats with a little cargo room. Then we could ride together or whatever."

"It'll be heavier and more work." He sees tents, campfires and starry nights overhead.

"That's ok, with you doing the paddling it will be easy." She sees, cuddling, s'mores and Sadie at their feet.

The shop owner is listening and motions them into another room to show them a high performance touring kayak with a special convertible cockpit for two adults and a child or dog, or one person with tons of gear.

"This boat is only two pounds heavier than that other one, but by moving the seat you can balance it for one or two people," says the owner.

"Let's look at paddles and then put one of these in the harbor," says Josh.

"We have a pool out back, you can try it there."

"Ok, sounds great, and then if we like it we can take it down to the harbor, and see if she really likes it." Josh looks at the owner like it is a nonnegotiable detail; of course we will pay you a large deposit first. I use PayPal Visa, but I can go get cash after lunch if you prefer to wait."

"No no, Visa works. Follow me, I have graphite paddles out here by the pool."

Outside at the testing pool the shop owner starts to lift a kayak, but Josh stops him saying,

"Let Sammie to do it." She has no problem lifting and moving the longer kayak, the owner anxiously watches as she sets it in the pool. He is concerned she may ding his expensive inventory. She runs up the steps with paddle in hand and quickly plops into the seat and adjusts kneepads and foot stops. With real difficulty he climbs in next, the snug cockpit and familiar feeling triggers his memory, his mind fills with visions. His chest tightens and muscles ache, for a moment he wants out of the kayak. He sits still with eyes shut and his hands resting on the smooth deck. Josh forces himself to imagine Sammie and him paddling to Rock Island, he sees Pepper swimming alongside and Sadie barking at her. When he opens his eyes he is back in the present. The right knee pad hurts him, and for the first time he feels anger, the boat that ran him down came from the right. He rubs his hand over his right arm and shoulder, everywhere on the right side hurts. *Stupid ass! Someone should run him down.*

"I like it," says Josh, "But I'm not making the decision, what do you think Sammie?"

"I think I want to try it in the water so I can do some paddling."

"Ok, she's the boss, like I said were going to buy two boats, but we need to try it in the harbor." Josh climbs out of the kayak, and rolls onto the small deck sorely reminding himself he has not healed in just one day. Sammie simply stands in the boat and then steps onto the platform next to Josh.

"Did I do it wrong," she laughs at his struggles, "it seemed easiest to just stand up and step off."

"You're very funny, but I'm not laughing."

"I'm sorry, I can't imagine how much pain you're in. Let's get an in the water test." Says Sammie to the owner. "What do we do?"

"No problem, says the shop owner, lets head down to the kayak dock, I have one of these ready to go. Bring that paddle along if you like it, the ones down there are rentals." The water test goes fine, Sammie and Josh try the kayak separately and taking turns being in the back and front. They talk about carrying Sadie and camping gear and try to imagine different combinations.

"Have you thought about how we will get them home," asks Sammie.

"Well I figured I would try paddling again, but I'm kinda sore, I don't know if a long trip will be much fun."

"We don't have life vests anyway, why don't we just carry them over to the ferry, and then have Charley pick us up at Orcas Landing. You know—if we get going soon, we will have plenty of time for a campfire, or we could paddle to Rock Island. Last time you were there you were a wanted man."

"I'd like to spend some time with Pepper too, I guess I owe her big time."

"Sadie would like some attention too."

"Ok, it's a deal skipper," says Josh to the shop owner, "let's go write up this sale."

ORCA BOY

Chapter 51 - Coming Home

Sammie and Josh carry the two identical kayaks between them. They tossed their backpacks and paddles into the cockpits and with Sammie in the lead, a bow T-handle in each hand she leads the way down Front Street towards the ferry terminal. Josh holds the stern T-handles bringing up the rear. Seeing kayaks carried down the sidewalk is normal in Friday Harbor as is seeing them lugged on and off Ferries. The fare is $1.50 extra per kayak, the same as for a bicycle. The next ferry is in forty-five minutes, they stop at the Burrito Bandit's mobile shack.

"Hey my man Joshua, you look terrible dude.

"Thanks, that's how I feel."

"You were right Peppers revenge is my biggest seller, and my sales have doubled, all because of you."

"That's great Bandit, but Chet is the guy to thank, not me. He talks it up everywhere on the promenade."

"What do you want today, on the house my friends?"

"That's a generous offer, but we only need a couple cups full of ice and coke."

"That's all! Okay, you got it hombre." Josh tucks five bucks into the tip jar. The Bandit watches and nods.

"Why did you pay him anyway, you gave him more than the cokes cost." asks Sammie when they are out of earshot.

"I got some extra, and he can use it. It's the right thing to do."

They set their kayaks on the grass lawn next to the burrito wagon and sit down leaning against backpacks to wait for the next ferry. Small talk about the new kayaks quickly falls silent, Josh has fallen asleep. Sammie sets the drink cups to one side and makes sure he is comfortable. She leans her head on his while he sleeps on her shoulder. A single tear works its way down her cheek. Closing her eyes, she cradles him. Soon she nods off too.

ORCA BOY

When the ferry clears the corner coming around Shaw island, Orcas Landing comes into view reminding Josh to call home for a lift. The two of them have immensely enjoyed being with each other since leaving the hospital. Unlike when they met on the same boat a week earlier, Josh has mostly gotten over his fear of pretty girls, and Sammie in particular, except when she looks into his eyes, and then he still falls apart saying the occasional dumb thing to her, but he no longer lets it define him. Sammie has fully embraced their friendship, confident that Josh and her share a special bond. She doesn't wonder or question his motivation with her, and is less surprised each time he reveals a new talent or knowledge.

"Hey aunt Maggie, do you think Sammie and I could get a ride home from the landing, were coming in on the ferry in about ten minutes or so with a couple of kayaks."

Maggie brings them both back to Pearson Cove, they carry the kayaks down to the wharf and set them next to the gear shed. Charley is at the barbecue, its too late for lunch and too early for dinner, but he has burgers on the grill.

"I threw something on as soon as Maggie said you were on the way," says Charley.

"I'm suddenly very hungry," Sammie's drooling look and tugging arm say the rest, "Sammie too," adds Josh. "Hey, you should call Sandy, she may be worried and knowing you are back will make her feel good."

"Yes daddy." She bats her eyes at Josh. *Oops, you're not my daddy.*

"I'm not your mommy either, but she might also cut you some slack from work if you include her in your life." Adds Josh.

"Hi Sandy," Sammie raises her hand for quiet before Josh can say something embarrassing, "I wanted to let you know Josh and I are back, were over at the cove... yes, he's a little sore but he's fine... I'll be along later... ok, I'll call Sadie if she's outside you can let her go... ok bye."

Sammie pulls out her silent dog whistle and gives Sadie four short blasts.

"Five minutes, you two, burgers in five."

"Ok, I'm going to sit right here and wait for Sadie."

"Give her about thirty more seconds," says Sammie, "Right now she is waiting for another clue to where we are.

"Here's a clue, c'mere Sadie," yells Josh with a shrill two-finger whistle, "I figure she's on the other side of the house.

Sadie comes bounding around the house, barking with every stride, she runs up Sammies front and then tries to run up Josh. Sammie heads her off by stepping in front of Josh blunting her excitement and protecting Josh's bandaged legs.

"Sit down Sadie," says Josh, "we need to rub your neck and relax a bit. Oh, I'm happy to see you too. I owe you some boat rides and I'll toss a stick for you down on the beach a little later."

"Don't forget Pepper." Says Charley

"Where is she, do you see her?"

"She's right there in the middle of the cove," says Maggie, pointing, "it's her favorite spot since you've been gone." Pepper is motionless below the surface, probably not aware of any activity on shore. Her normal routine is to leave the cove on a rising tide when fish are active in the channel returning at ebb tide and then napping. She breaths at the surface and looks around periodically. When kayakers from Sandy's *Islander Resort* come by she will tolerate their presence for a while, but becomes wary of noisy groups slinking off into deep water and leaving the cove.

"I see you strung a line with some floats across the entrance out there, what's the sign say."

"It says, *Sleeping orca – No Power boats*—I put that out there after we had too many gawkers and big wakes from inconsiderate boaters looking for a glimpse of Pepper. Sandy's people in kayaks entertain Pepper, probably cause she's looking for you, but she doesn't need the others."

"That sign is a good idea, you know when word gets around, there's liable to be a lot more traffic here in the cove."

"Wait a sec." says Charley alarmed, "what word are you talking about Josh?"

"Well you know, just with time and all, the words bound to spread. Have you ever thought of re-opening the marina. Maybe kayak rentals or something. With Pepper as an attraction you might have a gold mine cash cow."

"Would you like to see a steady stream of people out in the yard, on the wharf and paddling around in your cove," says Charley.

"Not really."

"Me neither, let's leave the tourists to the *Islander Resort,* Sammie can bring guests over and then take them away. Besides, Pepper could leave tomorrow if she has a falling out with you or Sadie."

"Hush your mouth," Maggie jumps in, Pepper is family, so is Sadie."

"You think so huh," jokes Charley, "What's her last name, when's her birthday, and where's her mom and dad.

"Easy," says Maggie, "It's Pepper, daughter of L21 and her birthday is the first day with a rainbow in April. Her parents are fishing in Alaska. Anything else you want to know."

"You guys finish without me," says Josh, "I'm grabbing a burger and going out on the dock, I think Pepper needs a hug."

Josh heads down the gangplank, Sammie, Charley and Maggie stay on the upper entertainment area. When Sammie and Sadie start to follow Josh, Maggie with her ever present camera at the ready asks her to hold back to see how Pepper reacts to Josh. He picks up his staff leaning against the gear-shed where he I left it the morning Rogers tried to arrest him.

Standing still where Pepper has a clear view of him he stops walking and raps a piling—bam bam—bam bam. Pepper immediately raises her snout and eyes above the water to hone in on the familiar sound, she spots Josh facing her, scratching stick in hand. Recognition is instant and she responds with a shrill trill and some clicks, but mostly she lunges forward launching her body up to her pectorals out of the water as her powerful tail propels her in an Olympic style Dolphin Kick. Pepper pulls up short of crashing into the wharf's pilings sending a tsunami wall of water harmlessly over the planks. Her momentum carries her partly under the dock where she effortlessly stops under Josh's outstretched arm.

Maggie records it all, the scene not only removes all doubt there is a unique friendship between them, but an almost familial bond is apparent. Josh moves to a dry spot and sits on the dock leaning over the edge. She raises her snout allowing him to easily touch her and then rolls partly on her side. Josh rubs her eye patch. The sound she makes can only be described as purring.

"How've you been Pepper girl, I've missed you the last few days, sorry I ditched you at Rock Island, but I couldn't risk you following me to Friday Harbor. You saved me, so I guess you're over it. Have you been hanging some with Sadie?"

He changes position with his legs dangling over the edge, his feet touching her side and reaches her dorsal fin with the stick. Chirps interrupt the purring when Josh scratches her favorite spots. She really revs up the purring as he rubs the area on her back at the base of her dorsal fin, it reminds Josh of scratching Sadie's back causing her to shake a leg. Rubbing her eye patch seems to be the orca equivalent to massaging Sadie's neck. Sammie and Sadie announce their arrival with Sadie barking hello. Sammie reaches down and for the first time Pepper allows her to rub her eye patch. Maggie is getting it all while Charley takes the role of director telling her to zoom in and pan around the dock.

"Let's throw the stick, you guys." They all walk down the dock to the lifting slip that has become Peppers home base in the cove. The stick and rope are hanging with the float on a rope. Sadie can't contain herself when Josh lifts the stick by the rope. Pepper is following six feet away, her snout high, blue and green eyes watching every move. With each stream of clicks she drops her mouth open showing her yellowish white teeth and pink tongue leaving no doubt she is speaking her mind in her own orca language.

"Hang on you two, lets get down by the beach so Sadie has a chance, ok Pepper." By the time the foursome gets to the beach Sadie is her normal excited self and Pepper is staying close by in two feet of water, her dorsal fin in the air and her belly occasionally dragging bottom in the smooth gravel. Sadie's excitement is contagious. Pepper keeps slapping her pectorals creating poorly aimed water jets and whopping sounds. Finally, Josh clears a circle keeping Sammie safely out of the way and winds up an Olympic hammer toss. He wings the log stick on a rope and float far out into the center of the cove. Pepper is on it before it lands sprinting fast, her body half in the air. She does the maneuver she likes best and dives early making her turn underwater and breaching skyward with the rope clamped in her jaws. She heads back with the log skimming the surface banging along her sleek body. Twenty feet out she stops in deep water and with super tail strokes, lifts herself straight up. At the height of her breach she flicks the rope sending the log to Josh's feet. A few gravel pebbles fly up prompting Josh to jokingly say, *hey be careful,* but the log is so perfectly tossed to him that he merely stoops to pick it up for the next toss. His banged and bruised body is complaining, but not enough for him to hold back, so he heaves another toss toward the wharf this time. Pepper repeats only without the breach that with a killer whale miscalculation may have landed her on the planks. This time, she botches the return toss landing the stick-on-a-rope some fifteen feet away. Josh's next throw is into six inch deep water intended for Sadie. Pepper parallels Sadie and loses the race. She is in only shallow water and Josh is relieved that she didn't beach herself in her juvenile exuberance, a trait Sadie probably will never overcome no matter how much Sammie yells to calm down.

Sadie returns with the too big stick in her mouth, the rope dragging. Her barking resumes before it hits the ground. Josh can't resist playing the two buddies against each other and lands the next toss just off shore between them in about two feet of water. Sadie beats Pepper and bounds into the chest deep water biting on the oversize log. But before she can turn Pepper snags the rope as she flies by ripping the log away from Sadie. Sadie barks her indignation all the way back to shore until Pepper using a pec fin, splashes the log along with five gallons right to Sadie. Sadie eagerly gets it in her mouth and tears off for a dozen paces and then circles back and drops it in the water in front of Pepper. After barking her desires, she noses the stick into deeper water for Pepper to throw.

"I'm hurting all over," says Josh, "I gotta quit. I'm going up for a another burger."

"I'll come up too; these two don't need any help."

"This is unreal," says Charley to anyone listening, "We are watching something no one will believe."

"Oh yes they will," says Maggie, "I'm getting fantastic shots." Josh is standing at the railing watching and massaging his sore bruises with one hand, a hot hamburger in the other, his ear-to-ear smile proudly displaying huge pride in being part of such an extraordinary friendship.

"See what you started," says Sammie half hugging his arm trying not to look overly affectionate in front of Maggie and Charley.

"I haven't done anything; Pepper is the one to be credited. She is an amazing animal, look out there, without being taught she's leading Sadie around the same way we do. I wish she could talk to us, I mean in a way we understand. I think she's smarter than anyone gives orcas credit for. If she could talk, we would probably discuss global warming and salmon farming. Hey, after awhile, let's get the new kayaks down here, I'd like to paddle around with Pepper."

"I thought you were tired."

"I'm not tired, I'm sore."

"Last call for food," says Charley.

"I'm good, uncle Charley thanks. You and Aunt Maggie have been great; I know I've brought a lot of unexpected attention with me. I'm especially sorry for getting you arrested and hauled to Seattle."

"We'll get over it Josh," says Charley, "Maggie and I are very proud of you and what you have done, your mom would have been too. By the way, are you keeping in touch with Ray, we've e-mailed him a few pictures but didn't want to worry him so we haven't said anything about the accident."

"Danny said it wasn't an accident, and I told dad all about getting run down. You can tell him everything."

Sammie and Josh carry the new kayaks down the gangway and set them on a half submerged float. Sammie is off and floating free in a matter of seconds, but Josh is sore all over and can barely bend his legs, so it takes him some effort to get going. Ultimately, the two of them race across the cove with Pepper following them. Sadie keeps pace along the beach; only barking once or twice. Sammie turns seaward with Josh close on her tail and angles through the coves' entrance into choppy water. She arcs a long sweep putting her new kayak through a short trial. Following Sammie and watching her moves, Josh is impressed with her ability and skill. She effortlessly maintains a pace that he struggles to keep up with. A quarter mile offshore she coasts with her paddle lying across her lap, Josh nestles his boat next to hers, their paddles tying them together and holding them stable in the small swells

"I love my new boat, how are you doing, are you ok," she says, "are you glad we brought them on the ferry instead of paddling?"

"I could've made the paddle ok, but I'm glad we took the ferry, hanging with you is fun."

"Are you sort of saying you like being with me?"

"Yes, I guess." *Bad choice of words, dumb ass.*

"Oh—you guess—well I guess I like you too," Sammie and Josh lean together and kiss between rocking waves.

"I shouldn't have said I guess, I really like you a lot."

"Me too." Sammie beams, and then they kiss again sealing their budding romance. Josh gives a thumbs up toward shore.

"I caught them kissing, this 10X zoom lens lets you sneak in where you don't belong," says Maggie.

"That's called snooping," says Charley, "you shouldn't be sneaking secret pictures."

"I know, I know, but there's no secret, Josh looked right at me and gave me a thumbs up. I'm sending this one to his dad." Charley wraps his arm around Maggie giving her a hug triggering their own romantic kiss. The two kayakers agree to race back. The finish line is the cove entrance. Sammies lighter weight puts her in the lead off the blocks, and catches Josh by surprise. She continues to pull away for the next five strokes, but he is stronger and his longer reach overcomes her lead by the time they reach the entrance. The two are side by side matching each other stroke for stroke.

With a few hundred feet left, Sammie bears down hard taking back a slim half boat lead. She has effortlessly retaken the lead, but Josh is not done yet, with superhuman strokes he manages to catch and stay even with her. The two kayaks streak into the cove, each oblivious that Pepper has been pacing them underwater. Orcas have been clocked swimming thirty miles an hour, easily twice their speed. Pepper flashes under them and then jets to the surface breaching in front of the kayaks, showing off for sure, but mainly saying look what I can do.

With a killer whale suddenly exploding to the surface and then careening in front of them, both kayakers put on the brakes and swerve around her effectively ending the contest, or at least leaving it as a draw.

"I was ahead—I slowed for Pepper," yells Josh across the water to Sammie."

"No you weren't," Sammie yells back, "we were tied because I slowed and let you catch up, look at you, your sweating and panting, I'm not even breathing hard."

Sadie's barking ends the argument, she excitedly bunny hops on the last finger float trying to get Sammie and Josh to pay attention to her. Sammie turns toward Sadie and the dock, closing the gap in seconds. She comes to rest next to Sadie and holds the dock steadying the kayak. Sadie needs only one encouraging word giving her permission before she jumps into the front cockpit. She immediately lays down with her chin on the coaming watching Pepper.

"I'll take Sadie, you take Pepper," says Sammie joking.

"That's ok, you paddle Sadie around, and Pepper will pull me—maybe!" Josh climbs out next to the submerged lift boards, for a moment, he tries to remember being rescued, but he comes up blank. The only memory he has of the hoist slip is of Pepper when he cut the cables girdling her.

He attaches a fifteen-foot scrap of the floating rope he used for the throwing toy to the front of his kayak and then forms a loop in the free end and gets back in his new flawless blemish free kayak. With a few paddle strokes, he joins up with Sammie and Sadie, in the middle of the cove. Using the bam bam—bam bam code, he calls Pepper and she obediently surfaces next to him. Josh dangles the loop so she can see it. He jerks the rope taught showing her it is tied to the kayak and then hangs it from his paddle holding it in front of her snout. Pepper doesn't need more prompting or explanations, she clicks twice as if saying I got this, and opens her mouth a little. Josh drapes the loop across her head and over her snout. He pulls the paddle back when she closes down on the rope.

"Lets go girl, you can do it, go, go." Pepper doesn't move. "Come on pull the rope." Still nothing. Josh takes the paddle reaching under water and pokes her big tail fin causing her to make a single swoosh of a stroke moving her forward. The rope stretches out and gently tugs the kayak along. *Now what Pepper, we don't have any signals, only come to me and emergency run away.*

"Go Pepper," he yells, "pull me, go." Sammie paddles in front of Pepper attempting to lead the way. Still nothing. Next Sammie spins her kayak in place and paddles backwards leaving Sadie facing Pepper.

"C'mon Pepper, swim." She yells as she paddles backwards. Sadie barks at Pepper and that does the trick. Pepper can't resist her friends challenging encouragement and using her pectoral flippers moves her and Josh forward after the barking dog. Sammie increases her speed and pulls her and Sadie backwards further across the cove. Pepper immediately swings her tail jerking Josh's new kayak up to speed and alarming him.

Oh boy this may not be a good idea, he says to himself realizing he has no control after he just hitched his kayak to a colossal powerhouse with no way to release the rope. At the far side of the cove Sammie coasts and then dips her paddle braking to a stop. Pepper glides up beside an excited Sadie. Momentum propels Josh's kayak to run into Peppers back with a minuscule bump.

"Sadie sit down," scolds Sammie fearing she may jump out, "sit down and be quiet."

"Guess what," says Josh as they float near shore, "I didn't paddle once." He reaches out and barely catches the line on the tip of his paddle. With some juggling he manages to pull himself around to Peppers snout where they look each other eye to eye while Josh holds the rope loosely in his hand, the loop still clenched in her teeth. He tugs the rope pulling them together.

"I know what you want Pepper girl, it doesn't take a trainer to understand you." Sammie is nervous and wide eyed, she and Sadie watch from twenty feet, Sadie is whining her desire to play or at least be involved. Josh strokes Peppers eye patch eliciting clicks and a new twirtling sound she has begun since his rescue.

"Let go," he jiggles the rope and raps the kayak twice with his other hand and repeats, "let go." She opens her mouth just enough for Josh to pull the loop away, and then he vigorously rubs the white patch above her eye while saying good girl. Sammie watches, no longer fearful, but in awe of Josh's innate ability to talk orca talk. His kayak is bobbing against her sleek body and over her pectoral fin, any large tail movement or flick of a fin will disrupt the stroking party, tipping the kayak and throwing him into the water.

"That's enough Pepper, it's not like you saved my life or something—oh yeah—you did." He reaches across her head and rubs the other patch, but as he leans on her his added weight begins to sink them both so he makes it quick getting his weight off her and back on the kayak. "That's it, Pepper girl," he shoves the kayak sideways and reaches for her dorsal fin with the paddle.

"Just a few scratches in your secret hot spot and then were all racing for the other end. Are you and Sadie ready? Is Pepper ready?— three bangs and we go. He hits his paddle three times and Sammie digs in, Sadie barks her approval, Josh easily out sprints Sammie with Sadie's weight holding her back. The surprise is on Pepper, she is caught enjoying a good personal rub when everyone takes off without her, but she catches on right away. She swims under water and does a half broach beside Josh, her tall dorsal fin and the top of her body break the surface just fifteen feet away. Her sleek hydrodynamic body arches back under water, and with a resounding tail boom propels herself forward. She broaches several more times stopping before crashing into the floating wharf.

When the kayakers pull up to her, she is clicking and whistling, it's obvious she has won the race fins down and wants everyone to hear about it. In her excitement Sadie is half out of the cockpit with her front feet on deck, Sammie is sure she is about to jump in the water so she swings next to the dock and says jump off, Sadie jump. Once on the dock Sadie runs from finger pier to finger pier trying to get nearer to Pepper. Josh and Sammie paddle near the beach with Pepper trailing close behind. Sadie runs up the gangway and follows them along the gravel beach. She repeatedly runs into the water towards her friend as she glides along shore toward the steep section of beach where she is able to safely ground herself without being stranded.

The two unlikely animal friends finally touch noses, or snout to nose is more accurate. Sadie stands in chest deep water, her barking subdued to an occasional yelp, her tail swinging her rear end in slow motion water dampened arcs. Pepper is excited as well, she shows it with a stream of clicks, trilling, and squeals. What Josh calls purring seems to be reserved for when she is much much calmer. Sadie and her half ton buddy are dissimilar as can be and yet share the common bond of all juveniles. They are motivated to play and having fun.

Sammie and Josh rest side by side, their paddles interlocked stabilizing the kayaks as they watch their charges. Sammie sneaks her hand into Josh's, he holds her hand tightly, the two are lost in thought watching Sadie and Pepper play.

"Your bleeding," says Sammie in a non-alarming, I'm getting used to it way while she looks at bright red blood oozing through his pants.

"I know, I've been rubbing the side of the cockpit, it must've been too much, I'm pretty sore too, I guess I should cool it and elevate my leg for awhile."

"You guess," says Sammie, "don't you want to know what's wrong."

"I know what's wrong, I'm bleeding—and it will stop when it clots. I can help it by elevating it, or you could put emergency pressure on it and save my life, or are you chicken to touch my blood?"

"Nooo... I just think you should be concerned. C'mon Josh your bleeding a lot."

"It's not a lot, and I am concerned, It's just not a big deal, but you are right, lets head up." Josh walks with a limp so he can hold his hand on his thigh. The blood has run down his leg to his ankle and is leaving a steady droplets trail on the walkway. Walking is aggravating his wounds. By the time they get back to the barbeque area, his bleeding has become serious. He grabs a mostly clean but ratty looking towel rag from the outdoor shelf and plunks down in a low slung arm chair. Then he lifts his leg over the arm resting his foot on the picnic table. He folds the towel several times and lays it across the middle of his stitched up leg and pushes with firm overall pressure.

"There," he says looking at Sammie, "that's all it takes, satisfied?"

"Yes, provided you stay put, you probably shouldn't have left the hospital."

"Correction nurse," says Josh, "I shouldn't have banged my stitched up leg on the kayak while racing you and a killer whale while a big dog runs alongside barking encouragement."

"When you put it that way, it sounds more like a team effort. Just keep your leg up, your grounded anyway."

"Yes ma'am, but if you would get some of that ice over there in the cooler and wrap it in a paper towel for me. I could chill it and speed up clotting."

"You remind me of your dad," says Charley, "I remember once he cut himself messing with his jack knife and they couldn't get him to stop playing baseball, blood was everywhere, on the ball, all over home plate, on the bat. He made a real mess that day. He said to everyone, *just relax, It's just a little blood.*"

"Ok, here's your ice-pack, can I trust you to stay put while I run home for awhile."

"Yes ma'am."

Sammie and Sadie jump into their kayak and push off. Sadie has tired from all the running and sits panting in her forward cockpit. Pepper follows along as they pass through the coves entrance and over the floating line. Outside the cove Pepper holds back letting the kayak pull away from her, she hangs around a little, but soon turns back, swimming under the rope she returns to the cove. Josh has been watching from the terrace hoping she would not follow, but then he texts Sammie.

Text: *Call Pepper, use two double taps.*

Sammie doesn't answer, but she received the message and calls Pepper. Meanwhile Pepper hears her call loud and clear. Josh watches as she sprints out of the cove. In her excitement, she jumps over the floating line. Using good racing form Pepper breaches just enough to clear the rope by inches reentering the water with hardly a splash. Her dorsal fin cuts a wake heading to Sadie and Sammie like a cat chasing a string.

Text: *She's on her way, have fun at home with your guests."*

Pepper races to catch up to the kayak announcing her arrival by surfacing and clicking beside Sadie which elicits happy yelps and a stern *sit down Sadie—hi Pepper,* from Sammie.

Sammie calls home, "Hi Sandy, I'm paddling up to the lodge right now, Pepper is with me, the guests may want some pictures."

"You mean you're in the water with that killer whale, honey are you sure that's safe, I thought you stayed on shore."

"Don't worry, just get your camera, we will be down on the north side beach in a minute."

Sandy's concern has got Sammie thinking about her own safety, she has only been on the water with Pepper one time, and that was with Josh earlier today. Without Josh's calming presence, she has only Sadie. Just then, Pepper explosively spouts unexpectedly right beside her sending a gut wrenching fright jolt through her. She grabs the kayak coaming for support and closes her eyes. In her head she knows there is no danger, but her body's instant reaction is to involuntarily contract every muscle. Sammie forces her hands open, and takes an extra deep breath trying to regain composure and control her mounting fear. A second deep breath does the trick.

"You scared me to death Pepper, and you—Sadie, you never barked once, what kind of protector are you." Pepper responds with her head up and mouth open, a string of clicks flows over her pink tongue. Her pearly almost white teeth are in stark contrast to her jet black body. She is one boat length away off to the side spewing a long vocalization. "If you are telling me to calm down, you can just knock it off, you scared me, I didn't scare you—and you better not be laughing either. Scoot over here, and I'll pat you on the back with my paddle."

Sammie reaches out and softly taps the water's surface between them, Sadie barks something only she and Pepper understand, but Pepper gets it, she swings a pectoral fin pushing her closer. Sammie easily reaches her arched back laying the paddle on it in front of her tall dorsal and then rubs back and forth. Pepper's clicks slow and stop, leaving a moment of silent calmness on the water around them. *You know, I don't think it's scratching that you want, I think all of us crave companionship and touching. The same way I pet Sadie, and hold hands with Josh. I'll bet you miss your mother and your pod, they're your family. Where are they?*

Sammie noses the kayak into shore and swings it sideways just as it touches the beach. Sadie jumps out and runs down the beach at full speed with Pepper chasing her. Sammie smoothly picks up her new boat using the handy carry strap designed with her in mind. She heads up the stairs to put away her kayak threading her way past Sandy and a throng of guests milling about watching the dog and killer whale on the beach. At Sammies request, Sandy asks guests to stay off the beach. She returns from the kayak shed helping herself to a plate of finger foods laid out by the *Islander* staff. She settles in at the observation wall next to Sandy.

The guests excitedly point at Pepper, cameras and smart phones record non-stop. Sadie is wading into two feet deep water coming nose to nose again and then tearing off. The two don't seem to tire of chasing each other. Sammie takes her paper plate and walks back down the stairs to the beach. On the way guests ask to follow her onto the beach but she still says no, fearing a group of people may scare Pepper. Sammie finds a stick she knows Sadie can carry and waves it in the air to get Sadie and Peppers attention. With Sadie jumping at her feet and Pepper waiting she heaves it over the waiting orca . Sadie dashes after it but stops at ten feet out barking. Pepper does just what Sammie hoped, broaching straight up and flinging the stick to her feet. She toss's the stick back over her frantic dog, landing it a few feet from Pepper for a repeat, but Pepper simply bats her pectoral fin sending a wall of water and the stick right to Sadie. Sammie dashes for the stairs when she see's what is coming, she retrieves her plate off the bottom step and rejoins the group up above.

"How did you train her to fetch?" asks one of the guests. The question bothers her,.Sammie is surprised how defensive she became when he suggested Pepper is trained like a dog, like Sadie. In her short time knowing Pepper Josh has never treated her as anything less than equal, and now she was getting her own hackles up over a simple and honest question.

"Pepper is an orca , the largest member of the dolphin family," she says mater-of-fatally, "She is very smart, training is not needed, simply asking her is all that's required."

"What—yeah right," says a smart-ass guest, "you talk to her, ask her to do things."

Sammie takes a lesson from Josh and turns on the smiles and charm. "Of course I don't talk to her silly, she's a killer whale, she reads my mind, and then she does what I'm thinking. Would you like to go down there and throw the stick for her?" Sammies curt yet caustic remark causes laughter from the others and a stern look from Sandy.

"Look, they've both got a hold of the stick." says another guest. All eyes are watching dog and orca play tug. "How come the whale doesn't just rip it away from the dog."

"They are playing," says an astute guest, not fighting, look how the orca lets the dog have it."

Sandy asks Sammie about Pepper being dangerous, she is concerned Pepper may attack a guest when they kayak or accidentally knock someone in the water with her big fins. Sammie assures Sandy that she has no idea what Pepper may do, but Josh would say to be safe, they should tell guests to stay away from her for their own safety. But the truth is that Josh would be more concerned about Peppers safety amongst a bunch of unpredictable strangers. Josh would approve her warning for Peppers sake. She feels good following his lead, as if they are a team. She pulls out her phone and texts him.

Text: Pepper and Sadie are playing fetch the stick, you are wonderful, miss you already.

Eventually Pepper stays further off shore, not interacting as much. It would be easy to think she is napping. At Sandy's insistence that guests want to walk the beach, Sammie decides to have Josh call Pepper home. Even though he is stiff and sore and prone to bleeding, he makes his way down the gangplank and out to the old boat lift slip. They all refer to it as Pepper's slip now that Charley has rigged up a thick piece of steel creating an underwater gong and a striking mallet. Next to the sunken planks are low profile camp chairs and Josh plops himself in one. He rests his problem leg in the other. His hand easily reaches the water. His hiking/scratching stick lays on the dock half under the chair.

It's just before dark, the famous San Juan sunset is about to perform its evening ritual. Using the mallet, he hits the gong four times, bong bong—bong bong. Sammie has her phone to her ear while watching Pepper snooze a hundred feet offshore.

"Ok," says Josh, "anything yet,"

"OH YEAH, she turned seaward before you said ok, it looks like she's leaving me and Sadie without even saying goodbye, Sadie must have heard it too though because she yelped and stood up, but she's not whining. I think I'm the only one that can't speak orca ."

"Will I get to see you tomorrow?"

"If you're lucky."

"Here she comes, I guess I gotta go so I can say hello to her."

"Hey Pepper, how's my girl, did you have fun visiting at Sadie's beach? Maybe you can go again tomorrow. I'll figure out something Sammie can use to call you." Pepper slides onto the sunken ramp coming to rest inches from Josh's hand. With little more than bending his wrist he strokes her eye patch, he can feel the rumble deep inside her as the low purring makes its way to the surface. Josh leans back in his chair to have a comfortable chat. One sided small talk soon gives way to an equally one way discussion about young orcas and their family units, Soon he tires of keeping the conversation alive and falls asleep with his hand on her head. He misses the crimson sunset but gains another short shot of needed rest.

Chapter 52 - Blood

"**J**osh, honey," says Maggie, Josh, wake up,"

The sun is completely gone and the floating dock has become lost in the dark cove. With a little coaxing, Maggie and Charley help their beat and tired nephew walk up to his room in the old lodge. Maggie says they need to change his dressings, but Josh sleepily insists on waiting until morning saying the bleeding has stopped and he needs to sleep. Charley agrees the bandages can wait, and helps him get blood his soaked pants into the wash to soak. Josh zonks out seconds after laying down. It's not yet ten o'clock, the western sky is still aglow. In spite of grabbing six hours of sleep in spurts, he is still exhausted.

Morning comes early in Pearson Cove, but early is relative to when one goes to sleep. Josh is awake at 3 am, the eastern sun won't be lighting the horizon for two more hours, roosters are silent, the night still belongs to bats, owls and mischievous sea otters. He scans screen after screen, absorbing orca research almost as fast as his finger depresses the key. Studies indicate orcas sleep with half their brain, does that mean Pepper is half awake he muses. They also live shorter lives in captivity, have excellent memories, harbor grudges, and show affection.

Lying in bed on his side, head on his elbow, he one handed clicks open Peppers e-mail and goes through the required security steps to retrieve his last datamaster 24 financial inquiry targeting Eloise Thompson. *Very interesting,* muses Josh. *Kirstin's mom has an overseas benefactor paying her way at the rest home.* International World Bank pays San Juan Acres Village monthly payments like clockwork, and has been for eight years. *I wonder what happened eight years ago.?* He goes back through the orca deaths report Dave Johnson supplied him and verifies what he remembered reading earlier. Digging yet deeper into the latest Datamaster release, he zeroes in on earlier cash deposits made directly to Eloise Thompson's bank account. Small low resolution image files allow him to look at all her deposit slips. Some of the dated fuzzy renderings, reveal notes, and some are initialed. VM, Vicky, V Masters, the flashy calligraphic hand writing is easy to spot as he scrolls endless documents. It is obvious to him that the earliest payments aren't from International World Bank, but from Victoria Masters, her ex boss, they predate world bank payments and then end when the banks begin. He goes back over Victoria Masters accounts, there are no records of withdrawals from her accounts at the same time. *Why was she making cash deposits directly to Thompson's account, and where did the cash come from? Was she making payments to others? I can't follow cash, and I can't look at every financial record of every person remotely involved with Friday Harbor or WU. I need to make something happen, ruffle some feathers. Dad said to watch out, someone is getting nervous. I guess if that someone is nervous enough to try to kill me once, they will really be nervous if I start asking questions that should have been asked ten years ago.*

4 am—Josh opens a new word doc. and titles it orca Study.

Companionship and Bonding Study between Orcinus-orca and domestic Canine-dog

Breadth of Study

One juvenile orca   appr 18 months – One 18 month Golden Labrador Retriever.

Land based observation and in the water one on one contact during friendly playing periods and intense competitive interactions.

Observations of note: Neither dog nor orca display any aggressive tendencies, however both exhibit a high level of competitiveness. Orca appears to manipulate dog, acts with empathy, compassion and shares rewards. Dog reacts to orca as equal, but displays human like expectations from orca ie dog repeatedly brings toy to orca expecting it to be thrown. O rca will throw toy or race away with toy suggesting thoughts of sharing or fairness. Both animals appear to be comfortable and relaxed while resting in close proximity.

4:10 am—Google search "Killer Whale behavior" Josh reads screen after screen of data, he follows links to old research, new research, and bad research. *What a crock, they can't say that, where's the evidence, you need to spend five minutes with Pepper and learn something, then you can write your thesis paper.*

ORCA BOY

5 am—Google searches "orca weaning, orca abandonment, orca maturity"

6 am—text message to his dad - Dad, it's unreal how smart Pepper is, but I'm concerned that she seems to have adopted me, or looks to me as her surrogate family. We haven't seen big momma since the first day. I'm feeling good but am sore. I got the bleeding to stop, it's hard to stay still, I have much to do, I plan to go back to FH and ask questions today that may lead to uncovering everything, I know be careful. Maggie and Charley are great. I bought Sammie a new kayak, 28 lbs -100% Kevlar, one for me too.

6:30 am—Josh strips and eases into a tub of warm water, it's a strange feeling sitting on the bottom of an antique bathtub after being raised taking showers. The stitched up lacerations on his legs stopped bleeding yesterday afternoon when Sammie made him sit down and raise the problem leg, but the stiff bandages are a mass of dried blood. It's difficult to get his legs completely under water. *How the heck did they do this? People must been shorter back when this old lodge was built.* After only a minute he lifts the edge of the white tape, at first he makes progress, but the dried blood takes time to loosen, and his impatience results in tearing open the partially healed lacerations. Small amounts of blood flow out from under the loosened bandages tinting the tub water pink. Pink turns to red and the water takes on a crime scene look as gross as on TV murder shows, except Josh is very much alive. *Oh crap, this is not working out well, I hope this old tub doesn't stain.* He sloshes the ring forming around him, the porous old ceramic surface is eating up the blood. Turning on the water and pulling the drain plug dilutes it back to a weak pink. Refilling the tub works for awhile until he notices the hot water is cooling off. *Well at least cold water helps clotting. I hope uncle Charley isn't planning on a hot shower right away.* Sitting still doing nothing while soaking is not in Josh's playbook, he looks around the spacious bathroom for something, anything to either help quench bleeding or occupy his mind while doing nothing. *If I could sneak down to the kitchen I could dig out some corn starch or tea bags, even an ice pack.* In frustration, he gently pushes his palm on the offending area and leans back resting his head and staring at the ceiling. He starts out to meditate but switches to deep thinking and planning as soon as he takes a cleansing breath. With eyes shut, he runs down the events since meeting Sammie on the ferry. A smile comes to his relaxed face when he looks for common denominators. *What's the common denominator here,* was what his mother used to say when injecting humor into an unpleasant situation. *It's Sammie, she's involved in everything, but so is Pepper and Sadie. Guilt by association.* Another smile.

He focuses his thoughts again, and runs down the list of players he knows about. Game Warden Rogers, A whole bunch of bit players at the Fish and game department. With a spark of insight, he mentally check marks ex Fish and Game employees as an unknown but viable group of common denominators. Dave Johnson, Kirstin, Kirstin's mother Eloise Thompson, Victoria Masters, the entire WU research group past and present. The middle eastern bank angle with unknown players. Danny O'Brien, Roberta Wilson and her brother the camera guy—not likely. Brad or Carly—no, Chet and his sister Christy—no, but maybe one of his protest groupies—maybe. He sifts through what he knows, not eliminating anyone but narrowing choices.

When he narrows his thoughts to people from ten years ago when orcas started missing the list shrinks to the fish and game bunch with Rogers at the top, Eloise Thompson, Kirstin, Victoria Masters, her late husband. Nasel Peterson may be involved if he inherited a problem and has kept quiet, which puts Dave Johnson back in the mix, except he has been forthcoming and helpful. Kirstin forwarded his phone call misdirection ploy to Rogers, which puts her and Rogers squarely involved with trapping orcas, but not necessarily the top bosses or even calling the shots.

Josh runs a line of thinking in his head and then changes a detail and runs it again. He comes back to some of his favorite sayings for clarity. Not because cute sayings are fun, but because they are rooted in logic and mostly originated with very smart people that history has proven correct. *Follow the money - The golden rule - Keep it simple – Confucius sayings.* The money trail highlights Victoria Masters and Eloise Thompson, and the Middle Eastern World Bank. The golden rule means, *He who has the gold, rules!* Once again, World Bank, Masters and Thompson are at the top of the golden rule list. *I can't ask World Bank any questions, at least not directly,* thinking of datamaster 24, *but I can go visit Victoria Masters and Eloise Thompson.*

Josh open his eyes, he has managed to kill thirty minutes and satisfied himself that he has a good action plan. In his head, he puts it aside and works on removing the water-soaked bandages. The adhesive still grips quite well but the blood has mostly softened. He sloshes in the tub, pink gives way to crime scene crimson and the tub acquires a definite red ring. *Maggie's going to kill me.* The last attempt at stemming the bleeding is holding. The layers of gauze peel off and for the first time he sees the ugly curved five-inch gashes and the emergency room stitchery. His left leg is doing well, but at the time of the attack his right leg was elevated on the kayaks foot rest and his thigh took most of the spinning propellers vicious slicing.

"Oh man, this is worse than I thought. That boat did a number on me." I can't go to Friday Harbor, I need to stay off this leg and let it heal. No wonder I keep bleeding. He carefully cleans away dried blood and loose adhesive. The hard to clean areas, he leaves for later. To keep from straining the stitches and opening the cuts, he holds his leg straight and hops around on one foot putting on his cutoffs. Under the sink he finds a can of powdered cleanser with bleach and works on the tub as best he can.

7:30 am Josh makes his way downstairs to the kitchen, on his way by the hall closet he picks out one of his grandfathers old canes and using it for added support hobbles his way to a chair. Maggie and Charlie, each with a cup of coffee, are sitting at the big oversize table. He plunks down with his leg stretched out like he's plans to trip someone. The hospital sent him home with a *to-go care package* of sterile pads and tape, Josh dumps the contents on the table. No one says anything, the usual *good morning sunshine, or did you sleep well,* comments are on hold while the image of his chopped up legs sinks in.

Maggie speaks first, "Oh honey, you must be in pain, did they give you any pain killer, do you need some aspirin?" Charley gets up and comes around the table to get a close look at Josh's legs. He leans forward with his hands behind his back signaling he has no intention of touching or contaminating what are essentially open wounds.

"What do you think Josh," says Charley, "are you going to make it?"

Laughing, "Yeah, I got this handled, but it's becoming darn inconvenient. I wasn't really mad or pissed about what happened until this morning in the tub cleaning up the blood. I know it's not good to harbor hate or seek revenge, but I really would like the person that did this to me to get what they deserve."

"He'll get caught, but I don't know about getting what he deserves, I wonder if Danny could use some pictures of your injuries, Maggie, why don't you take a few pics of him before the bandages go back on. Try to get gory ones, and get a close up of the bruising on Josh's face. They might be helpful later for sentencing when this guy is caught."

Sadie's barking announces her and Sammies arrival even though Sammie is still way back in the woods. Seconds later Sadie is at the side door bouncing up to see in the window.

"You better get covered up," says Maggie, "you don't want Sammie to see those cuts do you."

"I think it's okay, Aunt Maggie, she's already seen them. Apparently, while I was getting my fifteen-hour beauty sleep, she was with the nurses bandaging me. There she is, COME ON IN." yells Josh.

"Hi everyone, Sadie no, stay out—go see Pepper, right now, go see Pepper." Sammie closes the door behind herself, but Sadie is already racing around the lodge for the gangplank.

"What's in the sack." Josh asks for everyone.

"Sandy wanted me to bring muffins over for you guys." Then taking a close look at his legs, "Eew! you looked better at the hospital, some of these stitches have pulled, no wonder you've been bleeding, you're going to have some awesome scarring."

"Thank you, you look pretty too. Have a chair, let's eat."

Charley gets up, giving Sammie his chair, "I'm going to check out the back window and see if Sadie found Pepper."

"Don't drop crumbs on your legs," says Sammie, "what are you—a caveman?"

Chapter 53 - Forensics

Deputy Danny O'Brien finds the forensics report on his desk first thing in the morning when he arrives. The tech must have worked all night, but he found prints all over *Black Widow*. He lifted prints, and smudges that are unreadable plus several that have matches on file. Victoria Masters prints are on file as are all WU staff, the boat is covered with hers and Kirstin's. Dave Johnson's for some reason are missing from the WU fingerprint file. An unknown that resemble Kirstin's are included. *I'm betting the unknown are Ryan's.* The shifter and throttle handles have smudges on top of prints. Typical of when a perp wears latex gloves.

Damn, nothing here I didn't already know. Danny flips to the Fish and Game boat. It's a positive match, the Fish and Game boat is the one that ran down Josh. The paint on the kayak matches, the bottom paint on the aluminum sled, the Kevlar thread picked off the rivet from underneath the water matches the kayak skin, and the coup de grace is, grooves cut into the kayak top deck framing, match the propellers on the Fish and Game boat. *Forensic Science has proven the boat is the weapon, yes—got it!* The finger print analysis matched up a single partial thumbprint on the ignition key. Plus multiple matched prints from all over the boat belonging to Fish and Game employees. *Now we're getting somewhere.*

Reading down the file, Danny scans the usual unexplained discoveries and disclaimers, including one about footprints and an unidentified sugary black substance staining floorboards in both boats. The file contains an enhanced printout of a person's footprint, the tech estimates it to be a man's size 10. *That's interesting, moving along what else have we learned?* He continues skimming to the end of the report, and then reads it again, page by page.

Danny parks in an empty spot by the promenade and the marina office. The tide is down, boats and floating docks are eight feet lower than six hours earlier. He can see over the top of most. For a moment he scans the entire moorage tracing in his mind the maze of floats necessary to run an operation the size of Friday Harbor. The steepness of the gangplank speeds his descent down to the main concrete float. The floating dock has a course anti-slip texture, and is more than wide enough for groups of people to walk side by side. If he had a sense of deja vu it would be alerting him that the same pair of binoculars are trained on him as before. The person watching purses his lips, and waits, contemplating what Danny knows, guessing what he doesn't. He shakes his head in affirmative when Danny, as expected turns onto the float that leads to *Black Widow*. The police hold is lifted, the yellow tape is gone, *Black Widow* sits calmly in her slip ready to take her owner for a ride. The black stain in the report is hard to spot but with some careful studying he manages to see the unknown substance on the carpet. Getting down on his knees and sniffing accomplishes nothing but he had to try it.

Stepping off *Black Widow* requires him to stand on a rubber pad in order to reach the float. *Unless you have wings everyone steps right here getting on and off this boat.* He slides his penknife along one of the rubber grooves that provide extra traction. Wiping the blade on the tip of his finger is a mistake, it takes an alcohol towelette to get the goo off the knife, his finger remains black.

The walk to the breakwater from *Black Widow* is not the longest walk possible without going back on land, but it is close. Danny takes his time, at every intersection, at every turn he pauses and looks for a black substance. The newer floats are made of concrete encased foam and get regular power washings, the older floats of pressure treated wood are half black and tarry from years of hard use. He works his way toward the breakwater, at the floating bathrooms where the surveillance video showed the person changing coats he carefully inspects all the way around the building and goes inside finding nothing.

Just past the bathrooms is a picnic float with tables and a gazebo, along one side is a barrel barbecue, and there on the planks is a puddle of black goo that has been dripping from the barbecue. The catch tray is hanging loose, apparently burned barbecue sauce from overzealous chefs is the unknown black substance. Since he now knows the source, the rest of the walk to the breakwater goes faster. *It sure would be nice if I could pin down when that mess happened.*

The Fish and Game boat has been released back to the state, and is tied to the dock after having been unceremoniously jerked out of the water to have its bottom looked over, like *Black Widow* the tape is gone, and the humiliation of being impounded as a crime scene is no more. The commercial indoor outdoor carpet running the length of the sled is not as luxurious as the carpet on *Black Widow* but it still picked up a little of the carbonized sauce. Danny picks at a spot with his penknife and again smears his fingertip. *Yep, same stuff as the picnic float, I really need to find out when they used the barbecue last.*

At the harbormasters office, Danny asks the girl behind the counter if she knew when the last group used the picnic float, and gets a blank stare. After explaining what he is talking about she admits that they don't schedule it, people just use it whenever they want to. *Who cleans it with a pressure washer when it needs cleaning* he asks next. *Ah yes—maintenance—of course,* is her answer. *And where would that person be right now,* he presses for a more helpful answer, convinced that he just needs to ask her the right question correctly. As she is about to point him towards the gas dock and maintenance sheds, she remembers Jorge is upstairs.

"Just a second," she stabs an intercom button on her phone, "Jorge could you show the deputy where the maintenance office is?" Asks the girl.

"Hey Jorge, good to see you again," says Danny, "I wanted to talk to you anyway, maybe we could step outside and you can point me in the right way." Danny leads the way out to the promenade, they run a few feet dodging over spray mist from the irrigation system. Water puddles along the walk so Danny leads them to a dry spot where he stops. Both their wet footprints are clearly visible, and Danny takes a second to verify that Jorge's shoe size might be a size ten, but the tread design is totally different than the forensics print out. When he looks up, Jorge is also looking at the wet footsteps, and then at Danny. He shows no indication of concern.

"What did you want with me," says Jorge.

"Oh, it's probably nothing, but I noticed the picnic float down there with the barbecue on it?"

"Yeah, it's for boat owners that rent slips, what did you want to talk to me about?" Danny has to make up a story, he hadn't wanted to talk to Jorge until after interviewing the maintenance staff.

"I wanted to know if you saw anyone using the picnic float last Tuesday at around dinner time?"

"No," – he says quickly, his answer is curt and short and Danny's cop radar detects fear, he (Jorge) doesn't want to talk, or he just doesn't want to talk to a policeman, a common occurrence which makes people look and act guilty. "That building you're looking for is the one down there," pointing. "Right next to the fuel dock." He takes a step backwards, his body language says he is uncomfortable and wants to leave. "Is that all?" says Jorge, edging away.

"Yeah sure, thanks, you've been very helpful." Danny doesn't head for the gas dock just yet, he watches Jorge walk away down the promenade. The last time they spoke down on the floats, Jorge had been friendly, almost talkative. *I wonder what has changed Jorge.*

"Nice place you got here," says Danny to the maintenance foreman behind the makeshift desk just inside the door. The tin roof and creosoted timbers are beginning to heat with the days sunshine giving the ages old work shed its own special atmosphere. A large fluorescent shop light with four, four foot tubes hangs from rusty chains defining the office from dark mountains of old and new marina gear. To one side unplugged for the summer is a portable heater, the kind that glows orange and shoots an invisible beam of infrared energy from a parabolic reflector.

"I like it, it's home, help yourself to the coffee, it's fresh." Pointing to a glowing light on the front of a Mr. Coffee pot in the shadows. The foreman leans back in his rescue chair and hooks both hands behind his head. Danny takes one of four mismatched chairs scattered about the desk.

"Looks like a good place to play cards?"

"It is on a rainy day, that's for sure." The foreman is not the least bit intimidated, nervous, or concerned by the man half his age in a sheriffs uniform. Secure in his position, secure in his wisdom he patiently waits for Danny to get around to the purpose of his visit.

"You probably heard about that kid in a kayak that got run down last week."

"Yeah, I saw Billy pulled out that Fish and Game boat, was it the one?"

"I can't verify anything, but let me put it this way—I'm through looking at boats. You know that picnic float with the gazebo and barbecues, down past the restrooms."

"Sure."

"It's got some sticky goo dripping from the barbecues onto the dock and getting tramped around, any idea when the mess happened, or maybe when was the last time that picnic float got scrubbed down or cleaned."

"That's hard to say, probably three of four weeks. We power wash as needed, not on a schedule. A lot of the time the people that make the messes just hose it down when the barb's dump their guts. But the last time we power washed the docks it would've been looked at, mostly we just going after goose crap. You might try asking some of the boat owners down there. Some of them are livaboard and see everything that goes on." Danny didn't find out anything useful, but sifting through useful and useless information is what investigating is all about. He heads out on the dock, joining the streams of people moving about like bees in a busy hive, each worker with a special task.

Standing on the main walkway facing the picnic float, he watches the surrounding boats for any activity. He studies curtains blocking prying eyes and the suns damaging rays. Some forty five foot yachts have planter baskets with flowers hanging over the water, their colorful blooms competing with king-size flags that are a part of every serious yacht. Water hoses are neatly coiled on the dock near strategically placed faucets. One nearby boat sports especially prodigious flower baskets that are dripping from recent watering. The boats hundred pound chrome anchor projects out over the dock, Danny reflexively ducks, as it clears his head by inches. Walking down the narrow finger float it's hard not to be impressed by the boats sheer immensity. The boat blocks his view of the promenade, and most of the waterfront, creating its own private space. Standing at the foot of the portable boarding stairway, he considers knocking on the pearly white hull but then jogs up the half dozen steps bringing himself back into the daylight and face to face with an ageless elegantly clothed yet casually dressed lady in a sunbonnet.

" Hello—your flowers look great, you must have a green thumb,"

"Thank you, this year for a change, they are doing very well and giving me great satisfaction."

"I'm sorry to interrupt you, I know your time is important, would you mind helping me out, I won't take but a minute."

"Well deputy, I guess that....depends." Her eyes settle on Danny, her expression is one of amusement, and interest.

Her comment registers with him, and causes him to flash to Roberta Wilson, he hesitates, and maybe his face flushes for just a second. "Ah—you know that picnic float next door with the barbecue and the gazebo."

"Yes—is there more?" her hint of a smile, and glint in her eye suggests she has affected him as intended.

"I'm trying to pin down when the barbecue over there dripped that black gooey substance on the float, would you happen to know when that happened?" She simply stares at him, as if she doesn't comprehend what he said. Danny is about to rephrase the request when she answers.

"Deputy, that is the one question I did not expect, come on board, I want to show you the view from the fantail, my back deck." She leads him down the side deck and up two steps to the raised aft entertainment area. Overhead is a partial shelter of striped canvas, across the back is a stainless railing capped with highly polished teak, scattered fashionably about are teak lounge chairs.

"Wow," says Danny, "this is impressive." The picnic float is only twenty feet away, he can see all of the gazebo and barbecue area plus a good portion of the main walkway leading to the breakwater.

"Thank you, it's my home, I was sitting right here that night. You are investigating that kayak hit and run aren't you, I certainly hope so. I saw you and Billy's crane lift that park department boat."

"Yes, I'm looking into the hit and run, did you want to share something with me?"

"Well like I started to say, I was sitting right here, it was dark, and I saw a person stop right there on the dock. Coming down the H float was a group of men from Fish and Game, you know they have to wear those awful green outfits and the black baseball caps, anyway this person ducked onto the picnic float and stood behind the gazebo, you know it squeaks when you step on it. After they went by, he waited and then kept going. It looked to me like he was hiding."

"Can you describe this person?"

"He had a big floppy hat that covered his face, and some sort of long jacket, like a rain coat or something."

"Was he tall, short, fat, thin—how did he walk."

"Sneaky, he walked like he was sneaking around, I think he was not fat and not short, and something else, now I remember who used the barbecue that afternoon, it was a Canadian group. I remember their boat, it was a sailboat named -Au Revoir- from Vancouver. They were in that slip, right there. They put some sort of smokey sauce in the barbecue, and then they must have burned it, you can see where it ran over that dinky little cup."

"Any Idea when they were cooking, do you remember any ferries coming or going maybe?"

"No, not really, I'll guess around 4 PM, I'm sorry."

"That's ok, I can figure it out from the harbor camera, I just wanted to narrow it down a little. You've been very helpful."

Danny walks away from the sumptuous live-aboard yacht with plenty of new information to digest. On shore, invisible binoculars follow his progress as he inspects the picnic float and gazebo again. He stands in front of the barbecue contemplating why a person would be hiding from a group of Fish and Game employees, and then he looks up scanning the waterfront buildings. He settles his eyes on the harbor camera and then steps behind the gazebo blocking coverage, when Danny reappears on the other side still looking up at the camera the binoculars reflexively pull back, invisible or not, the person prefers to remain anonymous.

In his darkened office, Danny crowds close to his monitor; the harbor camera footage begins at 6 PM and is beginning to look familiar to him after multiple views. This time he zeroes in on the picnic float and barbecue, one man is visible carrying sacks stepping off the float.

Danny watches the man walk to the Canadian boat Au Revoir. That's it, sometime before 4 and 6 is when the black goo appears. *Thank you Canadian visitors for leaving your mess in Friday Harbor.*

Chapter 54 - Eloise

Text: "Let's go! I'm ready if you are." Five minutes later, Maggie and Josh pick up Sammie and follow the winding road from the Islander resort to Orcas Landing. Maggie avoids the ferry loading lanes and drops the kids and Sadie at the bottom of the foot ramp to the waiting ferry. Their timing is perfect; the morning ferry is still loading the last of the Orcas Island cars and will pull away in minutes. Sammie and Josh head straight up the stairs for the cafeteria.

Josh's three days of forced rest have done wonders. He takes the steps one at a time, but only because Sammie is intentionally holding him back by stalling in front of him. She treats them to Caramel Lattes and they settle in the glassed in observation area below the pilothouse for the twenty minute ride to Friday Harbor.

"Are you sure about this?" asks Sammie, holding his hand between hers.

"Look, nothing is for sure, but just because some whacko idiot runs me down out in the ocean doesn't mean something is going to happen to us today. All I want to do is visit the rest home and talk with Eloise Thompson, and then see if we can talk with Victoria Masters, or Jacobs."

"I know, I just feel helpless, you know, not knowing."

"You've got Sadie to protect you, besides what can happen at a rest home, it's a bunch of antiseptic smelling old people."

The ferry docks at Friday Harbor while they are still nursing their Lattes. Sadie drags them off the boat ahead of the first wave of bicycle pushing foot passengers. Traveling light with nothing but a dog and backpacks has an advantage, that's for sure. They cut diagonally across the street to the Harbor Coffee Shop where they have arranged to interview with travel writer Roberta Wilson and her brother. Roberta and Sammie have become close since meeting at the Islander Resort, almost like sisters sharing secrets, but it was Roberta's idea to meet and tag along when Sammie shared with her that Josh intended to pay a visit to Thompson and Masters.

"Wow, look at both of you," says Roberta. Sammie and Roberta do girl hugs and Josh fist bumps with Pete. "How do you feel Josh?" presses Roberta. "Sit down, we saved this table and watched you come in."

"Compared to last time I was here," says Josh, "I feel great. I won't be doing any flips today, but I bet I could."

"Really, you can do flips?" Roberta is genuinely impressed if its true, and Sammie knows better than to be surprised anymore, so she just says, no you won't—and then smiles and cocks her head at Josh.

"I do a little Gymnastics as a sport, it's not all monkey flips and cartwheels, it's more disciplined, but yeah I can do a flip when I need to. You guys eat, but I'm saving myself for a Pepper's Revenge at lunch time, so I'm just having water for now."

"What is a Pepper's Revenge?" asks Roberta.

"See that food cart across the street," says Sammie proudly, "that's the Burrito Bandit and Josh created a monster burrito he named Peppers Revenge. They are really big, so big Josh is going to share his with me—aren't you?"

"Anything new with Pepper you guys, is she still Queen of the cove?"

"Absolutely—Charley strung a floating rope across the cove entrance to warn boats, but she treats it like another toy and swims under it or jumps over it. Any strange whales or sharks get the boot, err tail."

"You are joking of course, Pete rented us a car, so we can head out anytime." Soon they file out of the coffee shop and are driving on San Juan Valley Rd.

The retirement community where Eloise Thompson lives is situated on a rolling hill with an expansive view of the surrounding islands. A weathered gray sign marks the entrance, a long gravel driveway connects the road to the sprawling single story complex. Gravel gives way to black top and a parking lot emerges adjacent to manicured lawns, gardens and fountains. Seating benches and tables with umbrellas line meandering paths and trails. The morning is light and airy, several seasoned citizens, some using walkers and wheelchairs make their way about. The front entrance to San Juan Acres is served by a circle drive to bring tenants within a few feet of the door. Pete parks the rental car off to one side with other visitors cars.

"Roberta," says Josh, "I hope you don't mind me springing this on you, but may I enlist your help here."

"Go on." Roberta grins because she had already considered Josh would be asking for her help.

"We are uninvited, unexpected, and may be asking to visit an invalid suffering memory loss or even someone incoherent. I look a lot like a seventeen year old kid that is up to who knows what. You on the other hand could easily play the role of a university orca researcher with an intern tagging along. Mrs Thompson was in the Orca program so it all makes sense.

"Ok, I'll do it, but how about if I play the role of a writer, and you will play yourself."

"Sounds great, I'm sorry but I think you guys will have to hang tight out here and see what develops. Ok lets go."

Roberta and Josh, walk through the front door of San Juan Acres. Josh holds the door for Roberta, she holds a pen and notebook, and her purse is shouldered. Josh follows to one side and a step behind. Inside is a large commons with comfortable furniture groupings. Hallways fan out in multiple directions like spokes. Straight ahead is a reception desk. Somewhere between the car and the desk, Roberta has fished out a pair of glasses and now wears them.

"May I help you," says the all business, woman at the desk.

"What a wonderful place you have here, you must be in charge. I will get right to the point, my name is Roberta Wilson and I am writing an orca   paper for the university archives. We have many famous people here in the islands that were instrumental in our killer whale research and my job is to preserve some their history before it is lost. If we don't pay attention to our elders and listen to their wisdom we are destined to make the same mistakes over again. It is very important to give credit where credit due to energize the younger generation to keep the program strong and save the whales."

"Ms Wilson," says the receptionist holding up her hand, "I get the picture." Josh keeps a smiling straight face but hadn't expected what he just listened to. "Are you talking about Eloise, she's our resident orca   expert."

"Yes, I am, may we visit her?"

"Of course, but she hasn't recognized anyone for several years, I don't think you will preserve much history, I'm afraid your too late, but I will call her out. She sits outside by the big fountain every day, why don't you wait out there and she will come out. Under the umbrella."

Josh and Roberta sit outside on the broad bench encircling the fountain. Cascading water rushes endlessly to the soothing tranquil pond below. Colorful fish call the pond home, some gulp air and bugs at the surface risking becoming a passing heron's meal, older wiser ones lay in wait near the bottom.

"What are you going to ask her Josh?"

"I don't know, I thought we would just start with hello."

"Good plan."

"Your speech inside to the receptionist was quite impressive, was it planned?"

"No, you gave me thirty seconds warning, but I knew to talk fast to avoid an engaging conversation with questions. In retrospect, I don't think it mattered, the staff may be grateful to have any visitors they get. I think some of these places are dumping grounds for the living dead. Some seniors are real modern day zombies, except with walkers and canes." While they are waiting Josh fills in Roberta on what he knows about, Thompson, Masters, Kirstin and the orca program.

"How do you know about agent Rogers financial history" says Roberta with an accusing slant, "and the payments from World Bank, isn't that stuff confidential?"

"Simple, I asked online acquaintances for help."

"That's it, you just ask?"

"Yep, just ask the right people. You probably should not include in your writing anything that might raise a question of impropriety." Josh's unblinking stare conveys to her more than his words.

A large side door on one of the building's spokes slowly opens and is held wide by hidden electric arms. A young girl, or perhaps they call them staff or helper, pushes a wheelchair out into the morning's fresh breeze. They stop at the bottom of the short ramp and she arranges a handmade wooly scarf around Eloise Thompson, draping the end in her lap and tucked under clasped hands. The girl looks up and points to Roberta and Josh before pushing the wheelchair toward them.

"Ellie," says the helper, "I'm going to leave you right here under your favorite umbrella, these nice people are here to see you. Would you like to …."

"I know who Vicky and Jorge are she snaps—you can leave now." The young helper meekly smiles at them and then backs away as if trained to melt away and disappear once her menial task is completed. "I didn't want to say anything in front of that girl," says Ellie, "you know, our secret." Josh and Roberta trade looks, each assessing what they have heard.

"We got another orca ." Says Josh diving in.

"Oh goody, how big is it?" Asks Ellie.

"It's about eight feet, I think." Both of them are paying carefully attention to Ellie's demeanor, looking for clues to steer the conversation.

"That's too small, it will starve, if it's still nursing."

"What should we do?" asks Roberta.

"Gorge knows, ask him."

"I'll find its mother," says Josh, "I also know of a nine footer, a female."

"That's perfect, "Ellie looks around and lowering her voice says, "they'll be thrilled." Then she spots a big goldfish in the water next to her wheelchair, oooh, there's a big one and a female too, at least nine or ten, what do you think Jorge?"

"Ellie are you talking about killer whales or goldfish," says Roberta.

"Well, Orcas of course, you should know that."

"Well than who takes them after we catch one."

"I don't know, Robert takes care of that."

"Of course—but do you remember where we take them?" says Roberta.

Josh takes out his phone and texts Sammie: *Bring Pete and come over to the big umbrella, but don't say who you are or your names.*

When Pete and Sammie walk up, Josh says, "Look Ellie, here's the rest of our team. Come over here you guys, I told Ellie about the nine foot orca we got." Ellie remains silent watching their approach, Pete sits on the concrete bench staring into the water, Sammie takes the last chair at the umbrella table.

Ellie eyes Sammie, and then hesitantly asks, "Do I know you?" Before Sammie answers,

Roberta says, "Of course you do Ellie, who do you think she is?" No one speaks, all are watching Ellie, Josh is biting his lip knowing what happens next may put them on track for discovering the truth or simply entertain an unfortunate resident living out a lonely life at San Juan Acres care facility.

"My daughter lives in Friday Harbor" Ellie lowers her voice and leans forward so just those around the table can hear, "that man over there is Agent Rogers, we need to keep our voices down." Pete is listening and watching, Josh catches his eye, and motions for him to move around to the backside of the pond.

"Why should we be quiet," says Josh whispering, what will Rogers do?."

"He will put us in Jail if he finds out about the money."

"What money Ellie," pushes Josh.

"Vicky's money," she nods at Roberta, "shh."

"Okay," he says, he leans in close to Ellie and asks, "where does Vicky get the money."

"From Robert of course, he loves me and Vicky, he gives all the money to her."

"Does Robert know about the orcas, is he in on our secret?" Says Josh.

"Of course, it's his secret, that and the other one."

"What other one?" Everyone around the table is enthralled and huddled, waiting for the Ellie to reveal the next secret.

"I can't tell you, it's just between Robert and me and Vicky and Kirstin," she reaches out for Sammie and Roberta's hands. The three of them form a triangle at the table. "It's our family secret."

A large goldfish breaks the surface ending the moment. The three way huddle dissolves. Josh looks across the pond, and Pete raises a questioning eye brow, Josh shrugs his shoulders. Pete nods back. Roberta and Josh end up staring, *now what,* at each other. Unspoken words and head shakes, convey agreement, there is not much more to learn by continuing the pretense of being friends and family, besides the willful subterfuge on a person with limited memory capacity goes against their sense of what's right. All of them, except maybe Pete share some lingering self-disgust or shame over the sham. They haven't really been tricking her, more like letting her talk in hopes of getting her to spill the beans, bringing down the only people that care about her.

"Well that's about it," says Josh, no longer considering that Ellie still thinks he is Jorge. "Anyone think of a something to ask Ellie before we go."

"Ellie, does anyone come to visit you." asks Sammie.

"Oh yes, I have lots of visitors." With that, Sammie bends over and hugs Ellie for as long as Ellie hugs her back. "I will come and see you again." Sammie's tears are flowing when she catches up to the group. Roberta holds back near Ellie, she faces the building, and the girl that brought Ellie to them steps outside and waves to her that she will take care of Ellie. *Thank you*, yells Roberta. Sammie turns around and walks over to the helper.

"Does she get any visitors."

"No, not really, did she think you were Kirstin?"

"Yes."

"It's her daughter, I've never met her, she calls me Kirstin too."

"What's going to happen to her?" Sammie realizes as soon as she spoke, she already knew the answer. San Juan Acres is where old people go to die.

"Nothing, she lives here."

Chapter 55 - Four Corners Casino

Victoria Masters and her husband Robert, bought the house on the hill overlooking the harbor two decades ago. They moved to San Juan Island so he could take over the WU whale research department. The grand old house is one of the older Victorian homes that turn of the century ship captains and lumber barons preferred. Pete parks the rental car alongside the cobblestone lane and kills the motor. The four of them have been discussing and rehashing their visit with Ellie for thirty minutes.

The emerging picture confirms what Josh has suspected all along. While connecting the dots he drops tidbits of what might be confidential information, but he always cloaks his source by saying, *if I were to guess,* causing Roberta to grimace shaking her head, and to cover her ears trying to unhear what she shouldn't know about.

ORCA BOY

"My guess, says Josh, is that Vicky Masters dead husband was the person that started orca dealing. I'm guessing that some offshore bank connected to a buyer is supporting Ellie Thompson, and that Ellie, Kirstin and Victoria kept it going, and now, thanks to Ellie, I think Jorge, whomever he is, is in on it. It looks like that jerk face, Agent Rogers was kept out of the secret. I don't know who this Jorge fella is, any ideas."

Roberta and Pete have become drawn into the orca poaching scam and are eager to learn more. Roberta is filling her notebook with short story and magazine article notes. She has ideas to keep her busy writing for some time, but the biggest developing story is orca thefts, and she hasn't touched yet on Josh's personal story, saving Pepper, his attempted murder, or Sammies and his blossoming romance.

"How do you want to handle Mrs. Masters," says Roberta. "She won't be easily fooled and will possibly rebel if we try to trick her or accuse her of wrongdoing."

"Let's tell her the truth, we are researching juvenile orcas, namely Pepper," explains Josh, "and you are writing about it. Let's knock on her door and play it by ear, shall we," Josh motions, *after you,* to Roberta with his outstretched arm. The two of them walk up to Vicky's ornate, black iron adorned front door, Sammie, Pete and Sadie stay in the rental car.

"Wow," says Roberta, after Josh drops the heavy anchor shaped iron weight. "That's a serious knocker."

"Aw, wait until you see the ones at Pearson Lodge, heck even Sammies are bigger than this little one." Roberta turns and looks at Josh as he hears his own words. He averts his eyes. *Oh crap, I'm toast.* His face burns red, he can't look at her. *Why couldn't this happen to Chet.*

She snickers a little and says, "Josh, it's ok, I know what you meant."

"You won't tell Sammie will you?"

"Oh yes I will, you can count on it," more snickering. Just then Victoria Masters opens the door

"Nooo—she'll kill me."

"Why will she kill you young man," says Vicky.

"He just said her knockers were bigger than your little one here." Pointing at the door.

"No no—no, that's not what I said. Ok, I said it, but not like that." His redness deepens, and he kicks at the ground unable to look at the two laughing women.

"My name is Roberta Wilson, Mrs. Masters, I'm a misguided travel writer off on a tangent."

"And what is that tangent that brings you to my house?"

"First let me apologize for showing up announced, Josh can make his own apologies. Since you are right here in town, we thought we would take a chance. Your tangent answer is orcas, they are not the same as travel writing, but I happened to show up in Friday Harbor in the middle of some demonstrations and well, here we are. Our easily embarrassed local hero and Internet researcher here, tells me you are WU's resident expert for the last decade."

"Well, thank you for not calling me old, or orcas—*whales,* yes I once played the role of department director, but nowadays I just lecture and hang around. I would be happy to help you out, what can I do." Roberta looks at Josh, his cue to say something.

"Mrs. Masters, is there any evidence orcas communicate telepathically."

"Oh my, that's not what I expected, but call me Vicky. Evidence—no, incidents and believers yes. Why do you ask, most people ask If they talk."

"Of course they talk," says Josh matter of factly, "all you gotta do is listen, Pepper talks more than Sammie." He looks at Roberta, "Oh boy, I suppose, you have to pass that on too," she nods.

"Who is Sammie?" asks Victoria, "and is Pepper an orca?"

"Sammie is his de facto girlfriend, even though neither admits it. She's waiting in the car along with Pete, my photographer brother."

"Why don't you invite them to join us out back on the veranda. I'll get us some ice water and we can all sit down and enjoy the view. Bring everyone around through that black gate, and I'll meet you out there in a few minutes." Victoria closes the door, they hear the latch click and then silence.

Victoria pushes her hip against the door and backs out carrying a large tray with five ice water filled glasses and a pitcher. Pete hurries over to assist her in time to catch the door before the spring slams it shut. They all take their pick of outdoor chairs and lounges. Pete hangs back fiddling with his camera. Introductions are quickly dispensed, and Sadie briefly becomes the center of attention, followed by Sammie.

"Do you mind your picture being taken, I won't publish anything without your approval." Says Roberta.

"Pictures are ok. So then Josh, we left off with you asking about esp. That is interesting, tell me what prompts you to ask."

"Sure," says Josh focusing on Vicky, "there's a juvenile orca I have been around lately, and she seems to understand me and Sadie much better than you would expect. Her level of perception is uncanny, but if they read minds and project their own thoughts it would explain my observations."

"Can you describe some specific instances." Asks Victoria

Josh and Sammie go on to explain Peppers many antics and activities shared with them and Sadie. Both Roberta and Vicky sit entranced. Roberta writes notes, and Vicky asks questions. She is particularly interested in hearing about Big Momma and the experience Josh's grandfather had with her almost forty years earlier. The net entanglement and Peppers rather docile acceptance of help does not surprise her since there are many documented cases of marine mammals holding still while humans cut them free. The apparent friendship and bonding between Josh and Pepper while unusual does not surprise her either. Big Mommas absence concerns her though.

While talking and learning like a student sitting rapt in front of their professor, Josh has not forgot the real reason for being at Victoria Masters home. Once he has gleaned from her, mountains of orca knowledge, he decides to level with Vicky, but avoid confronting her.

"Mrs. Masters, we, err mostly me I guess have been asking about care and feeding of pet *Killer Whales*, but make no mistake, Pepper is not my pet. I am deeply concerned that she remains wild and lives out her life as intended. Which brings me to the second part of our visit. Certain factions in our government have tried to capture her, which has led to some unwarranted arrests, and some probing research. Earlier today the four of us visited San Juan Acres and met with Ellie Thompson. I am sorry for her condition. We had an interesting exchange for an hour or so. Ellie mistook Roberta for Vicky, you I assume. She thought I was Jorge, Sammie was Kirstin, and she called Pete Agent Rogers.

"You had no business going there," Victoria stands and takes a step toward the black gate, it appears the party is about over.

"Wait," Josh stands, "I'm are sorry, I didn't know her condition, we developed a list of people associated with the WU whale program and are simply making the rounds. Dave Johnson, Kirstin, Jorge, Agent Rogers, World Bank, San Juan Acres, Four Corners Resorts of the world, these are all names my research has uncovered, and a bunch more, Nasal Peterson, Victoria Masters, Whale World of the Med. We can't talk to everyone, like the late Robert Masters, but wouldn't you agree it makes perfect sense to talk with whomever we can right here in the San Juans."

Vicky is quiet, she caught some troubling names, *Robert Masters, World Bank, Resorts of the World.*

After a lengthy silence, where Vicky stares out over the city and the water beyond, a much reserved, tired sounding Victoria Masters quietly says, "what do you want."

"I don't want anything except for orcas to be left alone. I know World Bank is supporting Eloise Thompson, and I'm guessing the payments will stop if someone doesn't get what they want, am I right so far."

She nods.

"What's the person's name and company called?"

"All I know is a Wilson Hernandez from Four Corners Resorts was Roberts contact, and then when Robert died, somehow they got their hooks into Nasel. It all started with a gambling debt, Robert incurred when traveling, but I always thought it was a phony set up to force his cooperation."

"Who is Jorge, and what's his involvement?"

"Jorge is in charge of security down at the marina, but ten years ago he worked for Rogers at Fish and Game."

"Is Jorge in on it? Is Rogers involved?"

"Jorge was doing captures in the beginning, Robert was paying him, since he passed, I haven't been involved."

"You made cash payments to San Juan Acres, before World Bank took over. Where did all the cash come from.

"Robert had money in a box, I had to take care of Ellie, I think his death triggered her breakdown, she never recovered."

"Mrs. Masters," says Josh, "from what I know, it is apparent that someone local is still in the orca selling business and I will speculate that Hernandez is still the money man. The only players are Rogers, Kirstin, Jorge, and Nasel Peterson. Who do you think is Hernandez's contact?"

"If Kirstin is involved.."

"Excuse my interrupting you, Kirstin is positively involved, she called Rogers when I called in a tip, she made the call, she is definitely involved."

"She may not be willing," snaps Vicky, "she can't afford to support her mother." Josh is carefully watching Vicky's constricting dark eyes and her subtle body language, she seems at ease, but he knows that as a speaker lecturer, she is comfortable fielding questions and quick retorts. He is leaning towards believing she is being honest with him, but not because she plays a good act, but because her answers make logical sense. Roberta is a silent note taker. She is jotting notes about Vicky and the orca mystery, but writes even more about Josh, she is fascinated by his methodology and ability to control what is an apparent investigation, and yet she remembers with a chuckle, that just forty five minutes earlier he had fallen apart over a big door knocker comment. Her thoughts and eyes wander to Sammie, *it's true young lady, women do have ultimate power over men, use it wisely.*

"What do you think Roberta, shall we thank Mrs. Masters and go visit Kirstin, or do you have any thoughts you care to share."

"Yes I do, what do you plan to do, once you have it all figured out?"

"I don't know for sure, but ongoing orca abuse must stop, that means poaching must end, and possibly repatriating orcas in captivity if it can be done without further cruelty or abuse."

"What about retribution," asks Vicky, "or redress." Josh notes her self-concern or possibly, she is more worried about Kirstin and Ryan.

"Punishing people that do bad things does not help orcas or rectify a situation, it probably won't change who they are either. My only interest is in helping Pepper and her kind. Big Momma brought her baby to my grandfathers cove for help, and that's what I'm doing. As far as Mrs. Thompson is concerned, I have a few ideas how to get *Four Corners* to continue their support indefinitely.

"How," says Vicky, "what can a kid on San Juan Island do to influence an international gambling syndicate,"

"Simple, I know how to expose their complicity through social media, the publicity will be devastating, and that will cost them a fortune. On the other hand, they can cooperate and run their resorts and life goes on."

"Do you think threatening a bad review online will have get their cooperation." Vicky scoffs. "You're naïve young man, sorry."

"Well Mrs. Masters I'm just guessing, but if someone inside their operation wanted to, say, *prove a point;* they could disable their credit card reservation system for a couple hours. If they were being downright nasty, they could at the same time start rumors on face-book that they were bankrupt and that's why their system is down, social media will spread it across the world causing mass cancellations at all their casinos. If you want to short sell some stock and make a bundle, that would be a good time to do it." Josh glances at Sammie and gets an approving nod back, she knows better than doubting what he says even though she has no idea what short sell means.

"Listen, you asked what a kid can do. I haven't given it much thought yet, but doing something is incredibly easy, doing something effective takes some thinking." Roberta smiles and scribbles something in her notebook.

Josh stands and faces Vicky, "Mrs. Masters, thank you very much, your candid admissions are going to help set things straight, I promise, and I won't forget Ellie."

"You asked me if orcas have esp., perhaps you can do some thinking and then ask Pepper."

"Perhaps."

Chapter 56 - Kirstin

Sixth street looks much the same as when Deputy Danny pulled up in front of Kirstin's house a week earlier. The watchful lady across the street is first to see the rental car. Her wispy curtains do little to hide her interest.

"So," says Roberta, "If you are correct."

"He is so far," interrupts Sammie.

"As I was saying, if you are correct, this person, *Kirstin,* is almost the top person and is not likely to appreciate being accused of complicity, and have you considered the possibility that she may be the one that ran you down?"

"It's hard not to suspect everyone, heck, I'm not convinced of Vicky's innocence, all these people have motives, even Ellie, except she seems pretty unlikely in view of what we saw this morning."

Once again, Sammie and Pete wait in the car while Roberta and Josh make their way up the broken sidewalk to Kirstin's gravel driveway. Muddy tracks mark the edge of the driveway where cars have strayed into the yard. Avoiding mud, they step lightly skirting the driveway. Two cars sit end to end, a newer looking shiny red Toyota radiates engine heat as they squeeze between them. Footprints lead from the driver's door to handmade stepping-stones ending at the porch. A speckled pathway made from gravel and crushed oyster shells leads to the backyard. Josh stands on the first of three weathered plank steps and knocks on the door and then retreats back to the broken shells and stepping-stones beside Roberta. Ryan Jacobs, Kirstin's teenage son answers the door, he takes in Roberta in front of him like a gift from heaven, her stunning good looks bridge the age gap leaving him gawking, not even registering Josh's presence. When the testosterone driven spell breaks and he does look at Josh, his eyes widen, he recognizes Josh.

"Hi, my name is Josh Pearson, this is Roberta Wilson, we've come to see Kirstin, is she around?"

Seeing Kirstin's son Ryan, floods Josh with mental images and thoughts to process. Ryan is tall and slender, much like Josh, and they are about the same age. Ryan ogled Roberta, the same way he had ogled Sammie when they first met on the ferry. Josh knew about Ryan from the first datamaster24 data dump. What he had envisioned was a geeky kid with bottle glasses, born of an academic researcher. What he witnessed of Ryan for the twenty seconds so far, is a kid much like himself or even a younger skinnier version of Chet. He probably plays Warcraft, GTA and knows all the secrets of Dungeons and Dragons . Josh's eyes drift to a skateboard cruiser leaning in the corner of the shallow porch, they could share tricks, he used to have the same model board before he lightened his load when moving to Orcas Island. A smiling Kirstin appears behind Ryan.

"It is you," says Kirstin, "I heard your name but it didn't register who you were. You are better known around town as, *That orca guy*, or *The guy that got run down*. How are you, the last the news people have is that you snuck out of the hospital and disappeared, what did you do."

Laughing, "That's funny, Sammie and I rode the *Island Transit down* to the marina and went for a kayak test ride, and then we carried two new kayaks home on the ferry. Not really very sneaky."

"No, not sneaky at all. So you look pretty good, are you ok, how is Sammie?"

"Sammie's fine, I gave her quite a scare, I guess I looked pretty bad when she dragged me out of the water in the dark that night."

"The news reports are sketchy," says Kirstin, "some credit you with leading protests, others say you are on the run still, but there's nothing about what happened." Kirstin has moved beside Ryan and is comfortably resting her hand on his shoulder. Ryan, eyes averted, has been looking away, since she came to the door.

"Pepper saved me, she witnessed the crash," Josh and Roberta intently watch Ryan and Kirstin. "I don't remember anything, but she must have pushed me and the smashed kayak two miles into the cove and then shoved me onto the lifting ramp. Somehow Pepper communicated with Sadie. Just like Lassie—Sadie brought Sammie and my aunt and uncle. Do you think orcas and dogs share some sort of esp., I asked your aunt Vicky the same question." At the mention of Victoria, Kirstin stiffens, removing her hand from her sons shoulder. Ryan looks up for a fleeting glimpse into Josh's searching eyes.

"Why are you here?" says Kirsten. Dave Johnson comes into view behind her; it's his Red Toyota in the driveway.

"Hey Josh," says Dave excitedly, "we heard what happened, I hope you are alright, what's going on." Two people have asked Josh why he is at Kirstin's house. Roberta can't jump in, she is the outsider holding a pencil and notepad still to be introduced.

"Hi Dave," says Josh, and then returning to Kirstin's cold question, "several reasons. "When we met on Rock Island, I was a soon to be exonerated fugitive, but I sensed a certain kinship and sense of purpose with you, as well as a load of semi-legitimate suspicion on my part. I've been somewhat out of commission for a few days, but now I'm trying to learn all I can about the University research program to figure out how to protect Pepper and her kind. That's why we, oops, let me stop right now and introduce my writer friend Roberta Wilson," Josh motions with an arm wave to Roberta, "as I was saying, that's why we met with Vicky Masters and your mom Ellie earlier." Josh intentionally stops talking without mentioning anything Ellie or Vicky told them. He carefully watches the three people in front of him. Roberta, her pencil at the ready, watches all four in front of her. Like the proverbial elephant in the room, the silence is unmistakable as Josh deliberately waits.

Dave anxiously breaks the quiet. "This is great Josh, we're glad you're alright, tell us what you need us to do so we can help?"

"That's right," says Kirstin, following Dave's lead, but her hearts not in it. It was a bombshell to the gut when Josh said he visited her mother and Aunt Vicky. "Why don't we all go inside and sit, I want to hear about this esp."

They traipse across the cheap entry vinyl leaving new muddy tracks on top of the last ones. The front room is small but comfy like in all the houses on the street. The furniture is dated, but there's room for all of them. There is an unmistakable old feeling to the house, a feeling of mustiness and old age. After being in Vicky's spacious backyard with a view, it's an eye opener to see how the rest of the family lives. Dave and Kirstin take the sofa, sitting at opposite ends. Ryan heads for his corner and loses himself in his computer. Roberta takes a love seat sofa leaving Josh sitting on a bench seat in front of an old secretary with a roll top. When he sits he gets a whiff of familiar perfume.

"So, esp. Let me explain a little, I've become aware of an ability for Pepper and Sadie to connect with each other over long distances, but I've also seen an intriguing amount of understanding on the part of Pepper. It makes sense that an intelligent animal like her would be a fast learner, but she goes way beyond being a quick study, it's as if she already knows what I want her to do. Dave, I was thinking there might be a paper here, maybe several if you are interested."

"Are you kidding—of course I'm interested, this is fantastic." Dave leaps up with his hand out to shake, Josh stands to meet him halfway and he bumps the bench seat, knocking it over backwards against the roll top secretary desk.

"Whoops, sorree" he shakes hands and then turns the bench upright, but then remains standing in front of the secretary. "This house was where your mom lived wasn't it?" he asks Kirstin.

"Yep, right up until she moved to San Juan Acres."

"It has a certain feel to it, like past generations are still present. I like this roll-top desk is it your moms?, does the roll top still work?" Without waiting for an answer he lifts the handle and raises the top. The concentrated perfume smell hits him in the face, and for good reason, laying open is a half full box of perfumed stationary and envelopes. He carefully closes the lid, while turning back to sit on the bench he takes note of their expressions. No one is showing any concern, Ryan has his face twelve inches from the monitor and is apparently not paying attention to them, except Josh notices the game clock is ticking down and Ryan's not working the keyboard, mouse or joystick.

"Alright—I talked to Mrs. Thompson at San Juan Acres, and I spoke to Victoria Masters, between the two of them I have the whole story." No one speaks, Josh looks at Roberta and winks at her, and then picks up the bench seat and moves it in front of Kirstin and sits down facing her.

"I know that Four Corners Resort Casino is paying Ellie's rent, and that before them your uncle Robert was paying her and Jorge, and others that you don't know about. I know you have somehow been roped into carrying on. I'm guessing you feel like you have no choice because of Ellie, am I right so far. You don't need to answer, I know that's asking a lot of you after I come over here and spring everything. I wanted to see your reaction in person. The whale watcher group is going to make sure no more orcas are poached, and there is a plan to get the surviving ones back or have them released. Someone is making sure Four Corners Casino's keeps making support payments to San Juan Acres." Kirstin slouches and stares at the floor, Dave looks at the ceiling, his mind racing.

"Well, says Josh, "I guess we should leave, but first I want to see this game Ryan is playing." He leaves his bench and leans over Ryan. While looking at the screen and lightly touching his shoulder he whispers to him. "I know you made that dumb ass letter and delivered it to the hospital, do you want me to tell your mom?" Ryan shakes his head no. Josh can feel him shaking.

"Ok, I won't tell her, but you need to wise up, ok?" Ryan nods.

Roberta heads out the door first, followed by Dave Johnson. Kirstin puts her hand on Josh's wrist stopping him inside.

"You're right about everything, but we didn't try to hurt you, please believe me."

"Who did it, do you know?"

"No."

Outside Dave and Roberta are talking San Juan Island tourist spots and restaurants.

"Speaking of restaurants," says Josh, "I've got a girl in the car that I need to make amends to."

"Just a second Josh," says Roberta halfway to the car, "Listen, Sammie doesn't care about making amends or restaurants, do you want to thrill her and make her happy."

"Of course I do."

"She just wants you, not your obsessions and investigation. She wants to hang out and talk about you and her, not Ellie and Pepper. You should take the rest of the day off and just hold hands." Then Roberta stands on her tiptoes and kisses him on the cheek. "She wants that too."

"His hands were wet." Whispers Josh before Dave gets back to the house, "and his excitement seemed contrived."

"Are you listening to me." Roberta stops in front of the car. "Well, did you hear me."

"Yes of course, but..."

"No buts, just get in the car and pay attention to Sammie."

Chapter 57 - Second Man

Danny O'Brien is (figuratively) banging his head on his desk, and pounding his fists in frustration. All his leads are luke-warm. For the umpteenth time he watches the unidentified person skulk from *Black Widow*, to the restroom, to the Fish and Game dock. He stops the video every ten seconds and studies the background looking for the one clue that will bust the case open or set him on a path to the truth. It's pure wishful thinking, but he decides to pursue his most promising lead and see if he gets lucky or shakes something loose. He has positively matched Jorge's fingerprints to the Fish and Game boat, but that's not enough, he can think of a number of legitimate believable reasons for his prints to be there. In fact as security chief, Jorge's prints could be on any boat in the marina. Nevertheless he heads out the door for the marina to interview Jorge a second time.

"Welcome back officer O'Brien" says the counter person at the harbormaster office. What can we do for you today."

"Can you direct me to Jorge, is he out there somewhere?" pointing to the docks.

"Just a second, I'll find out." She pushes the transmit button on her desk microphone. "Jorge, come in please, Jorge."

"Jorge."

"Deputy O'Brien is here to see you."

"Ok, I'm on *C dock,* I'll be right up."

"Thanks," says Danny, "I'll meet him on the way." Danny waits in the open door while she radios Jorge.

People step to one side on the promenade when he approaches. Most are cordial and say hello, some go silent or drop to a conspiring whisper, as if he might overhear some illegal plot. The protest group is manned by a few hard core whale lovers taking naps on benches. Danny makes his way past the Customs building and down the second gangway. He can see Jorge turning off C dock.

"Hey Jorge, lets walk out to the breakwater."

"Sure Danny." The two walk in silence, each pondering what to say. Jorge has every reason to sweat, he knows his involvement in orca poaching makes him a likely suspect in the hit and run. Danny must investigate, his job is plain and simple, follow the evidence, get to the bottom and arrest someone the prosecutor can convict. While Danny's job is clear, he also has to live on the same island, shop in the same stores, raise his family just like the people he investigates. Running around falsely accusing citizens or even the hint of an accusation is extremely bad PC for himself and the sheriff's office. In a small island county with only a handful of tiny tight knit communities, gossip is rampant and deadly.

"See that black mess at the barbecue," says Danny, stopping for a second at the picnic float, "we found traces of it on the Fish and Game boat." Danny leaves out the fact that he has a print of a footprint. "I've been able to narrow it down to the last user that afternoon. That means that someone tracked it on their shoes and then boarded the game boat that evening." They continue towards the breakwater float.

"That really could be anyone," offers Jorge.

"You mean anyone that happened to be down here on that night, even you."

"I was at home, if that's your question."

"Anyone vouch for you?"

"No." Jorge exhales loud and long as if saying, *bring it on.* The ice is broken, Danny can carefully choose his next question.

"Is it possible your footprints are on this boat?" He motions to the aluminum Fish and Game sled tied up with three others at the breakwater beside them."

"More than likely my fingerprints too." Danny perks up at the implied admission.

"Is that so—why would that be."

"If it's the same boat, and I don't know which is which, but I climbed on one last week to put the keys back on the dash."

"Explain that, give me the details, what were you doing with the keys."

"I was making rounds and found one of those key floats laying on the dock right about here. I picked it up and it had a single key attached to it, so I figured someone from one of these boats dropped it."

"How did you know which boat it went to?"

"I didn't, I just tried the first one in front of me and the key worked so I left it on the dash with all the others." Jorge looks up at the taller deputy with a hint of smugness. He just explained away stray fingerprints and footprints that might point to him.

"So you tried the key and turned it."

"Yep, the lights and warning buzzer came on, so I switched it back off and removed the key."

"You're positive you removed the key?"

"Absolutely—look, we don't like them leaving keys on the boats, but we can't stop them, I just tossed it up with the other stuff in the tray."

"Were there other keys in the tray that fit the boat?"

"Could be, but I don't have any reason to go through their stuff or organize keys for them. I worked for them once years ago, that was enough." Danny sifts through everything he has learned in the last ten minutes. Jorge is still a viable suspect on his radar, but he has a good story.

"Why did you leave Fish and Game."

"Personality conflict reasons."

"Such as?"

"Rogers."

"Funny!—your still both at Friday Harbor Marina, and you provide security for his private boat fleet."

"The irony is not lost on me, but I've moved on. Speaking of moving on, are we done here?"

"For now."

Danny has not ruled out Jorge, his explanation for his fingerprint on the key is possible, but not being anywhere near the suspect boat would be a better story. Jorge got Danny thinking about other keys though, and he walks back to the Game dept. boat. Wearing latex gloves and using a pencil he digs through the pile of floats in the tray and discovers two other keys that fit the ignition and will run the boat. He bags them for printing. His earlier discovery when he was going frame by frame through the video uncovered a second man and completely rewrites the possible scenarios that went down that night. All this time he had been under the assumption that someone took out *Black Widow* and then switched to the Fish and Game sled. Wrong, wrong, wrong. Now he knows that two people passed each other in the shadows of the bathroom, one of them coming in, the other going out. One of them ran down Josh Pearson.

Chapter 58 - Ambushed

"**N**ow what are we doing?" says Sammie. "You got rid of them, and now were walking, smart move."

"Oh, I don't know, do you want to just walk around town?" Josh motions Sammie down the sidewalk and then cautiously reaches for her hand. Sammie responds just like Roberta promised, she clutches his hand and leans against him dropping her head against his arm while pulling him tight with her other hand. It's pretty much impossible to walk comfortably that way, so in a minute they are strolling and holding hands the way young and old have done it since dating began when the first cave boy and cave girl ventured out of their parents rock houses.

"Sadie come here," yells Sammie, Stay with us, you're not allowed here off leash." Sammie yells at Sadie but never loosens her grip on Joshes hand, she is not about to give up any gains or allow Josh's unexpected respite from shyness to be a one shot effort. With Sadie dealt with, she crowds him enough to switch hands and send a searching arm around his waist. He drapes his arm over her shoulder pulling her tight again. They walk arm on shoulder, hand on waist, matching steps stride for stride, squeezing every bit of air from between as they walk as one. The total side-body hug walk lasts all of fifty ungainly feet, before they go back to holding hands, but the mood is hot with subtle primal messages. At least in Sammies head.

"I'm going to make sure Four Corners Casinos keeps paying for Ellie at the rest home," announces Josh. "And make them give up captive orcas." Sammie is thrilled to hear the news.

"How will you do this," she asks, settling for holding his hand, keeping his interest will have to wait.

"I don't know yet, partly money disruption and partly system disruption, but what about you, are you glad to be on Orcas Island?" Josh's clumsy attempt at changing the subject to be about her, comes off rather poorly.

"What are you talking about Josh, who cares about Orcas Island—wait a second — holding hands, sending our ride away, insisting we walk." Sammie stops and stands in front of him, she holds his other hand so they are face to face and almost eye to eye. "This is Roberta's work isn't it? she talked to you didn't she—didn't she?" Sammie wont let it go. "Tell me Josh, tell me?" But then she sees the same shy nervous look come over him. The same look she saw the first day on the ferry. She promptly stops grilling and pulls him to her in a hug. She wraps her arms around his waist and he wraps her up in his arms. She lays her head on his shoulder and they just sway for a long time. "I asked Roberta for advice. After meeting Carly at the hospital, I told her I was afraid of losing you. I don't want you to change, I like you and I like being with you. Tell me how your plan to help Ellie works, maybe I can help."

Just then a passing beat up 4 x 4 skids to a stop beside them.

"Looky you, you punk, getting all nasty in public, is this your new girlfriend, does she know you been messing around with my Carly?"

"We got nothing to talk about Brad, Please just leave us alone. Come on Sammie, lets walk."

"Brad pulls forward, "Your buddy the sheriff isn't around to save your skinny ass this time, you better run. Or maybe I'll just take that pretty dog and well call it square, a bitch for a bitch."

"Shove off you moron," says Sammie, stretching Josh's arm when she turns toward Brads rusty Ford Explorer. "Sadie wouldn't even piss on your tires."

"Whoa baby—listen to you, I like that in my women."

"Bite yourself jerk-face."

Brad is starting and stopping, keeping pace with them, dissing Josh and throwing sexual innuendo at Sammie, the traffic light has changed and cars are piling up behind him. Josh spots an empty parking space up ahead and glimpses the immediate future. He pulls her into an about face and heads them back the other way. Leaving Brad at the head of a line of busy travelers and islanders.

"He's an ass. I feel sorry for Carly."

"Jeez Sammie, that's not how you calm things down. Let's go this way, maybe he will get stuck in traffic." Josh guides them into a pedestrian only path between buildings and they emerge in a back parking lot used for Saturday Markets. "Crap, if he turns the corner and cuts back through here were toast, c'mon—hurry." He drags her and Sadie into a painful full run out the far side just as a car accelerates into the gravel lot.

"That was close, lets head for the ferry, I think I'd like to leave the island now." They do a fast paced, half walk half jog while looking over their shoulders, watching and listening for the rattling 4 x 4. A block up from the promenade they slip into San Juan Latte's coffee shop, a little three table, four stool mainstay of the tourist industry for four months each summer. The next ferry hasn't pulled in to the terminal yet so they have at least an hour to kill. The other customers fawn over Sadie while Josh keeps an eye looking out the open door and one ear on the street sounds.

"Do you think he'll find us?" says Sammie, taking a table when someone gets up, she is nervously caressing Josh's hand, the other is wrapped up in Sadie's short nylon leash. "What will he do."

"Don't sweat it, he's just blowing off steam, he's probably long gone." Josh's controlled coolness calms Sammie, he can feel the change in her one handed hand wringing. Inside his head, he is assessing brad's immediate threat. He feels good but it's a little painful when he puts pressure on his barely healed thighs, he's not sure he could stand up to a well placed kick or have the leg strength to do what may be required. Preparing to fight a nut-cake in a back alley is not something he has ever done, its not the same as a title match where mental preparedness is half the battle. In his fight competitions, nobody ever cheated, or at least not, out and out tried to kill him. He takes a deep cleansing breath clearing his thinking. Sammie watches him exhale and relax.

"I see what you are doing, you don't believe he's left—do you?" her hand clenches into a fist of white knuckles. Josh is barely listening to her, his focus is mentally preparing and imagining possible scenarios. Brad knows that at the whale Museum he was out maneuvering and getting the better of him, which made him, look foolish, but he probably thinks it was a fluke. Never the less, now he has to prove himself so he won't risk losing. That's it, he silently concludes, while Sammie stares at him waiting for his answer.

"Well?"

"Look, it doesn't do any good to freak out, I'm simply analyzing the situation, we'll be fine."

"Analyzing, well that's anal." Says Sammie in frustration and fear. He pats her hand calming her. "I don't see how you can be so cool, aren't you nervous?"

"I'm fine, and so are you and Sadie." Says Josh, totally believing what he just said. He's mentally ready for Brad, he expects an ambush somewhere secluded, he expects Brad to be wielding a gun or knife or club, possibly a stick or metal tool, maybe a rod or pipe. Knowing Brads from a fishing family, he considers a fish whacker number one. He probably has it under the car seat just for teaching people like him lessons they need to be taught. His plan is simple, he mustn't let Brad hit him, it will only take once to decide the outcome. Josh knows he is fast, so he will bring the fight to brad when he telegraphs his move. At the museum he had tried to fend away and not hurt Brad. Perhaps that was a mistake. He will put an end to it before Brad can utter a word or even catch his second breath, his first breath will be wasted.

"Shouldn't we call Deputy Danny." Asks Sammie.

"We could, but he can't really act until after Brad does something illegal. If he just warns him away, then the issue isn't resolved, its only put it on hold."

"You don't seem to be afraid of him, aren't you worried a little."

"I am afraid, and I'm worried—I'm afraid I might be wrong, and I'm worried about hurting him really bad and..."

"And what Josh, tell me?"

"I'm afraid I might scare you out of my life, I don't want to be a violent person, but what I do is who I am, and I'm afraid you will be disappointed.

"I would be more disappointed if you didn't defend yourself or protect me, especially after coming to Carly's aid. What you did to Winnie The 3rd didn't scare me; I'm still here aren't I"

"Right in front of me," squeezing her hand, "but Winthorp wasn't a fight."

"What—do you turn into some sort of Grimm or something."

"No, Grimm's aren't real. You turn off the TV and they are gone. I'll still be here."

Sammie grasps both his hands, with hers and Sadie's leash into a big knot in the middle of the table and says, "I'll take that chance." In silence, her intense look drills into Josh, this time he does not look away. The un-stare-down does not have a winner or loser, they both cave, wanting to hug across the table. They settle for leaning forward and a flash kiss.

"I need to get a used laptop," Says Josh after a few seconds of reflection, "do you know of any thrift stores?"

"Are you for real, I don't believe you." Semi exasperated, she tears their hands apart.

"No, seriously, I need one, to work a deal for Ellie."

"Fine—last summer there was one up on top by the bowling alley."

They leave by the side door between buildings. Sadie leads the way but Josh holds her back so he can peek up the street. The coast appears clear so they double time up the hill staying back of the intersections until they can glimpse the cross streets. The next street over is where cars wait for the ferry. The waiting lanes are already full, four lanes wide, two blocks long. Trucks and trailers fill the outside lanes. Once the lines begin moving it will take about thirty minutes to load all the vehicles.

"There it is."

"Good, let's hope they have one with a charger cause you know the battery will be trashed."

Josh finds an old Inspiron in a bin stacked with chargers, phones and cameras. It boots and then reads low battery and shuts down. He takes it and a Dell charger and a canvas carrying bag with a handle. It's half price day, he gets everything for $40 and they take PayPal. Ten minutes after entering the store they are back on the sidewalk.

ORCA BOY

"The cars are moving over there, if we are going to catch this ferry we need to head that way." Says Sammie.

They fast walk one street over from the way they came up the hill and end up in front of the whale museum. The long stairway with switchbacks and viewing platforms comes out on the promenade, Sadie is eager to explore, she drags them down the stairs at a run almost pulling Sammie off her feet. Between them and the ferry terminal, the promenade crosses a couple access drives leading to marina gangplanks and small parking lots. A small park with ponds, fountains and gazebos separates the ferry terminal from the marina office. The last parking lot has a row of portable toilets creating a barrier, Sammie and Josh skirt the stink boxes and come face to face with Brad.

"I knew you would be walking along here, all I had to do was wait."

Brad stands squarely in front of them, legs spread, his hands behind his back. Sadie pulls on her leash trying to welcome the newcomer. If not for Sammie staying well back, Sadie would be licking him.

"What do you want?" says Josh, side stepping onto the lawn, only to have Brad match him, his hands still hidden.

"First I want you to say you're sorry, and then we'll see."

"Ok, I'm sorry—satisfied."

Josh moves back to the center of the path, and Brad follows still blocking the way. It's obvious, Brad is going to play a stupid game ultimately forcing a confrontation. The cat and mouse game is to Josh's advantage, he is judging Brads motions, reach, agility. Brad may as well be anchored to the ground wearing the heavy black boots street thugs seem to favor. Playing his game, and not showing either hand, Josh is sure Brad is holding something cross ways behind his back. Judging from how far back his elbows are pulled back he calculates whatever it is, is about one foot long. Josh has stopped back just far enough to keep clear of a sudden lunge. With one-step forward, Josh estimates Brad's longer reach could land a blow in the middle of a second step.

"Well—I said I was sorry, what do you want?"

Brad is so sure he is in control, he smarts off looking at Sammie while leaning forward baiting Josh. Josh checks his breathing never letting his eyes waver. If it were a match he would wait until his opponent repeated the amateurish lean in taunt and then clip him on the nose ending the match. He still hopes Brad may simply rant and rave, but the hidden hands tell otherwise.

"I want your dumb blond bitch to take back what she said or I'm going to waste you in front of her."

"Look, I don't know what part of what she said bothered you, why don't you tell me so we have it clear?"

"She knows,". . . . says Brad not sure where things are headed.

"What,?" says Josh, "tell me—oh do you mean—the *jerk-face* part."

When Brad called Sammie a bitch out the car window earlier, Josh had felt bad that he had not become her white knight defending her honor, this second time has sealed Brads fate. Until now Josh was hoping to diffuse Brad and go away with a truce. Not anymore.

"Look Bradley, may I call you Bradley, look Bradley, I can assure you, we are both very sorry that you are a *Jerk-Face.*"

Brad drops one hand to his side, his other forearm flexes as he tightens his grip. Josh reacts to Brad's subtle shoulder motion telegraphing he is raising his arm. Instead of stepping backwards and maintaining a safe distance, he steps forward taking away Brads own safety zone. In Brads hand is a short piece of steel rod with a wood handle and a leather lanyard looped on his wrist. Normally a club stored under a cars seat would be called a weapon bringing into question the owners lawful intentions. However a fisherman in Friday Harbor can stroll down main street with a fish whacker, and no one gives them a second look. Josh crowds Brad making it difficult to quickly raise his arm, which he must do before he can bring it crashing down with any force. By the time Brad raises the fish whacker above his belt, Josh is swinging his closed fist. His intended target since the bitch comment has been Brads soft neck area where a single tap touch in competition will win a match. At the moment he committed to the strike he knew he was throwing a death blow. He would not let emotions guide him and cause him to hit hard, too hard. Josh wanted to hit hard, at that moment he wanted to hit Brad as hard as he could. A primal scream leaves Josh's throat as his upper body follows his arm in a perfectly aligned power punch between Brads eyes. The sound of fist crunching nose cartilage and cracking eye orb is not familiar to him yet unmistakably damaging. Josh' second hammering blow is automatic, he has done the one-two sequence a thousand times in practice and hundreds of times in matches, but he has never intentionally landed a crippling blow nor ever tried to. The people he fights in matches are friends and athletes like him, involved in an ancient sport. When competitions are over they are still friends congratulating each other on their skill and tactics. The crossing blow develops maximum impact as he rotates his upper body. A fraction of a second after Brads face explodes Josh's second fist hits him in the side of the head below his ear. His dislocated and broken Jaw jerks sideways. Fleshy lacerated cheek and broken teeth spew a fountain of blood out his mouth. Brads not in pain, but he will be when he wakes up, his unconscious body falls and his head hits the pavement with a sickening thud and a little bounce, the fish whacker still looped on his wrist lies unused and ready.

Josh retreats to his ready stance, his actions automatic, his reflexes on high, Brads body is a crumpled mess on the ground beneath him. *Oh my god, this isn't good.* He kneels beside Brad, and places a hand on his chest.

"He's breathing—let's go," Josh backs away while nursing his sore fists. "The ferry is about done loading cars, we need to get out of here."

"Come on Sadie," Sammie shoulders her daypack with the laptop and Sadie leads her. She looks back at Brads body trying to process what just happened. Josh quickly scans the area, Brad had chosen well for his ambush, there's nobody around. The first person they encounter is a couple throwing penny's in a fountain. *Excuse me, says Josh, there's a guy over there by the portable toilets that looks like he's having a seizure, our phone is dead, please call 911, he needs an ambulance.*

It only takes five minutes to walk the short distance, they talk but don't say anything. Josh says *hurry up.* Sammie says *come on Sadie,* they both need to digest their thoughts. Josh is thrilled his expertise is real and now proven, not just real in competition, but in real life. When he was little his mother signed him up in a beginners martial arts class for six year olds. Now he doubts her decision and his own commitment. Taking down Brad was exciting, but hurting him is nothing to be proud of. He lost control, he let emotion drive him, all he wanted was to hit Brad as hard as he could, and he did. It's a good thing he didn't strike in the neck, but he almost did. He did what's right, but now he is running away, *what kind of winner runs away.*

From the top observation deck, Sammie and Josh have a clear view of the blue portable toilets, and the lawn next to them. An ambulance with flashing lights sits blocking the service ramp. A small crowd has gathered and is milling about the park while Emt's kneel beside Brad. Deputy O'Brien has walked down the promenade when saw the flashing lights. The emt's keep Brad on his back, both his eyes are swollen almost shut, the whites are swimming in bloody fluid. He can't talk except for a painful gurgling. Danny takes lots of photos before removing the fish whacker from his wrist, he also photographs the bottom of Brads shoes and then pulls a piece of paper from his case holding it next to the shoes. Danny takes pictures of the surrounding area getting as many bystanders as he can, and then points his camera at the ferry. *Oh crap,* says Josh, and he steps in front of Sammie while turning his back to the lens.

"Let's go inside, says Sammie, "I want to sit somewhere." They push through the heavy steel door and move to the front corner of the boat. They have the area to themselves, most passengers are out on the rail or lined up at the snack bar ordering counter. Sadie lays at their feet and pretends to sleep with one eye open. Sammie sits next to Josh and lifts his hand looking at the sore knuckles, he slumps down in the plastic seat and stares at the floor. He disguises the first sniffles, but soon Sammie looks at him and sees moist red eyes.

"I'm not scared of you," says Sammie, "I'm proud and totally impressed,"

He hangs his head, "I understand now, what they mean when they say, be sure what you ask for, is what you want."

"Shut up—you're feeling remorse for hurting that jerk face and blaming your skill and talent for being the bad guy. He's the bad guy, for a frigging genius you're making a pretty lame case for not excelling or doing your best."

"Did you see Danny, he was looking at his shoes, he even took pictures."

"Where is your head, can't you focus on one thing for more than ten seconds?"

"I'm sorry Sammie, you're right, I've been resentful blaming my mother for current events, she pushed me into martial arts to protect me from being a nerd, and now I'm blaming her for dying and leaving me. Brad got his sorry butt in the middle so I clobbered him."

"Are you listening to yourself? Brad got what he deserved because he was stalking us with a club and your mother saved *your* sorry butt today, because she knew one day you would need her smart thinking."

"Jeez orca Boy, why don't you hold me, and kiss me."

"Now who's not focusing."

When Danny sees that Brad is involved, he's not surprised, but seeing him the victim gives him something to ponder. The fish whacker club still hanging from Brads wrist is hard to miss. He knows Josh has an interest in martial arts, and he manhandled Roger's guy, but Brad is a street tough that's older and bigger. He looks like someone used the fish club on him, he doubts Josh could do the damage he is looking at.

"Come on, I'm going back," says Josh, "I'm not running away." He grabs the packs shoulder strap. "C'mon Sadie, wake up." The three of them tear out the door and sprint for the stairway at the far end. When he reaches the top of the stairs, he looks down on the car deck and sees the crewman dragging the safety chain across behind the last car.

"Hey hold up," he yells from the stairs, "were getting off." At that moment, the captain yanks the whistle cord and blows the single long blast signaling the ferry is underway.

"Stop, don't you do that"—yells the crewman too late and half heartedly because they actually have plenty of time, *maybe even five seconds to spare.*

The prop wash boils against the pilings pushing the ferry away just as they jump over the chain and step back ashore.

"Well that was exciting," pants Sammie, and not happy. "What are we doing back in Friday Harbor?"

"I'm not running away, that's not me. Let's go see Deputy Danny."

In the time they walk half a block back to the park, their ride home has cleared the harbor. Gawkers and bystanders are milling about watching, trying to see what is causing all the commotion. The emergency people are about ready to transport Brad. Josh edges closer until he gets Danny's attention. With a wave, Danny motions them over.

"Do you know anything about this Josh?" He guides them off to the side away from the EMT's.

"I did it, I…"

"He made you do it, Josh tell him." Blurts out Sammie, causing Sadie to bark in agreement.

"What happened Sammie?" says Danny, turning to her. "Start at the beginning."

"Okay, we were walking to the ferry and he came out from behind those toilets over there blocking us. Josh tried to walk around him, but he kept moving in front of us saying to apologize. He was hiding a pipe behind him and then he tried to hit Josh with it."

"How did Brad get hurt."

"I hit him twice," he holds up his hands showing the telltale bruising and scuffed knuckles.

"You didn't use something, or hit him with anything?"

"No, that club is his and was strapped on his wrist, I never touched it."

"Anything else.?" Says Danny.

"I didn't want to hurt him."

"What was this apology about?"

"Earlier today, up on the road, Sammie called him a *jerk-face*, so he chased us with his truck through some alleys, we thought we lost him. But he was waiting for us down here. Then he called her a dumb blond bitch, so I said he really was a *jerk-face,* and that's when he tried to swing on me with the pipe."

"It would be Josh lying there dead, if he hadn't defended himself," says Sammie.

An EMT yells over to Danny that they are ready to go, Danny waves them off and soon their whoop whoop siren can be heard heading up the hill.

"Am I in trouble?" asks Josh. "Can we go home?"

"Not with me, Brad may have something to say. If the DA charges him with menacing you may be called to testify, but you can do as you please."

"I saw you photographing his shoes and comparing them to a paper you pulled out, does that have to do with the person that ran me down?"

"I can't talk about details," says Danny, "but this is a photocopy of a footprint that I think may be our guy."

"I've seen that." Says Josh matter of factly, holding the paper and studying it, "yeah, I saw it today."

"Most likely you have, it's a popular tread pattern."

"No, I've seen that particular one, see the little mark here, that's a nick in the right sole, it allows mud to squish into the next cavity, that's why it has a smudged look."

"How can you be so sure, you just saw it for a second."

"I have a memory for details, and I saw that pattern in the mud today at Kirstin Thompson's house—and I noticed the nick."

"Are you sure, do you know who made the tracks?"

"Sure I'm sure; the tracks were on the ground outside of Dave Johnson's red Toyota, and on Kirstin's vinyl floor."

"When were you there?"

"A couple hours ago, we visited Vicky Masters and Ellie Thompson out at the rest home first, and then stopped by to see Kirstin."

Danny silently digests the fact that Josh has been conducting his own investigation. Sammie and Josh stand in front of the deputy as if they have just admitted to something and are waiting to be chastised. Sadie's dog ESP senses the impending lecture and with a whimper rests her nose on her paws. Instead of a lecturing them on staying out of police business, Danny sees an opportunity to join forces.

"What have you learned, if you don't mind my asking," asks the deputy sheriff.

Josh has anticipated the time when he would share or not share what he knows, but most importantly he mustn't put someone, not Danny or Sammie, in a position of choosing sides or right from wrong. He figures the best course is to shut up.

"Nothing much, Eloise Thompson thought Roberta was Vicky, she thought I was Jorge, she thought Sammie was Kirstin and Pete was agent Rogers. She's a nice person, it's sad."

"Did you Learn anything?"

"No," says Josh, but his lack of eye contact and body language gives him away. Danny waits for a better answer until, "Look, I can't blab everything I've learned that has nothing to do with your investigation, but I want the guy caught, I will tell you anything at all that is pertinent."

"I don't know anything," says Sammie raising her hands when he looks at her. "He's a one man show, I just handle the dog."

"And sometimes call people jerk face." jokes Josh with a laugh.

"Yeah—and that."

"What about you," says Josh to Danny, "do you have any solid leads besides that footprint, any witnesses, any smoking guns?"

"I can tell you that if the cut in that footprint lines up with one of the unidentified fingerprints, we have our guy. If he has a motive and no alibi, that will cinch it."

Chapter 59 - Evidence

"Mr. Johnson, I want to exclude you from the possibilities list. The easiest and fastest way to do that is for you to freely offer print samples, if you refuse you jump to the top of the list, and accompany me to the station. Any objections?"

Danny unrolls the butcher paper in front of Dave Johnson and instructs him to place both feet on it without twisting or scuffing. When Johnson steps off the paper Danny looks for the nick. He sees it just like Josh had said. He rolls up the paper making no comment to Johnson, next he pulls a clean water glass from a bag and holding it with two fingers at the top and bottom has Johnson take it from him with his left hand. He repeats the process with Johnson's right hand, and puts the glasses back in special paper evidence sacks.

"Do you remember where you were Tuesday night the 7th at 9 PM"

"Let me think for a minute," Danny watches him closely, "oh sure, I remember, I was at Kirstin Thompson's house, ask her, I'm sure she will tell you."

"Okay, I will, thank you." Danny's next stop is Kirstin's house, but Dave Johnson calls her first before Danny's cruiser is out of site.

"Hi Ryan is your mom there"

"Just a sec. . . . . mom, it's Johnson."

Before answering, she holds the phone in her hand and considers Josh's accusations, accusations that she admitted to as he was leaving. It felt good to tell him he was correct and a load was lifted that had been building for ten years. She wanted to believe him when he said he would make sure her mother would be financially taken care of at San Juan Acres. Ryan is standing in front of her, she can see the questions in his face, and she knows what she has to do.

"Hello Dave."

"Thank god you're still there, Deputy O'Brien just left, he's on his way there. You need to tell him I was there at your house that night." Kirstin doesn't speak for a long time, she knows what she is going to do, but she can't bring herself to say it.

"Kirstin, are you there, Kirstin?" Says a suddenly worried—Dave Johnson

"I can't do it, I'm sorry." Says Kirstin weeping.

"You're in it too, you can't back out."

"No—I'm not, Whatever you have done, you've done by yourself, good bye." She hangs up, and hugs Ryan.

"I saw him that night." Says Ryan.

"Who did you see."

"I saw both of them, please don't be mad at me."

Kirstin holds him at arms length, one hand on each shoulder. "What did you do."

"I took Aunt Vicky's boat out, and circled around Shaw, I saw Josh Pearson in his kayak. When I came back, I ran into Johnson by the bathroom, he borrowed my hat and Jacket. He said he was going out with some Fish and Game guys and was cold. He brought them back here the next day. Did he run over Josh?"

Deputy O'Brien arrives and interviews Kirstin and Ryan. Ryan identifies Johnson as the disguised figure boarding the Fish and Game boat, he also admitted taking *Black Widow* for a joy ride. Kirstin refuses to lie and be Johnson's alibi. Danny anticipated they would get a match on the prints, but with an eyewitness, it was time for an arrest.

ORCA BOY

Chapter 60 - Campfire

"You know," says Sammie, "we have some time to kill before the next ferry. Brads gone, now we can finally relax and walk around town. If I remember correctly your girlfriend advisor gave you some advice." Josh doesn't need to be reminded, he reaches out to hold hands, but then remembers on the ferry her saying *kiss me.* Using her hand he pulls her to him and then wraps his arm around her waist. She holds the back of his head and looks into his eyes. Only twelve inches separates them. Josh is about to lose it again. *I can fight off a bully, and wrestle an orca , but I melt in front of her.* He breaths deep, closes his eyes and leans forward, Sammie does the same.

The longish kiss and hug brings the proper mood back, but a horn toot snaps them out of it. They are standing in the roundabout crosswalk and a car has stopped, waiting for them to walk across the street. Josh timidly gives a four finger wave to the laughing couple in the car and leads Sammie and Sadie across in front of them.

Waiting for the next ferry, they lay claim to the same bench again.

"How much should we get for the whale museum, and what about funding Chet's group." Says Josh, his mind planning ahead.

Sammie doesn't care that he is thinking about something besides her, she's happy they are together, and lays her head on his shoulder.

"What about taking Pepper and Sadie and camping on Rock Island tomorrow." Answers Sammie.

"I was thinking ten thousand dollars initially, sure, let's do it." Answers Josh.

"Sandy won't let me go overnight by myself, do you mind going camping with some resort guests and their kids. You could be a guide and get paid."

"Are you kidding, I'll do it for free, we can have a campfire and tell ghost
stories."

Chapter 61 - Fire Alarm

The next ferry arrives and offloads a full load. A stream of cars and tourists swarm the turn around. The promenade stacks up again with people hurrying on their way. They let the crowd thin out and then jaywalk between cars. Sadie drags them back down the passenger ramp. Fortunately there is no captain or deckhand to recognize them, the ferry they jumped off is one of four and won't be back until tomorrow. They climb the stairs and find a spot at the rail to watch Friday Harbor settle down for the evening. They lean against each other for warmth in the breeze.

"You know what," says Sammie.

"What," says Josh turning toward her.

"Roberta is right. This has been a great afternoon, except the Brad part of course. Just hanging with you, just us being together with Sadie has been so cool. I wish it would last forever." She already has her arm around his waist, so she pulls him really tight leaning her head on him.

"Dow, that hurts . . . hey—that's him, that's the red Toyota, see it has that funny wheel." From their high vantage point, they can see all of the empty ferry lanes and beyond the turnaround up the hill on main street. "Look at him go, he darn near hit that guy. Look—he's racing across the parking lot trying to catch the ferry. He's going to be the last one on, the deck man is holding the chain for him."

"Are you sure its him, can you see his face?" They run down the deck and peak over the back rail next to the steps where they have a clear view.

"Call Danny," says Sammie, "he's trying to get away, innocent people don't run, now you know he is guilty."

Josh pushes connect. "Deputy O'Brien, this is Josh Pearson, we're on the ferry getting ready to leave, and I thought you should know that we just watched Dave Johnson race across the ferry lanes and board the boat."

"Yeah, he's in the red Toyota, we're leaving any minute, their hauling the chain now."

"C'mon what did he say."Says Sammie tugging his arm.

"He said he had to stop him."

"But how can he stop him—the ferry's leaving?"

The captain blows the long departure warning whistle, just as the chain is secured and the ramps are hoisted. The ferry shutters and its huge propellers start turning, sending wash against the pilings. The open gap behind Dave Johnson's Toyota grows. The ship is under way.

Suddenly the fire alarm pierces the air. Red lights along the walls flash and ringing bells seem to be everywhere. The ferry has barely begun to move, and the captain reacts swiftly. He kills the forward thrust and reverses the ferry back against the waiting pilings.

"Surprise, we're back in Friday Harbor again," says Sammie sarcastically. "I'm getting the feeling we are not meant to go home. How did you know the captain would back up if the fire alarm were pulled?"

"Lucky guess," says Josh looking around guiltily. What else could he do, if it was a real emergency, and they, I mean we have to abandon ship, what better place than at the dock? I hope Danny gets here before they figure out it's a false alarm."

In a few minutes, Deputy O'Brien, with lights flashing, fly's down the terminal driveway and onto the loading dock. He screeches to a halt half on the ferry and half on the just lowered steel ramp. The deck man lowers the chain and Danny sprints fifty feet to the last car loaded. Dave Johnson is still seated, he thought for a moment that he was home free, but when the fire alarm sounded his world came crashing in on him. All he could do was wait for Danny to escort him in handcuffs to the waiting cruiser. A minute after Danny backs off the ferry, the deck man backs the red Toyota off and parks it in a visitor spot next to the terminal office and dashes back on board. When the ramp clears the ferry deck the Captain blows the departure whistle one more time. The ferry gets underway while the deck man muscles the safety chain back in place.

"Let's go inside says Sammie, I've seen enough of Friday Harbor."

Chapter 62 - The Kiss

4 am—Josh is sitting up in bed at Pearson Lodge. The ratty old laptop has keys that don't work without wiggling them, *what a pain,* but he gets to work.

He composes and deletes the letter to Four Corners Casinos three times. *Pay up or else!* Is the theme of the letters. *Comply or suffer!* He envisions all the ways datamaster24 associates will hack the casinos, forcing them to their knees if they don't pay up. It was easy for him to snoop through personal accounts using hacked passwords supplied to him, all the time saying it was to save orcas, or save Pepper. Taking the next step is wrong and he knows it, it's inexcusable, crossing a line, an inner voice nags at him, holding him back.

"It's called extortion," he says it softly, whispering to himself. *Disrupting their business online is the same as throwing bricks through their windows.*

"Its' called cyber terrorism." He says it aloud again, so he can hear himself. His mother would've killed him, saying he wasted his talent. His dad would say follow your heart and do what's right, even if it's wrong. *That's it, that's the solution, thanks dad,* and then he deletes his fourth effort at demanding that they right the wrong they began a decade ago. *I'm not going to bully them or force them to do anything, I'm going to show them what's right.* He tosses the laptop and goes back to his tablet to compose an e-mail.

Dear Sir,
Recent events and protests in Friday Harbor involving orca poaching have grabbed national headlines, and Four Corners Casinos is smack in the middle of it.

ORCA BOY

I am offering my services to help you make things right. Your public relations and advertising folks may want to search "Orca boy" and "Saving Pepper" and then return my e-mail.

Josh Pearson - aka Orca Boy

This won't work either, they'll just blow it off—he deletes it like the others.

Datamaster24—that's the answer. He prepares a final request for submission to his willing hacker friends. Josh outlines a bogus plan announcing that Four Corners Casinos launch an advertising campaign offering free "save the whale," Orca Dollars and other rewards to visitors of their Casinos. He requests that press releases be sent to travel agents around the world. He wants social media swamped with news reports of the phony promotion. The coup-de-grace of his plan is to publicly announce that Four Corners Casino Resorts, will use the profits to fund the Whale Museum and San Juan Acres with annual $50,000 contributions. Josh anticipates the casinos will welcome increased tourist profits, and will eagerly jump onboard. He expects that potential negative public outcry will guarantee their cooperation, and Datamaster24 will keep the pressure on them if need be.

Text: Hi dad, you won't believe everything that has happened, but that will come out later. I want you to know that, thanks to you and mom, I'm doing what's right. Oh yeah, Danny caught the guy that ran me down.

Love Joshua.

"Good morning Josh," says Maggie, "You're up early. How was your day with Sammie in Friday Harbor."

"It was great, and very newsworthy, is uncle Charley up."

"Right here Josh, let er rip I'm all ears, what happened."

"Well—for starters Deputy Danny caught the guy that ran me down, it was Dave Johnson a staffer at WU. He made a run for it and tried to get away on the ferry, but the fire alarm...."

Josh keeps his aunt and uncle spellbound, but he leaves out details like kissing Sammie on the crosswalk. He covers the rest home, Vicky and Ellie.

After the news is dealt with, Maggie announces she is going shopping in town and Josh offers to tag along so he can pick up Tic-tacs and food for the camping trip to Rock Island.

"There they go," says Charley at the lodge's picture window, Maggie snaps away, seven kayaks make their way north outside the cove. Sammie and Sadie bring up the rear. Josh with camping supplies joins in beside her. Pepper is last out of the cove and takes position on the other side next to Sadie, all of them heading for Rock Island.

"Let's watch the sunset from on top of Proposal Rock," says Sammie, her paddling synchronized with Joshes.

"Sure," says Josh. "we'll watch the sunset." – *and this time I'm going to kiss you --*

Thanks for reading

Orca Boy